Beyond Resurrection

Beyond Resurrection

A. J. M. Wedderburn

SCM PRESS

0 334 02766 7

This edition first published 1999 by
SCM Press
9–17 St Albans Place London N1 0NX

SCM Press is a division of
SCM-Canterbury Press Ltd.

Printed in Great Britain by
Biddles Ltd, Guildford and King's Lynn

For Fiona and Martin

Contents

Foreword

Today there are many ways to approach and interpret the New Testament, in particular through the varied disciplines and schools of literary criticism, but also through sociology and social history, through a feminist critique, through psychology and social anthropology and the like. At times absolutist claims are advanced for these approaches, sometimes even that this or that approach has replaced the historical criticism which once was dominant in exegetical studies. For me, however, historical criticism remains indispensable and these various other disciplines can and must find their place within its framework. Otherwise – and this is perhaps not always recognized with sufficient clarity – the basic nature of the Christian faith, a Christian faith which finds its focus and its starting-point in a historical figure, is drastically changed. One can of course choose another starting-point, for instance the text of the New Testament as it is, and eschew all historical questions such as who wrote it and when and why, or what the respective writers meant to say, and what the relation is between what they wrote and what actually happened or was said at a given point in history long ago. But then the nature of the Christian faith has changed from faith in a person to faith in a book, with all the attendant questions about the reason for interest in this book and its importance, questions about the nature of its truth-claims. The text is then the focus of interest and it becomes irrelevant whether it points beyond itself to anything more important than itself.

For me, however, that text has little meaning unless it does indeed point beyond itself, and what it points to is what interests me: accordingly, I want and need to ask whether it points faithfully and clearly or whether its witness has been overshadowed or overlaid or obscured, deliberately or unintentionally, by other considerations, so that we are in danger of being pointed in the wrong direction, or of misunderstanding what is being said because we interpret it wrongly. To pose such questions and to pose them with all the rigour that the methods of historical criticism demand is an uncomfortable undertaking which constantly threatens to undermine cherished and established beliefs, and it is no coincidence that it has so often been New Testament scholars or theologians writing about the New Testament and interpreting the New Testament who in the course of the past two centuries have fallen foul of ecclesiastical authorities and incurred the disfavour of the pious. Historical criticism of later periods of church history, for instance, is a comparatively harmless undertaking: we are readier to recognize the human frailty and limitations of figures of a later period, even if they are the founding figures of a whole denomination, but when it is a matter of the founding figures of the church or even the founding figure of the Christian religion himself, who is regarded by many as God incarnate, then the limits of tolerance are suddenly far more circumscribed. Nowhere is that more true than when it is the resurrection of Jesus that is being discussed, for then not only is the very authority and status of Jesus himself at stake, but even the character and nature of God and our eternal destiny.

It is of the nature of historical criticism that when applied to events of this sort, so far removed from us in time, it can be expected to lead to nothing more than a verdict that this was more probable, that less probable, or both were to varying degrees possible. Such a conclusion, we feel, is a poor foundation for faith. But if that is and must be the critical verdict, and if there turns out to be no way around it, what are we to do, intellectually and practically? That question, too, therefore belongs to my present enquiry, even though I must readily grant that I am no specialist systematic or philosophical theologian (as a glance at the bibliography will show: it reflects simply those works that I have found it useful to cite and cannot therefore claim to be in any way a complete one, even in exegetical matters; this is a field where the literature is simply too extensive and the ramifications of the topic are too numerous). Yet it is, I feel, incumbent upon an exegete who comes to the sort of conclusion that I do to take account of the systematic and philosophical implications of her or his work and to seek to give some account of them, even if here it must be left to specialists to follow through the implications of such musings as these – the musings, it may be thought, of an exegete cast adrift in very deep waters indeed, an exegete whose powers of swimming in such deep and stormy waters are limited in the extreme and who possesses no life-raft, life-jacket or other ready-made means of survival.

The explorations and probings of the second part of this work have, I confess, a very rough and ready look about them, but I must also confess that, given the nature of the subject-matter, I would not expect, and indeed would be highly suspicious of, any neat and tidy answer. If in truth any talk of God or of ultimate reality must come up against a profound mystery, then does that not set a question-mark against the sort of theological studies where what God is and is not is declared with the greatest of precision?

In fact I had originally thought of a far shorter exegetical work which would leave the systematic and philosophical aspects of the problem to a colleague, but that possibility of collaboration was made more difficult by my move to Munich (and to a very different philosophical and theological climate and tradition from the ones to which I had hitherto been accustomed). Thus I have, perhaps rashly, embarked on further explorations of my own into the implications of this aporia into which historical criticism of this subject here leads us. I would still, though, wish to acknowledge and express my thanks to former colleagues in Abbey House, that little hotbed of theological thought in Durham, who provided the initial stimulus for this project (although most of them will thoroughly disapprove of its results!), as well as to the participants in a seminar on the resurrection of Jesus which I held soon after my arrival in Munich. This compelled me to dig rather deeper into the exegetical problems which these traditions present. A special word of thanks is due, too, to Leslie Houlden, whose helpfulness and influence will rapidly become apparent in the course of this work.

In preparation of this text for the press I am particularly grateful, too, to the staff of my Institute in Munich and above all to Frau Ingrid Imelauer, who has borne the brunt of the somewhat daunting task of preparing the index, and also for assistance at long, but electronically short, range with bibliographical and other queries to Dr Bruce Gordon of the University of St Andrews and Dr Bruce Longenecker of the University of Cambridge. And, to use an English expression that seems to have made itself thoroughly at home even in German usage, last but not least my thanks are due to Dr John Bowden and his staff at SCM Press, above all to Dr Bowden himself who has exerted himself far beyond the normal call of duty of the editor of a press in the task of improving and tidying up my typescript and curing it of a certain prolixity.

This book is dedicated to my children. I noted recently the foreword of a colleague's book, also dedicated to his children, in which he expressed the hope that some day they might be able to see something in their father's work. Mine are somewhat older than his and I hope that they may be able to see more immediately some value in the contents of this book!

Munich, January 1999   A. J. M. Wedderburn

Part I: A Historical Impasse?

I

The Resurrection of Jesus – A Question of History?

One need not apologize for yet another book on the subject of the resurrection of Christ or of Christians. It is a central issue for Christian life and thought and an ever controversial one. For many it is the bedrock and the *sine qua non* of Christian faith.[1] With this article of faith Christianity stands or falls: it

> stands or falls with the reality of the raising of Jesus from the dead by God. . . . A Christian faith that is not resurrection faith can therefore be called neither Christian nor faith.[2]

Or Thorwald Lorenzen asserts at the very start of his monograph on *Resurrection and Discipleship* that the resurrection of Christ is not '*a* question of faith, but *the* question of the Christian faith' (1). How much hangs on this is illustrated, for instance, by the centrality of arguments about the resurrection and its historicity in Petr Pokorný's *The Genesis of Christology*. For instance:

> without Easter Jesus' life would be a shipwreck that would reveal only the negative side of things – the limits of human possibility. In fact Jesus would be of so little importance that one would not take him seriously either as a question or as a model of shipwreck.[3]

And in the eyes of many, the apostle Paul settles the matter beyond all doubt: 'If Christ has not been raised (from the

dead), then our preaching is empty, and your faith is empty
. . . If Christ has not been raised, your faith is futile, you are still
in your sins' (I Cor. 15.14, 17). There can be no Christianity
without the resurrection of Christ, and without the resurrection
of Christ the Christian faith is empty, meaningless. Those who
question the resurrection of Christ have destroyed Christianity at
its roots. For Christianity to be possible the resurrection of
Christ must truly have happened, must be a historical fact. It
must be historically true that Jesus has risen if Christianity is to
have any validity at all.[4]

(a) A historical question with no certain answers?

However, if historical truth is indeed involved, then surely
historical questioning is also involved, and there the problems
begin. For the answers to historical questioning are rarely clear-
cut; they are given in terms of the more or less probable: this may
be regrettable, but it is an unfortunate fact that cannot and
should not be circumvented. For historians may be able to assess
the evidence and to state what the balance of probabilities is, or,
if they assert that something is certainly true, what they mean in
practice is that something has been established 'beyond all
reasonable doubt', that is, the level of probability has become so
high that the falsehood of the assertion is highly improbable. And
with much of modern history there are a great many answers that
are indeed 'beyond all reasonable doubt', and which can only be
doubted by the thoroughly unreasonable (as when the reality of
the Holocaust is called in question).Yet in dealing with something that allegedly happened in a remote corner of the Roman
Empire nearly two thousand years ago, it is unlikely that the
state of the evidence is often going to be such that the verdict
upon it is ever going to be 'beyond all reasonable doubt'. Perhaps
assertions like the statement that Jesus of Nazareth actually lived
in Palestine in the time of the Roman prefect Pontius Pilate and
was put to death by crucifixion might come into this category, yet
even this has been doubted; one must then ask whether that

doubt can be described as 'reasonable' or else dismissed as far-fetched, as mere questioning for the sake of questioning. More often in the case of such subject-matter we will be left with a choice between verdicts of 'more probable', 'less probable' and 'improbable'. Why should the resurrection of Jesus, if it is a historical fact, be an exception? Yet that, surely, is not enough to satisfy Christian faith's need for a secure foundation? Is one to base one's faith and one's life on a 'Maybe'?

For, if the evidence for Jesus' resurrection is subjected to historical examination, there is then the danger that one ends up with the verdict that, historically, there is considerable doubt about exactly what happened. It is perhaps symptomatic of this that the chapter on the resurrection by even so conservative a historical critic as the late Joachim Jeremias could give the impression that the likeliest historical verdict was that the disciples had stolen the body of Jesus:

> [Mary of Magdala's suspicion, in the story in John 20, that 'they' had taken the Lord away and laid his body in some other place] was a likely one because it was unusual for the governor to release the body of a man executed for high treason (Mark 15.45 par.), and fanatics could have remedied this decision by taking the corpse under cover of night to one of the criminals' graves (Sanh. 6.5f.). The account sounds most plausible; it is simple and free from any bias; as often, then, the latest literary text has preserved the earliest form of the tradition.[5]

The suggestion that the body of Jesus had been stolen met, too, with the approval of Hermann Samuel Reimarus in his critique of the resurrection traditions.[6]

If that verdict seems to leave readers in a quandary, wondering what they should believe to be true, and whether that belief is enough for Christian faith, the quandary is resolved for some by introducing a dogmatic solution. It is often so resolved, at least tacitly, by arguing that if Christian faith needs the resurrection of Jesus, then Christian faith must have the resurrection. In other words: *dogmatics provides the assured results which historical research cannot give us*. Few, admittedly, will do this as blatantly, or one might say honestly and openly, as Vincent Taylor did in his treatment of that other touchstone and shibboleth of Christian orthodoxy, the virgin birth of Jesus:

> the ultimate considerations which determine a true estimate of the Virgin Birth tradition are doctrinal. . . .If we attempt to confine ourselves to a purely historical inquiry, the verdict must be 'Not proven'.[7]

He then quotes, with approval, Gore's words:

> To clinch the historical evidence for our Lord's Virgin Birth there is needed the sense that being what He was, His human birth could hardly have been otherwise than is implied in the virginity of His mother.[8]

Taylor goes on to argue that if we consider that the virgin birth of Jesus explains his sinlessness, or is necessary for the doctrine of the incarnation, or is 'congruous with the doctrine of the Person of Christ', then this invests the New Testament tradition with a higher probability, 'sufficiently great . . . to make belief in its historical character reasonable' (129). If, on the other hand, it is not doctrinally relevant, it is unlikely to be true. With a singular candidness he concedes that we may be unable to say 'what is, or is not, congruous with His Person', at least not yet. Even if the story of Jesus' miraculous birth proves to be a legend, however, it would still be significant, for we would then have to ask what sort of person this Jesus was of whom such a legend came to be told (131–3). As I say, it is rare for the limitations of historical argument to be so candidly granted and made good, yet the same line of argument could easily be advanced for belief in the resurrection of Jesus: even if the historical evidence is at best uncertain, Jesus, being who he was, could not have been allowed to remain in the grave, but must have been raised to life by God. Or one could appeal to the needs of the Christian faithful today: he must have been raised from the dead, since only one raised to life is an adequate focus of Christian piety and devotion and worship.[9]

Such arguments will not do, for perceived theological or religious needs surely cannot answer historical questions. Arguments of the form 'I need it so, therefore it is so' only need to be stated in this way for their emptiness to be apparent. If theology and faith really need history, then theology and faith need to take history on its own terms: they need to listen to historians and to historical arguments. They need to cut their coat according to their cloth, and if the cloth that is needed is historical cloth, then they need to tailor their assertions in such a way as to let history be history. Historians must be allowed to practise their discipline according to the nature of their subject-matter and cannot be forced to become lackeys of another discipline; they cannot be press-ganged into supplying fodder for theological systems or fit objects of devotion for the pious. If theology or faith feel that they need to base themselves on something that is known to be historically true, and historical study cannot supply that knowledge of historical truth and perhaps even judges that there is considerable doubt about the assertion which they wish to hear from it, then the theologian and the believer have to re-examine their premises: can they in fact find another basis for their reflections and their piety than that bed of nails which is historical enquiry? Must they not seek another foundation if they are not to incur the charge of fantasizing, of building castles in the air?

Another way of tackling the problem of the precariousness of the historical evidence is to say, in effect, *'Give orthodoxy the benefit of the doubt'*. For, if history cannot by its nature do more than show something to be probably true, it could be argued that equally it cannot show anything to be more than, at most, probably untrue. Let us leave aside the question whether that claim is correct.[10] What historical enquiry, with the evidence which we do have, will be able to do is to evaluate the assertion that 'Jesus is risen' within a spectrum of judgments ranging from more or even most probable through to doubtful or even improbable. The probability that this enquiry can yield is unlikely to be beyond all possible doubt. Can the theologian or the believer take refuge in that doubt? Can they put the onus of proof upon those who question the truth of Jesus' resurrection, and demand that they prove their scepticism? Can they say, 'We will continue to believe in Jesus' resurrection until it is disproved beyond all doubt'? Why should an onus of proof be on either side? Can historical questioning and investigation ever take place freely and with a proper objectivity if such an onus is placed on either side of an argument? Certainly loading the dice in an argument in that way would allow, and does allow, all sorts of improbable and highly questionable assertions to be maintained, without fear of final and definitive falsification. But that is an abuse of historical methods: the game has been rigged from the start and the claim to objective historical investigation is a spurious one.

Van A. Harvey draws attention to another way of loading the dice: criticizing the arguments of Heinz Zahrnt for the historicity of the resurrection (although for him it is not a historical event which can be observed in the same way as other events in space and time, something that transcends the bounds of history), he notes that Zahrnt has so constructed his argument that it is supported both by the lack of positive evidence and by the admitted contradictions and absurdities in the accounts. For the fact that the resurrection-event itself is not reported speaks for its non-legendary character: had there been such a report, it could doubtless have been cited as evidence of an eye-witness account. The contradictions and absurdities show that there has been no collusion, but had the accounts agreed in all respects, this could of course be taken as proof of the certainty of the event.[11] The argument takes on a 'Heads I win, tails you lose' character – whatever the evidence, one way or other, it is all pressed into the service of the thesis that is to be proved. This game has also been rigged!

(b) Not a historical question at all?

Yet another, more robust, counter to the dilemma of trying to base theological assertions upon the unsure foundations of the historical is to deny that a belief like that in Jesus' resurrection is a matter of history at all. *'Jesus is risen' is not a historical statement and is not open or accessible to the historian's investigations.* That is implied by Dennis Nineham, among others, when he comments that the resurrection, which is at the very heart of the gospel, is not a '"historical" event' and falls outside the scope of the 'new quest of the historical Jesus'.[12]

His use of the term 'historical' here must be carefully noted, for he had earlier stated that 'the modern historian's method and criteria. . . are applicable only to purely human phenomena, and to human phenomena of a normal, that is a non-miraculous, non-unique, character'. That seems to be a definition which indeed excludes the event of the resurrection of Jesus. Or, as he puts it shortly afterwards,

> events can be called 'historical' only when the accounts of them have passed all the historian's rigorous tests; and since the historian's essential criteria presuppose the absence of radical abnormality or discontinuity, only those events can be described as 'historical' which are fully and exclusively human and entirely confined within the limits of this world.[13]

That is a plausible definition, if one so wishes it, but we need to ask a further question of it: for an event to be 'historical', *must* it be such that a historian can investigate it? In other words, must he or she be able to apply that method and those criteria to it? Even more significant is the further question: must the historical method and criteria be applicable in practice or possibly only in theory? If events, to be 'historical', must actually have passed the historian's tests, as the above quotation suggests, then that surely implies that the tests are not only applicable in practice, but have indeed been applied. That seems to leave no room for any merely theoretical applicability. However, Nineham subsequently seems to soften this rigorous definition of 'historical': Jesus' journey to Jerusalem *is* a historical event (unlike the super-natural, superhistorical event of his journey to heaven, his ascension), since it is one which 'we should *in principle* be able to verify by the ordinary historical procedures' (5, my italics). That surely implies that this event has not in fact passed the historian's tests. It is merely assumed that it (probably) would do so if they were applied, yet there has been no want of application of those tests to the Gospel material (an understatement if ever there was one!), which seems to indicate that in fact no final verification is possible because of the nature of the evidence. Verification in principle is unlikely in this case ever to be replaced by verification in fact, at least in this world.

The matter is complicated yet further by Nineham's listing of a number of 'historical statements' accompanied by other, 'supra-historical statements' which he marks by italicizing them: 'he was put to death *for our trespasses*'; he 'was raised *for our justification*'; he was 'conceived *of the Holy Ghost*' (8). If the italicized phrases are the 'supra-historical' ones which can only be verified by appeal to 'present Christian experience', then by implication 'he was put to death', 'he was raised', and 'he was conceived' are all historical ones. So is 'Jesus was raised' after all 'historical', and in what sense of 'historical'?

There is good reason to think that this latter position, namely that 'Jesus was raised' is at least in principle a historical statement in some looser sense than Nineham first suggested, may be a more satisfactory one than the one built upon a narrower defini-tion of 'historical'. However, one first needs to be clear about the ambiguities inherent in the word 'historical'. In the present context does it mean 'historically true' or 'of a historical nature, making a claim to be historical'? So, when we say that a statement like 'Jesus was raised' is 'historical', are we saying something about the truth of the content of the statement or merely some-thing about the nature of the statement? In the former case the statement has somehow passed the necessary tests and has been validated by historical investigation. In the latter case it is merely a potential candidate for historical investigation and historical verification or falsification, with no claim that it has in fact been investigated and verified. For there are many statements that can be recognized to be 'historical' in this latter sense, even if they have not actually been investigated by historians, or if the historians have not been able to reach a final, decisive verdict in practice because of the nature of the evidence available, as in the case of Jesus' journey to Jerusalem mentioned by Nineham. When we are dealing with events of the distant past this is often the case, since the nature of the evidence is very frequently so fragmentary or the factual is so mingled with the legendary that the truth is unlikely to be established beyond all doubt.[14] There are many events, too, both modern and ancient, whose nature is such that it is highly unlikely that we would ever be able to apply historical tests to them: what Julius Caesar had for breakfast on a given day or what Cleopatra wore on a particular occasion (if it was not a particularly significant occasion which has been recorded in some detail; for sometimes at least vague descriptions of persons' clothing are given on momentous occasions: e.g. Mark 9.3 parr.; Acts 12.21). We may still, however, be able to say that some answers to such questions are, to all intents and purposes, impossible: Julius Caesar could not, for instance, have enjoyed our favourite brand of corn-flakes, and Cleopatra did not wear a creation from one of the Paris salons.

And of modern events there are some that are past recovery, too: many are too trivial to have been noted by others or remembered by the participants. That is particularly true of private or internal events, but is not confined to them by any means. Neither I nor, *a fortiori*, any subsequent historian is likely to be able to say, for instance, what I was thinking about at 9 a.m. on 28 February this year. But such 'inward' events in the human mind are notoriously hard to fathom even under the most favourable circumstances; only when they are 'externalized', when one states or writes down what one is thinking or what is going on in one's mind, do others have access to such 'events'. And even then one must reckon with the possibility of deception or even self-deception. What went on, for instance, in Pilate's mind when confronted with the arrested Jesus and the charges against him is an object of (thoroughly legitimate) enquiry, but it offers scope for little more than intelligent or not-so-intelligent guesswork, based in large measure on what we know about the general situation at the time and Pilate's subsequent actions. But it is not only internal events of this sort that are in practice inaccessible to subsequent historical investigation. Neither I nor any subsequent historian will be likely to be able to say what clothes I put on on a given day in, say, the year 1950, unless some relative happened to take a photograph of me on that day and dated it, or to ascertain whether or not I had porridge for breakfast on that day unless a menu for the day turns up. Yet such questions are all by nature 'historical' ones, to be answered, as best we can, by historical enquiry, if we will. They are 'historical', but nonetheless trivial. What is claimed to have happened at Easter, however, is by no means trivial. Yet is it also 'historical'?

What happened to Jesus' body is certainly also a historical question. For if it is a historical question whether he was put in a tomb (and a real question, as we shall see, for there are those who have suggested that it would have been more usual for the body of an executed criminal to have been simply dumped in a common grave), then it is also a historical question whether the body remained in that tomb. Yet, *as far as we know*, no one saw what happened to the body; what the first witnesses experienced was not the resurrection-event itself, but an encounter with Jesus, an encounter which they then interpreted as meaning that Jesus was risen, had previously been raised so as to be in a position to encounter them;[15] it is only in the relatively late, apocryphal Gospel of Peter[16] that we find an attempt to describe the actual process of the resurrection itself, in an account that is manifestly legendary. For, regardless of the age of the traditions contained in this source, the level of palpable legendary embellishment is in general such that its claim to historical reliability is very low indeed. And even here, Kendrick Grobel maintains,[17] it is perhaps rather the exaltation to heaven that is 'mythically described', not Jesus' 'coming-to-life' itself. In theory, however, but only in theory, unless we are to believe this apocryphal Gospel, someone could indeed have stood, for instance, by the entrance to the tomb and have observed what happened. But we do find reports in the relatively more restrained canonical Gospels that at a somewhat later point of time followers of Jesus found the tomb empty. That discovery, if true, would also be a historical event, and so the reports of it look like historical ones: they are potentially historical.

Or we can, and indeed should, look at the question from the perspective of the accounts of the appearances of the risen Jesus to the disciples. It is an indubitable historical datum that some-time, somehow the disciples came to believe that they had seen the risen Jesus. This is, and must be, as already Ferdinand Christian Baur saw,[18] the basic datum from which all historical research into Jesus' resurrection starts. Paul Hoffmann is there-fore perfectly correct when he asserts:

> The object of historical investigation [of the resurrection of Jesus] can only be the early Christian belief in Jesus' resurrec-tion, not this resurrection itself.[19]

It is then perfectly legitimate for the historian to ask, as a histo-rian, what gave rise to that belief, just as he or she may ask what gave rise to the belief in some circles that the emperor Nero had not in fact taken his own life but would return.[20] Posing such questions belongs to the stock-in-trade of the historian: it is fully legitimate to ask what gave rise to such beliefs, even if it is mostly far, far easier to ask these questions than to give satisfac-tory answers! Indeed, historians may not be able to answer either of those questions. In the case of Nero the evidence is too fragmentary; in the case of the resurrection appearances one possible explanation, the traditional Christian one, passes beyond the historian's competence as a historian to deliver a verdict upon it. He or she may be able to weigh up the probabilities of natural, this-worldly explanations of both beliefs, like the theories that Jesus was not actually dead when buried, and revived in the cool tomb; or that the disciples stole the body; or that they looked in the wrong tomb. But there will remain the competing, alternative explanation of Christian tradition and belief, namely that God intervened to raise him from the dead, and that is beyond the historian's power to evaluate; it remains imponderable. But then so too in some measure does the belief that Nero was a 'divine' person. The most that the historian can do in either case is to say that the respective beliefs in Jesus' resurrection and Nero's survival can or cannot be adequately explained without recourse to humanly imponderable explanations.

A basic problem in both these cases is an absence of eye-witnesses, or at least, in the case of Christ's resurrection, of eye-witnesses who describe *what* they experienced, rather than simply reporting *that* they experienced it. Paul is our only eye-witness to the risen Jesus whose witness we still possess, but it is Luke who describes something of what the appearance of the risen Jesus to that apostle was like, though not without several discrepant features in his three accounts of the experience in Acts 9.1–9; 22.6–11; and 26.12–18; from Paul himself we have no more than a few tantalizing hints. So it is hard for the historian to judge how well-based the apostle's assertion is that Jesus appeared to him. Yet it remains a potentially historical claim, just as it is potentially historical that Pilate's wife had a dream about Jesus just before his trial (Matt. 27.19); by the nature of things – the nature of the evidence, the nature of the events, etc. – one cannot prove that either is actually historical in the sense of being historically true. But one can still pass historical judgments on the likelihood of their being true or not. The resurrection-event itself may be beyond the reach of historians, but they can still pass judgment on whether that event is needed at all to explain what *is* within their reach, namely the early Christians' claim that Jesus had been raised. In order to explain what is known to have happened, namely the disciples' coming to believe that Jesus had risen, was it necessary or likely that some such event occurred and impinged upon and occasioned the more obviously human events of which we do know? That *is* a historical question to which the historian can attempt to give some sort of answer.

Another objection to the suggestion that the question of the raising of Jesus can be approached by historical investigation, an objection that in many ways is similar to Nineham's claim just referred to, is the argument that *God*, the purported subject of this action, *by definition lies beyond the scope of such an investigation.*[21] If this explanation of the disciples' faith, that it was a response to an act of God, is true, then it lies beyond the historian's competence, and if the historian denies this explanation, then he or she is guilty of an arrogant reductionism which rules out such an explanation on principle: only that which can be investigated historically is true. A similar approach perhaps lies at the root of Alan Padgett's discussion of historical research on the resurrection: having correctly distinguished things which are open to natural-scientific explanations, and those which are open to historical explanations, he then suddenly offers a further category, something (the resurrection) which is open to a theological explanation, 'based on the causal powers of God'.[22] Hans Grass, however, has offered what is perhaps an adequate counter to this objection: even such 'metahistorical' events, as he describes them, have a side, a dimension, which *is* open to history and the historian; for there were certain persons who were involved in this event and were affected by it. Although God's revelatory act itself cannot be historically investigated and scrutinized by historical investigation, yet the fact that it is supposed to be a revelation *in history* means that human eyes have seen something and human ears have heard something; human hearts have been touched, and this event has come down to us in the form of a historicizing account. This side of the revelatory act that is open to history, that impinges on human history, must be scrutinized to ascertain its trustworthiness and credibility.[23] Even if one invokes 'the causal powers of God', one has invoked powers which supposedly cause things in history. Such a questioning is, accordingly, not inappropriate or out of bounds for the historian. For even if the experiences of the disciples that led to their faith in the risen Jesus are visionary ones, Jürgen Becker warns us,[24] that does not immediately make them into an unquestionable basic datum that possesses the special quality of an immediate and absolute intervention of God in history; the principle of the correlative interweaving of all events in history remains valid here too, and 'there should not arise the slightest suspicion in such an enquiry that one wants surreptitiously to wriggle out of a historical questioning'.

(c) A different sort of 'history' and 'historicity'?

In coming to this conclusion therefore I find myself in basic agreement, at least in this respect, with the recent and, at any rate in the German-speaking world, highly contentious study of the Göttingen New Testament scholar Gerd Lüdemann:[25] it is, he argues, appropriate and indeed necessary to treat the question of Jesus' resurrection as a historical one.

In that claim, however, Lüdemann is countering a different claim from Nineham's argument that 'Jesus is risen' is not a matter of history at all or the claim that God's actions cannot by definition be subject to historical verification: he is confronting the claim that there is a *type of historicity that is beyond the scope of historical investigation and yet offers a greater certainty than anything that the historian can provide.* Lüdemann is, however, rightly sceptical of attempts to evade the admittedly uncomfortable question of historicity and compares Barth's attempt to claim a historically privileged position for the resurrection of Jesus with Bultmann's retort to it: over against Barth's contention that there can be events the actual occurrence in time of which is far more assured than any historian could ever verify, and that Jesus' resurrection was one of those events,[26] Bultmann, whose view that Jesus' resurrection was no historical fact had provoked this claim by Barth, asked what Barth meant by 'occur' and 'history'.[27] How is the faith that Barth presupposes 'to be distinguished from a blind acceptance by means of a *sacrificium intellectus?*'[28] With justice Lüdemann sees that Barth has here eliminated the possibility of enquiring historically into the grounds of faith, a position which Bultmann also criticizes, but only at the cost of himself denying the possibility of questioning the validity of the Christian kerygma, as we shall see.[29]

Implicitly, too, Wolfhart Pannenberg distances himself from Barth's stratagem when he writes:

> There is no justification for affirming Jesus' resurrection as an event that really happened, if it is not to be affirmed as a historical event as such. Whether or not a particular event happened two thousand years ago is not made certain by faith but only by historical research, to the extent that certainty can be attained at all about questions of this kind.

Correspondingly he criticizes the views of Paul Althaus and Walter Künneth, affirming instead that:

> The only method of achieving at least approximate certainty with regard to the events of a past time is historical research. If one claims to possess other means in addition to the instruments of historical criticism which are given priority over historical criticism in case of conflict, then one is led to contest the right of the historical method in principle.[30]

On the other hand Lüdemann himself expresses surprise[31] at the strength of Pannenberg's own claim in his *Systematic Theology* [32] that for him 'historical' does not mean 'historically provable' but 'actually occurred'; nothing is 'historically provable', Pannenberg continues, in such a way as to be beyond all doubt, for in the case of Jesus' resurrection this will remain a matter of dispute till the eschatological consummation. The claim of factuality merely implies the expectation that the content of this claim will stand up to historical scrutiny. Does this mean more than that it cannot be historically falsified? For then we would be back to the problem of the rigged game. But in fact Pannenberg seems, in a public debate with Herbert Braun, to have laid down what in his opinion would falsify this claim:

The traditions of Jesus' resurrection would be subject to evaluation as unhistorical if:

(a) the Easter traditions were demonstrable as *literarily second-ary constructions* in analogy to common comparative religious models not only in details, but also in their kernel,

(b) the *Easter appearances* were to correspond *completely* to the model of self-produced *hallucinations* (owing to organic peculiarities or medicines),

(c) the tradition of the *empty tomb* of Jesus were to be evaluated as a *late* (Hellenistic) *legend*.[33]

Whether all this can realistically, or at least with any certainty, be claimed not to apply to the resurrection of Jesus is another matter, and Lüdemann asks pertinently what would happen if Pannenberg's expectation did not stand up to this scrutiny. Would that then be the end of the Christian faith? To the question of the falsification of the historical form of Jesus upon which Christian faith is based, Pannenberg's reply is a commendably honest and candid 'Yes, it would be the end', even if he sees no grounds for apprehension that such a falsification would emerge in the foreseeable future.[34] It is another matter, however, whether in his eyes falsification of the story of Jesus' resurrection would be enough to spell such an end.

Jürgen Moltmann's stance is in many ways similar to that of Barth, in that he adopts the strategy of questioning the very concept of history which historical criticism is wont to use and which has been developed on the basis of experiences other than the raising of Jesus from the dead. Such an approach makes it impossible to regard any person or event in history as absolute, for it works on the basis of analogies. As a result he proposes that 'the historical question as to the historicity of the resurrection of Christ' should be 'expanded to include the questionability of the historical approach to history as such'. Thus

theology has the possibility of constructing its own concept of history on the basis of a theological and eschatological under-standing of the reality of the resurrection . . . Then the resurrection of Christ does not offer itself as an analogy to that which can be experienced any time and anywhere, but as an analogy to what is to come to all.[35]

And yet the accounts of the resurrection of Jesus do seem to offer at least a partial analogy to claims made, both in ancient times and more recently, for the appearance of one dead to friends or foes.[36] It may be granted that, if historically true, the resurrection of Jesus would cause us to revise our views of history, but first there is that hurdle of 'if historically true'. This seems to be a veritable dilemma: if the game has really altered, then of course new rules of play must be in force, but first there is the question whether there really is a new game, since to all appearances it is still being played in the same old way. This gives the impression that the new game, if there is one, must be a very private one of the theologians, which no one else may join in, despite the absolutist claims of the theologians that it is now universally and eternally valid.

(d) Just the rise of faith?

However, there are accounts of what is meant by the 'resurrection' of Jesus which seem at first sight to relieve us of the necessity and indeed the possibility of asking what happened. One can after all *deny that anything happened apart from the rise of faith and of the proclamation of Jesus and claim that these are alone significant.* So when, for instance, Bultmann denies that the resurrection is a historical event, he means by Christ's 'resurrection' a way of speaking of the significance of Christ's death:[37]

> Christ the crucified and risen one encounters us in the word of proclamation, and nowhere else. And faith in this word is the true faith of Easter. . . . The event of Easter, insofar as it can be referred to as historical event alongside of the cross, is nothing other than the emergence of faith in the risen one in which the proclamation has its origin. The event of Easter as the resurrection of Christ is not a historical event; the only

thing that can be comprehended as a historical event is the Easter faith of the first disciples.[38]

How this faith arose is shrouded in darkness, enveloped in legend; moreover, it is materially irrelevant.[39] Bultmann himself did not shun the formulation of his position as being that Jesus had risen into the kerygma, the Christian message and its proclamation, in that he understands the kerygma as eschatological event.[40]

Rightly, however, Marxsen objects to this on the grounds that 'risen' is then being used in such a way as to bear little resemblance to the original meaning of the term, particularly in the context of Jewish apocalyptic writings. Or if 'Jesus is risen' means nothing more than that Jesus' cause lives on and did not perish with him, that his activity goes on, as Marxsen himself formulated it,[41] then there might be little cause to penetrate behind the faith of the disciples and to ask what gave rise to it. For one can see with one's own eyes that Jesus' cause still lives on, since the Christian church still proclaims him as its Lord. But even then the question can be asked, perhaps even must be asked, why the first Christians believed that Jesus' cause lived on. For neither this belief nor their interpretation of the significance of the cross are self-evident or self-authenticating. One would like to know how and why they came to this conviction. This wish is not a matter of idle curiosity, but a wholly natural and legitimate one, if one, is invited to share their conviction and to live by it.[42]

That question remains even when, like Marxsen, one limits the initial decision to the one disciple, Peter.[43] What led him to such a decision?[44] Did he or the first disciples simply decide that Jesus' cause should live on? But is not such a scenario, thus crudely formulated, anachronistic, even grotesque? Is it really conceivable, for instance, that the first disciples met together and decided that what Jesus had set in motion was too valuable to be snuffed out by a little setback like his crucifixion? If that scenario seems too deliberately contrived to be plausible, then one has to come up with an alternative that leads to the same result, namely

that Jesus' cause should live on. Such a scenario might be convincing in the business world of today when the directors of a
company may decide to continue their operations in a particular
market or in a particular commodity despite initial losses, but this
kind of reasoning would be worlds apart from the situation in
which Jesus' followers found themselves after his death. So the
question remains: why did they go on? What persuaded them,
induced them, to persist in their allegiance and devotion to Jesus
after he had seemingly been thoroughly and utterly discredited
and disposed of?

(e) Re-enter the question of history

The traditions about Jesus' resurrection are therefore neither
removed from, nor immune to, the enquiries of historians,
however uncomfortable for Christian faith the probings and
questionings of these historians may be, and attempts to circumvent that uncomfortable necessity must be regarded with suspicion. They give the impression of an unwarranted special
pleading. Despite that, the tradition lives on that 'genuine'
Christian faith 'is certainly not dependent upon the course' of
historical research and 'cannot and should not be dependent
on the change and uncertainty of historical research'.[45] Yet
Bornkamm, from whom this quotation is taken, at the same time
also insists that, as the Gospels proclaim, 'faith does not begin
with itself but lives from past history' (23). But what status has
this 'past history' in the case of the resurrection of Jesus? That is
unfortunately not a question to which Bornkamm's book itself
seems to give us any clear and unequivocal answer: he says only
that the accounts of Easter are 'testimonies of faith, and not . . .
records and chronicles'. In these stories we are to seek 'the
message of Easter', and so presumably we should not seek
'history' there (183).

Eugen Drewermann seems in some respects to go even further
in his handling of Mark's account of the finding of the empty
tomb:[46] the mystery of the resurrection cannot be externally

ascertained; one can but believe it, and it can only be communicated in images and symbols. Non-verifiability does not logically entail non-falsifiability,[47] yet Drewermann's reference to 'images and symbols' suggests that, whatever 'resurrection' is, it is something extremely elusive and not responsive to factual questions.

But is it enough to be content with the 'message' of Easter, and can this message be impervious to historical questioning, particularly if the message is that something has happened and therefore a certain human response is called for? For here one must distinguish the (changed) lives of the followers of Jesus and the way in which they lived after Easter on the one hand, and their warrants for living in this way on the other. These warrants involved statements that are apparently statements of fact, like 'God has raised Jesus from the dead', 'Jesus is alive', perhaps even 'we shall be raised from the dead'. If these statements are not statements of fact, then one has to ask again what the warrants are for the life that is to be lived by Jesus' followers. It is true that each of these statements needs to be interpreted before one can decide whether it is true or not in the sense that we have decided is appropriate, but if no meaningful or credible sense can be found that corresponds to what we can see to be true, then the statements are, for all practical purposes, as good as falsified. It is true that statements about what will happen (like 'we shall be raised from the dead') are different in kind from statements about what has happened (like 'God has raised Jesus from the dead') or what is now the case (like 'Jesus is alive'): statements about a future event are by their nature not open to falsification. But if the prediction is based upon, made plausible by, events of the past or present, then falsification of reports of those past or present events will cause the predictions based upon them to seem ever more implausible.

Attempts to remove a Christian faith based on Jesus' resurrection from the influence of historical judgments therefore seem to me highly problematic. What is the content of statements such as 'God has raised Jesus from the dead' if they are in fact immune to all results of historical enquiry? Is this statement in fact either so vacuous or so multivalent and infinitely elastic that it can never be either verified or falsified, at least with respect to its ramifications in our world and in the experience of our fellow mortals? The value of such a statement then seems to me questionable; a rather pointless and assuredly meaningless shibboleth. So what light does or can a historical investigation shed on Jesus' resurrection?

2

Historical Problems in the
Resurrection Stories

(a) Disunity – strength or weakness?

If the Easter narratives are meant to be historical accounts of historical events, then it is disconcerting that one immediately comes up against a plethora of differences in the various accounts, some admittedly trivial, some less so. Critics have long been aware of them. Already in the latter part of the eighteenth century Reimarus could look back upon a whole series of attempts to come to terms with these differences and with their implications for the credibility of the accounts. One's first reaction is, therefore, to say that these accounts cannot all be correct, that much of them is inaccurate or false, and that recovery of the true course of events is going to be, on the most optimistic of estimates, extremely difficult, even if one shrinks back from Reimarus' own scathing denunciation of their claims. For the accounts give different answers, for example to the following, quite factual questions:[48]

* *Which women went to the tomb*: Mary of Magdala and 'the other Mary' (Matt. 28.1), or Mary of Magdala and Mary, the mother of James, and Salome (Mark 16.1), or Mary of Magdala and Joanna and Mary the mother of James and the rest (Luke 24.10), or just Mary of Magdala (John 20.1).[49]
* *When she or they went there*: before dawn (Matt. 28.1; John 20.1), or after (Mark 16.2).

- *Why she or they went there*: to see the tomb (Matt. 28.1), or to anoint the body (Mark 16.1; Luke 24.1).[50]
- *What she or they found there*: there was an earthquake and an angel rolled the stone away (Matt. 28.2), or the stone was already rolled away (Mark 16.4; Luke 24.2; John 20.1).[51]
- *Whom she or they found there*: an angel sitting on the rolled-back stone (Matt. 28.3), or 'a young man' (Mark 16.5), or two men in shining clothes (Luke 24.3),[52] or two angels (John 20.12).
- *What she or they were told by the person(s) at the tomb*: Jesus was risen and was going before the disciples to Galilee (Matt. 28.7; Mark 16.6–7), or just that Jesus was risen as he had told them in Galilee (Luke 24.6), or simply 'Woman, why are you weeping?' (John 20.13).
- *What she or they did subsequently*: told the disciples (implied in Matt. 28.8–9; Luke 24.10?) or Peter and 'the other disciple' (John 20.1–2), or told no one (Mark 16.8; contrast the shorter ending added later to Mark's Gospel: 'And they delivered all these instructions briefly to Peter and his companions . . .' [NEB]).
- *Who was the first to see the risen Jesus*: the women (Matt. 28.9),[53] Mary of Magdala (Mark 16.9 [a later addition]; John 20.14–17), or Peter (Luke 24.34).
- *Where the risen Jesus was seen*: in Jerusalem by the women and on a mountain in Galilee by the disciples (Matt. 28.9, 16–17), in Galilee (Mark 16.7, but only foretold), or in or near Jerusalem only (Luke 24.15ff; n.b. 24.49; Acts 1.4 confining the disciples to Jerusalem), or both in Jerusalem and on the Lake of Galilee (John 20–21).
- *To whom the risen Jesus appeared in Galilee and where:* to the eleven on or by a mountain (Matt. 28.16) or to seven disciples by the Lake of Galilee (John 21.2).

These and other differences are considerable, but this has not prevented attempts at reconciling them, amongst the first of which was the later addition to Mark, 16.9–20, which tries to conflate a number of these traditions along with other elements not found in the canonical Gospels. One can perhaps make some headway by such arguments as saying, quite plausibly, that each author did not always give *all* the details and information that were available and did not have to do so; thus, for instance, one could say that mentioning only Mary of Magdala does not preclude the presence of the other women mentioned (although the scene with the dialogue between Jesus and her is more difficult to visualize with others present). Yet in the end such attempts to salvage the accuracy of the accounts in their entirety run into intractable problems like Luke's exclusion of the possibility of appearances to the disciples in Galilee. His Gospel and the Acts of the Apostles simply leave no room for resurrection appearances to the disciples there.

Thus those critics who are not concerned to press the texts into a fundamentalist straitjacket recognize the disunity among the witnesses here. David Friedrich Strauss can serve as a forthright spokesman for such a view:

> Thus the various evangelical writers only agree as to a few of the appearances of Jesus after his resurrection; the designation of the locality in one excludes the appearances narrated by the rest; the determination of time in another leaves no space for the narrative of his fellow Evangelists; the enumeration of a third is given without any regard to the events reported by his predecessors; lastly, among several appearances recounted by various narrators, each claims to be the last, and yet has nothing in common with the others. Hence nothing but wilful blindness can prevent the perception that no one of the narrators knew and presupposed what another records; that each again had heard a different account of the matter; and that consequently at an early period, there were current only uncertain and very varied reports concerning the appearances of the risen Jesus.[54]

For Strauss, as for Reimarus before him, such contradictory reports could not be a true historical record; for Reimarus it was a deliberate falsification, for the disciples had in fact stolen Jesus' body; for Strauss they are not historical reports, but a theologoumenon or mythologoumenon stemming from the spontaneous 'psychological necessity of solving the contradiction between the ultimate fate of Jesus and their earlier opinion of him' (742).

Sometimes, however, this disunity can even be used apologetically as evidence for the diversity of traditions which differ on minor matters, yet together point in a single direction, which display, in other words, an impressive unity in their diversity. This in turn strengthens their credibility: they are in some measure independent witnesses and their accounts do not all stem from a single original and are not a carefully concocted and rehearsed 'official version' of events. A classic example of this sort of apologetic is Frank Morison's *Who Moved the Stone?*, which exhibits a rich and vivid imagination that makes for easy and entertaining reading (hence the popularity of the work), but has considerable dangers when one is handling material and questions of this sort.[55] For a start, evidence has a way of being invented, in something of the same manner as the apocryphal Gospels added legendary accretions to fill gaps in the canonical Gospels' stories: for Morison it is 'certain' that Mary collapsed at the time of Jesus' crucifixion (65; cf. 71: Mark's language is 'conclusive'!), and somehow Morison knows that the 'whole training and sympathies' of James, the brother of Jesus, inclined him towards endorsing the official, priestly view of his brother's ministry (128).[56] No wonder, then, that Morison is ready to supplement the Fourth Gospel by appeal to the apocryphal Gospel of Peter, which expressly says that Mary of Magdala took other women with her when she visited the tomb (74); yet this later account need be no more than a subsequent attempt at harmonization similar to Morison's own. On the other hand, some other evidence which cannot be so easily harmonized is passed over in silence: there is no mention of the disciples' having to stay in Jerusalem in Luke; instead it is assumed that they departed from the city to return later (e.g. 111). In contrast to this, however, Morison expressly acknowledges the divergent accounts of the number of people or beings whom the women found at the tomb, and labels as later embellishments of the story Matthew's angel and Luke's two figures at the tomb (182).

Yet here, too, we have to retain a sense of historical perspective, which I fear is gravely lacking in Morison's account. He reads the story from the perspective of the subsequent history of Christianity as a world religion, but for the Jewish authorities at the time, and above all for the Romans, what was taking place in Jerusalem would not have seemed world-shattering or even especially significant at all: this was yet another instance of a public disorder, not unparalleled in Pilate's hardly over-sensitive or tactful administration of his admittedly rather troublesome province, an incident involving mostly peasants, mere nobodies in Roman eyes and not very much more impressive to the Jewish authorities (cf. Acts 4.13). Neither they nor Pilate would have seen Jesus as a 'first-class political prisoner', as Morison does (136); that is the language one would use of members of the Roman senatorial order or possibly of the provincial aristocracy, not of Jesus and his following of nobodies. Nor for that matter is the Acts of the Apostles an 'official history', 'universally accepted from early times' (104–5), at least to judge from the dearth of references to it or appeals to its authority before the latter part of the second century. And it is going rather far to claim that we know the eleven apostles better than any group in antiquity (113), especially considering how little we know about some of them. A sober historical assessment is not helped by inflated claims like these. But, equally, a 'sober historical assessment' is going to have to operate according to the criteria appropriate to the historical investigation of material of that period; Morison is by no means alone in having failed to preserve a sense of proportion or in having strayed into an anachronistic application of criteria that would be more appropriate to a better documented period of history when different expectations as to what was possible in history, and how history should be recounted, prevailed.

(b) An incoherent story?

If the harmonizing of the Gospels' accounts with one another is fraught with problems, it seems to me even more serious that there is, within each of the accounts, a measure of internal *incoherence* of one sort or another. By this I do not mean so much the puzzling way in which Mark's Gospel ends, with the women terrified and telling no one and no actual account of an appearance of the risen Jesus, but just mentioning the message that he would appear. There have been any number of attempts to solve that mystery, of varying degrees of sophistication.[57]

What concerns me more at this point is the way in which the stories of the appearances are told, particularly when one tries to visualize what these experiences might have been like to their human participants – and it *is* valid to pose the question like this, for the experiences did, after all, affect human beings: they were not so other-worldly as to bypass our world entirely, nor were they always so other-worldly as to bowl over those affected so completely that they were quite incapable of registering what they were seeing, even if they were usually and understandably filled with surprise and wonder. There is, for instance, the failure of Mary of Magdala, and more strikingly of the two disciples on the road to Emmaus, to recognize Jesus. Mary's failure *could* have been due to the early hour and inadequate light, and after it was all only an initial and perhaps momentary inability to recognize him, but the failure of the two disciples on the way to Emmaus to recognize him is much more puzzling.[58] Their contact with the unknown stranger is longer, ostensibly long enough for Jesus to explain to them all those scriptural passages in the Old Testament which referred to him (Luke 24.27). The light is presumably adequate, since evening is only approaching when they arrive at their destination and invite the stranger to eat with them (24.29). If they were from the ranks of the 'apostles' (24.10 with 13) who had known Jesus well, this failure to recognize Jesus is mystifying. What did Jesus now look like, that they failed to recognize him? Like another ordinary human being, but different in appearance from Jesus? But what of the scars of his recent ordeal, the results of scourging and crucifixion, the wounds in his hands and side which were apparently there for Thomas to touch in John 20.25, 27? Karl-Martin Fischer's attribution of the failure of the disciples to recognize Jesus to the fact that Jesus was disfigured through suffering is hardly satisfactory:[59] such a disfigurement must surely have raised further questions as to the identity of the stranger and what had happened to him.

In the light of these difficulties in the story it is small wonder that when a group of actors come to re-enact the story of the Emmaus road in the film *Jesus of Montreal* the actor who plays the risen Jesus appears in the dark and wrapped up more thoroughly than a woman in *purdah*; only so could the disciples' inability to recognize him at first have the faintest claim to verisimilitude or credibility. With this portrayal contrast Rembrandt's 'Christ at Emmaus' (a detail of which is reproduced on the cover of this book), in which the two travellers walk on, seemingly not yet having noticed the incandescently glowing figure just behind them! Luke 24.16 seems to refer to a miraculous blinding, which can be regarded as a tacit admission of the very real problem of credibility here. The recognition of this problem is also already implicit in a later addition to the ending of Mark's Gospel, where a summarizing version of the story of these two disciples is found: 'Later he appeared *in a different form* to two of them while they were on their way into the country.'[60] Yet it is not expressly said that this different form was the reason for their failure to recognize him; indeed, this failure is not mentioned either, for the next verse simply describes how they reported this news to the others, but they did not believe them.[61]

Or was Jesus transfigured and glorious, already partaking of a *new being* that is not of this age? But then the disciples' failure to spot this would have been puzzling. (And one would think that as soon as Rembrandt's incandescent figure just referred to had caught up with the two disciples they must have seen this immediately.) If he were transfigured and glorious, then his glory must have been incognito and hidden, only manifesting itself in strange features of incorporeality like the ability to pass through closed doors (John 20.19, 26), yet apparently compatible with such corporeal features as the ability to be touched (Matt. 28.9; John 20.27) or to touch (Luke 24.30, 38) or to eat (Luke 24.43).

The difficulties which these features of the various accounts present can all too readily be seen in the brave attempt to grapple with them in C. S. Lewis's classic study, *Miracles*: he fully recognizes the 'earthiness' of the Gospels' accounts of a corporeal Jesus who eats boiled fish (Luke 24.43), but, confronted by the stories of Jesus 'appearing' and 'disappearing' and passing through locked doors, he contends that this is evidence of Jesus' 'wholly new mode of being' (177). 'The New Nature is, in the most troublesome way, interlocked at some points with the Old' (183). This is no ghost from the underworld (174), although he concedes that features of the accounts like the passing through doors could lead one to think so (175). This risen bodily existence of Jesus transcends the mode of being of the old order, just as features of Jesus' earlier life, like his walking on the water and the raising of Lazarus (179), anticipated the final disclosure of the new order. And certainly he could appeal to Paul in support of his view that the new corporeal existence of Jesus was qualitatively different from what had gone before, for in I Cor. 15.35ff., as we shall see, Paul's stress is all on the difference of the new, 'spiritual' body from the old, perishable mortal body.

However, when Lewis appeals to the account of Jesus' transfiguration as another foretaste of the new order (182), questions begin to surface, for then the disciples had no problem in recognizing Jesus. In stories like the encounter on the way to Emmaus, however, it is apparent that, if Jesus is transfigured, he is transfigured incognito, and one has to ask whether a concealed transfiguration is a meaningful concept. Or is this an inward transfiguration in the midst of this apparently unchanged world such as Paul seems to contemplate for Christians in II Cor. 3.18 ('we are being transformed from glory to glory'; contrast Phil.

3.21)? And it is a consequence of Lewis' taking these accounts at face value that he feels that he has to insist that Jesus' ascension is also to be taken at face value: if the appearances of Jesus were real, 'then something happened to [Jesus' risen body] after it ceased to appear' (178). Yet the risen body of Jesus had apparently experienced no difficulties in appearing and disappearing again on a number of occasions previously; so why was some special disappearance called for? For it was not even the final disappearance, if we are to believe the account of Paul's experience of the risen Jesus on another road, that to Damascus. Luke's account, moreover, presents its own cluster of problems, which are further aggravated when one seeks to reconcile Luke 24 with Acts 1. Are we, for instance, to think of Jesus being permanently there on earth for forty days or constantly leaving and then returning to his heavenly existence after each individual appearance?[62] And was it forty days of appearances, as Acts suggests, or only one, which seems to be the impression given in Luke 24? But at least Luke's account removes the problem of relating these two versions of the resurrection appearances and the ascension to Paul's experience on the way to Damascus, for, as we shall see, he, unlike Paul, gives no hint that he considered these events to be of the same kind or order. It is the earthly realism of the resurrection appearances of Luke 24 that, if anything, makes the separate event of the ascension necessary; not, however, so that Jesus may just finally disappear, for he has disappeared more than once already, but to explain why this disappearance really is final.

So in the last analysis it is hard to believe that such fascinating speculations are more than that: they are an edifice built on foundations of sand or something yet more insubstantial; they are the stuff of which science fiction is made, but they seem to have left our world, the world of the crucified Jesus, behind.[63] If Hans Küng is right to insist that the reality of the resurrection is 'completely *intangible* and *unimaginable*',[64] and there is much to be said for the view that indeed it ought to be, if true, then such accounts, in the Gospels and in modern apologists, can well be considered thoroughly inappropriate. Nor do they solve the problems of the disciples' failure to recognize Jesus.

It is also possible to attribute these puzzling features to the *story-teller's art*. So, for instance, J. I. H. McDonald interprets this account of Jesus' encounter with the disciples on the way to Emmaus within his general treatment of the resurrection narratives, in which he draws upon literary criticism and especially reader-response criticism.[65] He points us to the structure of the Emmaus road story, artistically constructed to pivot around Luke 24.28–29, and to the concerns of Luke in telling the story as he does: he seeks to demonstrate the reality of the risen Christ and 'to recapitulate basic motifs of the Gospel' – the fulfilment of Scripture in Christ's suffering, death and resurrection, and the forgiveness of sins (107). The experience of revelation is 'accomplished through fellowship, through the interaction of speech and study', and leads to a new way of life (109). This whole account is part of McDonald's attempt to enter 'the world of the text, in which the reader is invited to participate' (2). But does one not have to ask whether this world is fantasy or not? Will fantasy save us and our world? Is it not still the task of the critic, having entered the world of the text, and having experienced that world, to exit from it again in order to ask whether what he or she has seen there is credible and has anything to say to the world around. It may be true that ultimately the resurrection of Jesus may prove to be paradox and mystery (143), but at least one must show that these rather more respectable descriptions are more appropriate than labelling the account as wild delusion. Has the narrator told a story that is merely entertaining or edifying, or does the story correspond to something in the world as it is? We may learn much from novels, but still need to sift out fact from fiction. That belongs, for instance, to the critical evaluation of historical novels, if not to the reading of them purely for the sake of pleasure. For we often hope not just to be entertained, but also to learn something from them about the way of life and the circumstances of a time other than our own, and there the question is relevant: was it really like that then?

However, it is appropriate to note what McDonald was setting out to do. He acknowledged the impetus given to his study by his colleague James Mackey, who had contributed to the volume a foreword more notable than most of its species. For Mackey set McDonald an agenda, as it were, being discontented with the view that resurrection life is something to be found in a life beyond the grave: if that better life is only to be found there why, he asks, has God given us our inferior life here? So Mackey wants to walk through this mortal life in the knowledge of Christ's risen life now, knowing that Jesus knew that life too in his earthly life and in his death, so that he too may 'live and die in the inestimable happiness of hope' (viii). But that leaves it unclear whether he is only really interested in resurrection life now instead of any resurrection life in an existence to come, or whether he seeks both the one and the other. Or, put another way, can he enjoy that 'inestimable happiness of hope' without that hope being for something beyond this life? For clearly, very clearly, the New Testament texts which McDonald handles, however much they may proclaim resurrection in our present earthly existence, also point to an existence beyond the grave. It remains, however, unclear whether McDonald, in seeking a witness in the texts to a this-worldly experience of resurrection life, is reinterpreting in this-worldly terms all that they say about a future, post-mortal life, or merely emphasizing a this-worldly dimension in addition to an other-worldly one. In other words: is his hermeneutical programme a reductionist one that reduces all statements about another, future world to this-worldly ones, or is he merely attempting to correct a one-sided concentration on the other world? Is the relation between this-worldly elements and the other-worldly ones an 'either-or' or a 'both-and'? At least it is clear that McDonald renounces any interest in the presence or absence of the bones of Jesus in the soil of Palestine. He also interprets 'the body of Christ's resurrection' in corporate terms as the community of the new age (44). But is it fair to claim that Mark is reinterpreting resurrection in somewhat similar terms, using 'the language of resurrection to denote transcendence', indicating that 'Jesus' effective power and presence are not located in the tomb but in continuing experience, in the ongoing life of the disciple-group in Galilee' (72)? Is this evangelist really saying that 'the transcendent Lord is immanent in "the body" of his followers' and nothing more?[66] I wish that I could believe that Mark really thought in anything like those terms.

Even less can I believe that Luke thought like that; as McDonald grants, one of the aims of this evangelist is to demonstrate the reality of Jesus' resurrection, and he does so in a way that, as we have seen, opens up all sorts of problems: problems of coherence and credibility. It is perhaps true that Luke is also concerned to show the meaning of Christians' eating at Christ's table at any time as an encounter with the risen Christ in which he is revealed as the crucified one who is now risen, and as the one to whose suffering the Old Testament pointed. But can one with integrity concentrate only on this dimension of Luke's account and forget about the crassly physical manner in which that encounter is portrayed, particularly if one admits that that way of portraying things is no accident, but has been deliberately selected by the author to make a point? One cannot then say that the author has left these puzzling features in the story because he was concerned to make some different point; what puzzles *us* is precisely something that Luke sought to emphasize. But is my concern with what Luke was trying to do here a legitimate one? Or is any reading of the text equally valid, however little connection it may have with the author's concerns? If not, if the text, and perhaps even what its author meant to say in it, exercise any control, then McDonald might have been on surer ground had he rested his case on his (far more plausible) reading of the Fourth Gospel as saying that the Spirit 'is the channel by which the risen Jesus appeared to his disciples' (133; cf. 139). But even here perhaps not only that is meant by the evangelist.[67]

Whatever we may judge that the Gospels' writers, and Luke in particular, were trying to achieve, it is still legitimate to ask whether the end they were seeking justifies the means which they used. Or was there the risk that how they tackled their task might gravely mislead their readers? For it is a feature of Luke in particular that what one might think were other-worldly phenomena take on a remarkably tangible form in his hands: the Spirit descends on Jesus at his baptism 'in bodily form' like a dove (Luke 3.22) and comes to the disciples at Pentecost in the likeness of flames and with an audible rushing sound like a gale of wind (Acts 2.2–3). That is vivid imagery, but it cannot be dismissed as just imagery. There is for Luke a bodily form for which the nearest image is a dove; there is indeed something visible at Pentecost which he likens to flames of fire: it comes with a sound which he compares to the wind, a sound which apparently drew a large crowd (Acts 2.6). But was there in fact something that could be seen and heard with the senses at all? This is surely 'myth' in the sense of describing the other-worldly in this-worldly, 'objectifying' terms; it is talking 'about the unworldly as worldly, the gods as human'; it is 'mythology in which what is unworldly and divine appears as what is worldly and human or what is transcendent appears as what is immanent'.[68] The mystery of the coming of the Spirit is something public enough to attract crowds.

Now it has very properly been pointed out that it is hard to dispense with 'mythology' in talking of the divine: if the other-worldly is too other-worldly to be described in this-worldly terms, at least analogically, then it cannot be described at all. But Luke's language, in particular in Luke 24, runs the grave risk of implying that this this-worldly language which he uses is more than just an analogy, more than just the nearest that we can ever get to describing the indescribable. He has made the other-worldly a part of our world, and we need to ask whether in the last analysis this is any more credible than when the Greeks described Zeus descending in animal form to satisfy his lusts, or whether Luke's story-telling instincts are any more to be followed than those of the Lycaonians when they assumed that Barnabas and Paul were respectively Zeus and Hermes come to earth in human form (Acts 14.12). If we believe neither the Greeks nor the Lycaonians, why should we follow Luke's account, or indeed those of Matthew and John, who can also describe Jesus' appearance to his followers in bodily, seemingly this-worldly terms, even if they do not place so much emphasis on its corporeality?

Yet for many the resurrection stories of the Gospels are normative. *They* represent what is meant by 'resurrection' or the 'resurrection of Jesus' in the Christian tradition, and to call their basic historicity and factuality into question seems to many to undermine the very basis of Christian faith. To refuse to take these stories at face value or to suggest that 'resurrection' might mean something different, not just to us, but perhaps even to other New Testament writers like Paul, can be seen as a thoroughly subversive move. But the stories cannot just, on the other hand, be written off or discounted as pure fiction: there are too many puzzling features about them which are unlikely to be sheer invention, and aspects of them seem to mesh with the historical in such a way that they are indeed woven into the fabric of the history of the early church. There seems to be more to the 'resurrection-event' than just a collection of stories.

3

The Reality of the
'Resurrection-Event'

As suggested in the latter part of the previous chapter, I do not think that the accounts of Jesus' resurrection can be written off as simply 'myth' (if one uses the term in a rather negative sense), nor can they be regarded simply as stories, as narratives which create their own world and invite us to enter that world and live and breathe in it. There is, in short, more to them than that, for there are certain features of them which tie them so firmly to their world, their real and historical world, and to their equally historical context, that they are anchored in this real world and in the real history of that time and of the Jesus movement, both before and after the time of Jesus' death. They offer certain answers to questions which that history poses, answers whose reality and historicity must be taken seriously, for they are answers which, if we do not accept them, may leave us struggling to find satisfactory alternatives. That means that to treat these accounts as mere inventions, mere flights of fancy or of the imagination does not do full justice to important aspects of them. They are meshed with historical reality and historical questions in such a way that their claim to tell a historical story has to be taken with full seriousness. For these events which we call the appearances of the risen Jesus to his followers, whatever they were, the happenings which these accounts purport to describe, were indeed also events of the real world, and like other events in this real world they left their indelible marks and traces in our world. Something really happened in our world that has left our world altered, that has shaped our world subsequently. These stories cannot be set aside as stories to be told just for the sake of the telling or for the sake of their impact on their hearers. They claim to explain this something that has altered our world as it has indeed been altered. For there are features of these accounts which defy explanation as mere story and which compel us to take them more seriously as accounts of what happened, features which seem in some measure to establish their claim to historicity.

(a) The coming to faith of the disciples

The Gospels portray the arrest, trial and crucifixion of Jesus as leaving the disciples in disarray and dismay: they run away (Mark 14.50 par.); they deny him (Mark 14.66–72 parr.); an outsider must assume responsibility for Jesus' burial (Mark 15.43);[69] they skulk in fear behind closed doors (John 20.19); they react with sceptical incredulity to the first reports of resurrection appearances (Luke 24.11; John 20.25);[70] they resume their previous occupation as fishermen as if trying to forget all about Jesus as a painful but now past episode in their lives or as if nothing had happened, as if they had never been commissioned by Jesus (John 21.3; contrast 20.21).[71]

Now it is true that some have argued that this gives a misleading impression: the disciples really expected Jesus' imminent resurrection, and the accounts of their dejection and despair are simply an artful ploy to offset the thrill of the resurrection appearances, a dark backcloth against which the brilliance of the resurrection shines more brightly. Belief in the resurrection is made prior to any traditions of appearances or the discovery of the empty tomb. The resurrection of Jesus was, it was argued by Klaus Berger and by Rudolph Pesch in 1973 (although ten years later the latter was to retract this suggestion as untenable, yet in his opinion fruitful), to be expected on the basis of Old Testament and Jewish expectations of the death, vindication and exaltation of the righteous prophet or the righteous wise man.[72]

Pesch summed up this view in retrospect in his 1983 article:[73] the concept of the resurrection of certain men of God was then current in the tradition of the martyrdom and resurrection of eschatological, prophetic figures, a tradition that had already been applied to the Baptist, so that Jesus' disciples were able to comprehend their master's fate with the help of this tradition. Antipas' fear that Jesus was John the Baptist risen from the dead (Mark 6.16) gave voice to a common expectation at that time which is known to us from many other passages. Or rather two common expectations, for, according to Berger, this tradition existed in two forms: martyrdom would be followed by the coming of the son of man, or the death of two prophetic figures would be followed by their resurrection and exaltation to heaven.

One problem with this theory was that hardly any of the evidence cited is pre-Christian and most of it is Christian. One possible exception is the Apocalypse of Elijah, in which the 'shameless one' slays Elijah and Enoch and leaves their bodies in the market-place; after four days they rise again (4.15).[74] Yet, while Nützel holds this account to be pre-Christian in origin, stemming from Egypt in the first century BCE,[75] others like O. S. Wintermute and K. H. Kuhn see here Christian influence, above all of Rev 11.8–9, in this section of this work.[76] And even if Nützel were correct, he rightly sees that a single piece of evidence from pre-Christian Egypt is hardly sufficient to establish that there was such a general and widespread expectation with regard to eschatological figures in Palestine at the time of Jesus (87). Some of the evidence does not prove what it was meant to either: the Lives of the Prophets (probably from the first century CE)[77] speak of the deaths of the various prophets and their burial, but not of their resurrection, apart from the hope of a general resurrection that comes to expression in them.[78] And one pre-Christian text which is of central importance for the concept of the suffering righteous one, the Wisdom of Solomon, mentions no resurrection of the righteous. The vindication of the righteous in this work consists in God's receiving their souls into the divine presence. And should Mark 6.16, where Herod Antipas, hearing of Jesus, supposes that he is the beheaded John the Baptist, risen from the dead, be historical or at least possess historical verisimilitude, then presumably all that is meant there is John's return to this-worldly life.[79] Nor was Antipas supposed to be predicting the future resurrection of John; he was ostensibly trying to explain the appearance of another figure, who seemed sufficiently similar to John to make Antipas' belief seem plausible.

Here, as in the question of the rise of the Easter faith of the disciples, it is important to distinguish between a tradition that is able to shed light on what has already happened and one that makes it possible to predict what will happen before it does. Had the latter existed, then the disciples could indeed have expected the resurrection of Jesus. Were this exegetical tradition, on the other hand, only able to illuminate the events of the end of Jesus' life subsequently, making the disciples wise after the event, so to speak, then the initial despair and hopelessness of the disciples and their apparent incomprehension become all the more intelligible. For the case for the existence of such an expectation which would have prepared them for Jesus' fate had to be built up by fitting together a variety of texts of different provenance and character, and it is far easier to see them as pointing towards such an expectation once one knows what the expectation is, namely that Jesus, who was both righteous and regarded as a prophet, did actually suffer death and was believed to have risen from the dead. It is debatable whether anyone without this advantage of hindsight would or could have predicted such a thing happening.[80]

Ulrich B. Müller, on the other hand, appeals to U. Kellermann's study of II Maccabees 7 and argues that there existed a 'special expectation of the raising of individual martyrs after their death, that had no eschatological significance'.[81] He therefore regards it as possible that, in the belief in Jesus' resurrection, this expectation of the immediate vindication of selected individuals was combined with the expectation of a more general resurrection at the end. Now it is true that in II Maccabees the martyrs have already drunk of God's 'everflowing life' (7.36); not so clear is whether the expectation of resurrection found in this book also refers to something immediately following death or whether the time of a more general resurrection is meant. Here Müller leans heavily on Kellermann's interpretation of II Macc. 7 as emending Daniel 12's promise of an earthly resurrection to the heavenly resurrection of the martyrs after death.[82] Nor does it help to compare here Wisdom 3.1–6; 4.7–19, for there it is, as we have seen, the *souls* of the righteous who are with God (3.1). Nor is the resurrection hope expressed in II Macc. 7 with features like an empty tomb (the chapter shows no interest in the burial of the martyrs or in the disposal of their mangled bodies) or appearances of the ones who had just died. Müller can, however, point to the dream-vision of the martyred Onias in II Macc. 15.12–16 (*Entstehung*, 62), Josephus' mention of appearances of dead heroes who have fallen in battle (*Bell.* 6.47), and the vision of Job's slain children in Testament of Job 40.3, as well as *CIL* VI.3 no. 21521, even though this last text has nothing to do with Jewish martyrs. The pious Jewish readers of II Maccabees must simply believe that a just God has taken the cruelly tortured martyrs up into heaven. But Jesus' disciples were evidently not content with that. Was that because it was so much disputed that Jesus counted as a pious martyr at all, or was it because their Jewish contemporaries (perhaps even the author of II Maccabees) only expected any resurrection at the end and they were claiming more than this?

At any rate, Müller's account offers a revised version of the theory of Berger and Pesch, a version which is less dependent on Christian and post-Christian sources. He sees a confluence of various traditions and influences, that of the exaltation of martyrs to heaven following their death, as just mentioned, but also that of the suffering of the righteous; that of the presence, in Jesus' preaching of God's reign, of something more than all that his predecessors had offered and that of the conviction that God's reign had come in Jesus' ministry – all of these, Müller feels, could have provided the context within which Jesus' disciples would have understood his death, and the shock of that death provided the impulse to pick up the tradition of the vindication of the martyrs through resurrection, even when this belief was not then current in all circles of Palestinian Jewish society. (And it is to be noted that in this account Jesus' death remains a shock, with which his followers must come to terms.) The parallels to the visions of the resurrected Jesus which Müller has cited are, on the other hand, of doubtful relevance in the milieu of Jesus' disciples, as he admits:

> The literary use of a dream-vision (as in II Macc. 15) or of some other account of a vision (Testament of Job 40) may be a means to express a 'theological idea' that is ultimately based on the possibility of a visionary seeing of a dead one which lay to hand in the ancient world, but a possibility which can hardly be taken as a reliable pointer to the categories of interpretation available in those Jewish circles from which Jesus' disciples come (63).

As a result he prefers to see the background to these visions in the activities of seers in that crisis-ridden time who claimed to have seen visions or dream-visions, or to have ascended into heaven. A similar combination to theirs, of reflection, interpretation and visionary claims, is to be found in Paul's visionary experience of the risen Jesus as the conclusion of a process of reflection which resulted in his deciding for that faith which he had hitherto sought to destroy (64).

Similarly, the disciples had sought to come to terms with Jesus' death, and their reflections are not only to be understood as a process of grieving (as in Lüdemann's account), even if this does not lead to saying farewell to the departed one but to a creative vision of the risen Jesus, but are also to be seen as in the first instance cognitive. It is at this point that expectations for the fate of martyrs and righteous ones flow together with the recollection of the message of Jesus that God's reign was already being realized in his ministry, and it is 'almost probable' that the resurrection of the dead was part and parcel of the disciples'

Jewish concept of the reign of God (70). But most of all it was what Jesus had already preached and done that paved the way for this new insight:

> the only plausible basis for [the disciples'] 'resurrection faith' is that glimpse which Jesus had already given them of the arrival of the reign of God who causes the divine power to prevail over all negative powers of this world (79),

just as Jesus himself had expressed his confidence that he would participate in the festive meal of God's kingdom (Mark 14.25).[83] If that is a historically plausible account of the rise of their 'resurrection faith', then it raises acutely the question of the validity of the cognitive insights that the disciples won through this process of reflection, and that is an issue that will loom ever larger in this study.

Or there is the remarkable account of Jesus' resurrection by the Jewish scholar, Pinchas Lapide, who was here heavily dependent on the views of Albert Schweitzer. He regarded it as so necessary that the son of man's rising and parousia should follow his death that Jesus' disciples were horrified, not at the death, but at what failed to happen immediately afterwards. For they had expected that he would be immediately transformed into the awaited son of man. Therefore the cause of their flight may not have been his death as such, but what failed to materialize on Golgotha following his death.[84] As Pharisaically schooled Jews, for that is how Lapide rather daringly, but misleadingly, views them, they could not believe that their beloved teacher would ever be deserted by the God of Israel, even in his death. Yet despite that, Lapide goes on to say that most of Jesus' friends believed his death to be the end of him (85) and that the desire to anoint Jesus' body proves that no resurrection was expected (96). That seems nearer the truth, for one would otherwise have to explain how this expectation could have arisen. No non-Christian text speaks of the resurrection of the son of man (which would imply the view, remarkable for Jewish ears, that the son of man had first died) or of resurrection as the son of man. Any appropriation of the son of man traditions to interpret the fate of Jesus involves a considerable reworking of those traditions to render them applicable to Jesus. That reworking and appropriation are only really conceivable after the events of Jesus' end had unfolded, including the rise of the belief that Jesus had appeared to them after his death.[85]

It is true that Jesus is portrayed in the Gospels as foretelling his passion and his resurrection (Mark 8.31; 9.31; 10.34; 14.28, etc.), and one would therefore expect the disciples to be eagerly awaiting the fulfilment of these predictions. However, not all are prepared to take those predictions at face value as the very words of the earthly Jesus; many see them, as well as the more detailed predictions of the passion (esp. Mark 10.34 parr.), as prophecies after the event, written with the advantage of hindsight. If there is a historical nucleus to these predictions, it may be nothing more specific than the bald prediction, with a hint of a play on words, that 'the son of man is to be given into the hands of men' (Luke 9.44).[86] That is hardly a particularly confident or hopeful assertion. It would, however, be consonant with the view that, although John the Baptist and Jesus may have known of the belief in the general resurrection of the dead, it played no role in their message(s); for them salvation or judgment concerned the living, and the proclamation of salvation or judgment concerned this world and the present life.[87] The coming of God's reign need not involve a new heaven and a new earth and the attendant resurrection of the dead; it can unfold in this world (as indeed could the resurrection, if one's vision of the future world is an earthly one). And perhaps in the light of this one can better explain that feature of Jesus' teaching to which Pheme Perkins draws attention, 'the paucity of resurrection language in the teaching of Jesus', a paucity which, in her opinion, 'makes it impossible to explain the centrality of resurrection in later Christian preaching by appeal to the teaching of Jesus'.[88]

There is, in short, much to be said for the Gospels' portrayal of the disciples as despairing and despondent, as very far from confidently expecting the resurrection of the crucified Jesus.[89]

And had they previously expected it in the manner of II Macc. 7, then it would seem that they had forgotten their martyrology in the heat of the moment (and Jesus too, to judge from the cry of dereliction in Mark 15.34 par.). Or was this expectation one that only occurred to them subsequently? The resurrection 'appearances' then become more like visualizations of an already present conviction about the present status of Jesus, a conviction that has arisen, not because of the appearances, but because of the appropriation of a particular theological tradition within Judaism as an interpretative key to unlock the mystery of Jesus' fate. Far likelier, therefore, is the assumption that the disciples were taken by surprise by the turn of events and that nothing that Jesus had said had really in fact prepared them for what was to come.[90]

That would be hardly surprising if Jesus himself had died without any such confident expectation of a happy outcome. The agonized cry of dereliction in Mark 15.34 par., 'My God, my God, why have you forsaken me?', speaks in favour of that. For Alistair Kee argues with a good deal of persuasiveness that Jesus died without any certainty of a happy outcome and 'without any belief that he would soon rise from the dead'.[91] The word 'soon' is, however, important here, for it is not so much open to doubt that Jesus could or would have predicted his ultimate vindication and that by resurrection;[92] that was, after all, an expectation which was widespread in accounts of the martyrs of the Maccabean uprising two centuries before. But there that vindication lay in the future, at the close of the present age, in the midst of, and as part of, a general resurrection of all people, or, in some traditions, at least of all the righteous; there was no precedent for the preliminary resurrection of a single righteous figure as the first-fruits of the coming general resurrection while the world still, to all appearances, continued on its usual, sin-laden course.[93] Had Jesus predicted such a destiny for himself with any clarity it would have been quite remarkable and attention-grabbing,[94] and the failure of the disciples to be prepared for it when it happened would indeed have been equally remarkable. So there is much to be said for the picture which Kee paints of

Jesus wrestling in Gethsemane with the fear of the unknown, a scene in which neither he nor his disciples expected any sequel, or at least any immediate sequel, to his death.

Yet there was a sequel: the Jesus movement, which had seemed to come to a halt, gathered momentum once more. It is, however, that starting up again which points to something having happened, rather than the progress made once things had got started again, for it has been pointed out that other movements, like that of Islam, made equally dramatic progress once they had been launched.[95] Where Christianity differs is in this dramatic recovery from what had seemed like a crushing defeat. Hans Küng makes this contrast explicit:

> we are faced with the *historical enigma of the emergence . . . of Christianity*. How different this was from the gradual, peaceful propagation of the teachings of the successful sages, Buddha and Confucius; how different also from the largely violent propagation of the teachings of the victorious Muhammad. . . . How different, after a complete failure and a shameful death, were the spontaneous emergence and almost explosive propagation of this message and community in the very name of the defeated leader. After the disastrous outcome of this life, what gave the initial impetus to that unique world-historical development: a truly world-transforming religion emerging from the gallows where a man was hanged in shame?[96]

Something must surely have happened to effect this change. Something must have happened in between, which in a short time not only provoked a complete reversal of their attitude, but also enabled them to engage in renewed activity and to found the primitive Christian community. This 'something' is the historical kernel of the Christian faith.[97] Yet, as we shall see, it is by no means certain what this 'something' was that must have occasioned this reversal.

*(b) The subsequent celebration of the resurrection by the church
on the first day of the week*

It could easily be overlooked, and often is, how significant is the
fact that the first Christians chose to celebrate the first day of the
week as their special day of celebration and meeting together; it
is true that many Jewish Christians may have continued to
observe the Jewish sabbath also, but we find the necessity for
the observance of the sabbath being disputed (Col. 2.16) and
references to Christians meeting together on the first day of the
week (Acts 20.7). In all probability this is already presupposed by
Paul's instructions in I Cor. 16.2 on gathering funds for the
collection for the Jerusalem church, although it is admittedly
each individual Christian who is to store up what she or he has
laid aside; at the very least this text points to the special
significance of this day for Christians, even if the instruction
does not necessarily presuppose that the Christian community
gathered together on this day.[98]

Yet at the same time it needs to be noted just how awkward
and inconvenient this must have been for the first Christians,
for it was not until the state recognition of Christianity under
Constantine that any official provision could or would be made
for the observance of the first day of the week as a special day for
rest or worship. It is thus no surprise that one early Christian
document, the Didascalia, has to urge Christians not to put the
necessities of their this-worldly life before God's word and their
duty to meet with the rest of the church on the Lord's Day.[99]
Similarly Tertullian had to warn his fellow-Christians not to give
the devil scope by giving priority to their daily business.[100]
Although these references appear at a somewhat later period, the
problem which they attest must have been there from the start.
Christians' neighbours – and in many cases their masters – would
have expected it to be 'business as usual' on Sundays. And if this
was a problem for those who were self-employed, it was an even
more acute one for those who were slaves, for, while most in the
Graeco-Roman world knew of the sanctity of the seventh day for

the Jews, and some concessions were made to Jewish scruples about violating this day, no such recognition existed for the observance of the first day of the week.

What impelled the early Christians to hold this day special? Other explanations have been offered, but they seem implausible in comparison with the very obvious explanation that this day was venerated because it was affirmed that on it Christians had first encountered the risen Jesus and had, moreover, experienced his presence as they ate together.[101] 'Therefore,' affirms the Epistle of Barnabas in the second century, 'we joyfully celebrate the eighth day, on which Jesus rose from the dead and, after being disclosed to us, ascended into the heavens.'[102] In the mid-second century Justin Martyr notes that Christians meet together 'on the day of the sun', for 'it is the first day, on which God . . . created the world, and the same day on which Jesus Christ our saviour rose from the dead. . . . [on this day] he appeared to his apostles and disciples and taught them . . .'.[103] The very name which Christians came to give to this day, the Lord's Day (κυριακή [ἡμέρα]), points to the associations which it had with the events of Jesus' life, for, as Ignatius puts it, writing to the Magnesian Christians, it is the day 'on which . . . our life arose through [the Lord] and his death' (9.1). It was that day on which 'he was declared to be God's Son in power by a resurrection of one dead' (Rom 1.4) and it was only fitting that the day should be named after him.[104]

It is the more striking that it was this day which was remembered and commemorated by the celebration of the Lord's Supper, since, as W. Rordorf notes, early Christians chose it rather than the Thursday, the day of the week on which Jesus had celebrated his last meal with his disciples. So, he infers, 'the Easter meal was decidedly more important for the tradition of the primitive community than the memory of Jesus' last meal'.[105] The evidence, too, seems to be that early Christians celebrated their communal meals on the Sunday evening,[106] and it is then that we find the Gospels describing the risen Jesus eating with his disciples (Luke 24.28–32, 36–43; John 20.19–29). It would be hard to argue conclusively that one was dependent on, derivative from, the other, but it is at least possible that the experiences of that Easter evening gave rise to and nourished the subsequent practice of the Christian church, rather than that the Gospel stories are simply a projection backwards of a later liturgical practice that arose for other reasons.

(c) The tradition that Jesus arose 'on the third day'

There is a persistent tradition, found as early as I Cor. 15.4,[107] that Jesus had risen 'on the third day', and this is not as easily accounted for as some suppose. For it is often suggested that this phrase is due simply to the desire to see in Jesus' resurrection a fulfilment of Hos. 6.1–2:

> Come, let us return to the Lord;
> for he has torn us and will heal us,
> he has struck us and he will bind up our wounds;
> after two days he will revive (LXX: ὑγιάσει) us,
> on the third day he will restore us,
> that in his presence we may live (NEB).[108]

Yet curiously nowhere is this text expressly quoted in the New Testament as fulfilled in Jesus' resurrection.[109] The text that *is* expressly quoted in this connection is Jonah 2.1:

> For, just as Jonah was in the sea monster's belly three days and three nights, so the son of man will be in the heart of the earth for three days and three nights (Matt. 12.40).

Despite the attractions of being able to find this text fulfilled in Jesus, Christians persisted in maintaining that their Lord had remained in the earth for what seems to be a shorter time, even if McArthur is right in treating 'on the third day' and 'after three days' as 'functional equivalents';[110] yet, of course, 'on the third day' is compatible with 'not more than three days'; 'after three days', on the other hand, is harder to reconcile with any shorter time-span. Furthermore, Hos. 6.1–2 clearly refers to the revival and restoration of more than one person: the first person plural is consistently used throughout, and that is, of course, thoroughly consistent with the interpretation of this text in rabbinic traditions as a reference to the general resurrection of the dead.[111] And what would be the implications of 'returning (Heb. *nāšûbāh*; LXX ἐπιστρεψώμεθα) to the Lord' in the case of Jesus? Would the term not imply repentance and consequently something to repent of? The application of this text to the resurrection of Jesus, who was regarded by the first Christians as righteous, would not therefore be unproblematic.[112] Without clear evidence that Hos. 6 exercised as strong an influence upon them as the story of Jonah,[113] we are left with the strong possibility that this tradition stems from the memory that the decisive event for the rise of Christian faith and the Christian church had occurred no later than 'on the third day', reckoned inclusively so that the Friday of the crucifixion counts as the first day and the period after nightfall on the Saturday counts as the third day.[114]

Another text which plays an important role in Karl Lehmann's argument and in that of E. L. Bode is Gen. 22.4, where Abraham and Isaac come 'on the third day' to the place where Abraham is to offer up his son; he sees the rabbinic exegesis of this passage as evidence that the rabbis regarded the third day as the day of salvation and of rescue from great danger.[115] Yet, quite apart from the question of the extent to which Gen. 22 figured in early Christian apologetics,[116] it seems to me a serious objection that this dating would more naturally apply to the crucifixion, the death of Jesus, and not to its sequel. (It would, accordingly, be easier to argue that it influenced Luke 13.32, but even that is perhaps going beyond what is really probable.) Slightly more plausible as a background is an old tradition which says that Israel's journey through the wilderness to the Red Sea lasted three days, the time for the journey into the wilderness that Moses had named to Pharaoh. That would perhaps better support the formulation 'after three days'.[117]

But can any other text be found as support for the belief that Christ's rising on the third day was according to scripture?

Perhaps not, if 'on the third day' also has to have a scriptural basis. But what if it was the rising of Jesus alone that was attested by scripture? That could find a wider support in the Old Testament, e.g. in those texts which the speeches of Acts and other New Testament writers cite in support of the resurrection of Jesus.[118] In other words, this credal statement is a lot easier to comprehend if one either denies that 'according to the scriptures' refers also to 'on the third day',[119] or if one assumes a certain looseness of thought and argument here: it was assumed that all that happened to Jesus happened 'according to the scriptures' (cf. Luke 24.25–27), and the raising of Jesus on the third day was also assumed to conform to scripture. This was all part of the divine necessity which comes to expression in the repeated use of the word δεῖ in connection with the events of Jesus' passion and its sequel.[120] One should, in other words, probably see behind this reference to the scriptures a threefold process of early Christian reflection: 1. the earliest Christians were convinced, thanks to their experiences at Easter and afterwards, that Jesus' fate was according to God's will. Because they also believed that God had revealed that will in the Old Testament scriptures, they 2. searched in those scriptures for the proof that the anointed one of Jewish expectations had indeed to suffer and die and be raised again, that his fate was therefore according to the scriptures (plural). As a result of this basic enquiry which convinced them that Jesus' fate did correspond to what the scriptures had foretold, they 3. sought for the confirmation of their basic search in as many details of the passion story and its sequel as they could, even if the supposed confirmation may seem to us at times somewhat tenuous. Even when only one passage could support, rather precariously, a detail like the third day, it confirmed that general character of the story as scriptural. But this analysis leads to the conclusion that the proof of the necessity of the third day belongs to the third and latest stage of Christian reflection on the scriptures and that the passage did not generate the date, as some have claimed;[121] on the contrary, the date led to the discovery of the text that showed its basis in scripture.[122]

It seems to me equally doubtful that this time-reference has its origin in the teaching of Jesus, for instance in that cryptic temple-saying of Mark 14.58 parr., as Lindars supposes.[123] It may be granted that some saying of Jesus may well lie behind this charge and that it was not therefore as innocuous or as easily disproved as the evangelists suggest;[124] if the dangerous part of the charge lay in the prediction of the destruction of the temple, and this may well be the genuine part of the saying, which was the basis of the charge, then it is to be noted that Jesus does indeed foretell this in Mark 13.2 parr., but there says neither that he will be the one who will destroy it (in contrast also to the charge against Stephen in Acts 6.14) nor that he or anyone else will rebuild it, let alone in three days.[125] It is John who makes out of this latter prediction a prophecy of the resurrection of Jesus (2.19), but this is more likely a later reinterpretation of the saying attributed to Jesus during his trial in the Synoptic Gospels. The use of a different temporal expression in all four Gospels from the one usually used of Jesus' resurrection makes it unlikely that this was meant to be a veiled reference to the resurrection or was composed for that purpose, but at the same time raises the question whether Jesus did in fact speak of a miraculously quick restoration of the destroyed temple. At any rate the readers of Mark (and of the other two Synoptics) who hear the charge at Jesus' trial will know that Jesus has spoken of the destruction of the temple, and the readers of at least two Gospels, perhaps more likely all three, will also know that it was not Jesus who destroyed it, but the Romans. (And as Jesus was in their eyes a true prophet, he would not and could not then have prophesied that he would be the destroyer.)

It has also to be noted, however, that if something so decisive did indeed happen 'on the third day' after Jesus' death and if this 'something' involved his disciples or some of them, then it cannot have taken place in Galilee, for there would not have been sufficient time for the disciples who had been present in Jerusalem during Jesus' last days there to have reached Galilee.[126] The nearest point to Jerusalem in Galilee is approximately fifty-seven miles away as the crow flies, and the disciples could not fly; to northern Galilee it was nearly a hundred miles and a seven- or eight-day journey;[127] indeed, if they were afraid of arrest, they would need to travel as inconspicuously as possible to avoid drawing attention to themselves, and any greater haste than usual could have been dangerous. Travelling in haste on the sabbath that lay between the day of Jesus' crucifixion and the third day would have been the worst possible tactic. Common sense would rather dictate that it would be better to mingle with the crowds of departing pilgrims leaving Jerusalem after the feast, if that were at all possible – as indeed the Gospel of Peter suggests that they did (14.58). This factor needs to be borne in mind as one weighs up the competing claims of Galilee and Jerusalem as the place where Jesus first appeared to his disciples. If one insists on Galilee, then one must dispense with the third day;[128] if the third day is retained, then only Jerusalem of the two alternatives remains. Was Luke then right after all and the disciples did not flee, but remained in Jerusalem? Or did they in fact flee and Luke's account is here theologically motivated? But in that case, to whom could Jesus have appeared in Jerusalem on that day?

So where did the resurrection appearances take place? Convincing is the logic of the argument that, had Jesus appeared to the disciples in Jerusalem, it is hard to see what their motives would have been for returning subsequently to Galilee and then going up once again to Jerusalem.[129] And to that city they (or some of them) most certainly did eventually return, for Paul's account in Gal. 1.16 and 18 shows how far it had by then (very few years later) become a centre for the early Christian movement in which leaders like Peter and Jesus' brother James were to be found. And in so far as Jerusalem became this centre and we really know nothing for sure about early Christianity in Galilee, it is hard to see how or why stories of appearances in Galilee would otherwise have arisen or have been transferred thither from somewhere else, namely Jerusalem, had it not indeed been there that some at least of them took place.[130] One might perhaps explain the references to Jesus' going ahead of his disciples to Galilee (Mark 14.28; 16.7) as foreshadowing the Gentile mission,[131] although I must confess that I find that often-asserted explanation somewhat lacking in conviction; but what is one to make of the scenes depicting appearances in Galilee? Simply misunderstandings of the saying found in Mark 14.28 and 16.7? But if there were no stories of appearances in Galilee to tell, would it not be simpler to follow Luke's strategy, for example, and turn it into a prediction that had been made in Galilee (Luke 24.6)? Yet the Fourth Gospel in its present form persists in telling of an appearance in Galilee, even though that account follows on most uncomfortably after the scenes described in ch. 20; despite them the disciples seem unaware in ch. 21 that anything had happened in Jerusalem. And Grass is right in saying that this chapter gives the impression that it contains old traditions – the disciples returning home after the seeming catastrophe of Jesus' death in Jerusalem; they, or at least a group of seven of them (instead of the group of the Twelve as in ch. 20), try to pick up their lives where they had left off, by resuming their work as fishermen (even though the Fourth Gospel has not previously mentioned their being fishermen).[132] Evidently, too, the Gospel of Peter contained a similar episode, for the present text of the fragment of that Gospel which we possess ends with Peter and Andrew and Levi setting out to fish on the sea.[133] But given that Jesus had died and been buried in Jerusalem, then, if resurrection stories were to be given a setting, Jerusalem would be a far more obvious choice than the distant Galilee. That means that, if one persists with the argument that something must have happened 'on the third day' in order to cause *that* particular tradition to spring up, then the resurrection 'happenings' are split in two: something happened in or near Jerusalem 'on the third day' and something else happened in Galilee, presumably somewhat later, if we are to allow time for the disciples who had been in Jerusalem to return home.

Yet, just as Galilee as a setting for appearances is difficult to dismiss as a pure invention, so there are, on the other hand, elements of the Jerusalem tradition which are equally hard, perhaps even harder, to explain if they have no basis in fact. Above all the very specificity of the Emmaus story is such an element. For this place is not mentioned elsewhere in the New Testament and indeed considerable doubt exists as to where exactly it was.[134] And the disciple who is named, Cleopas, is also hardly a central figure. Despite the objections of some,[135] it is still possible that this is the same person as the Clopas whose wife (if that is the force of the genitive here) Mary stands by the cross in John 19.25, and also possible that this Mary is the unnamed second disciple on the road to Emmaus in Luke 24.[136]

Once again, then, there seems to be good evidence, which can only with difficulty be explained away as a pure invention, that something happened both in or near Jerusalem *and* in Galilee following Jesus' death, although the precise location of such events in Galilee is far less precise (perhaps because the main witnesses moved back to Jerusalem shortly thereafter and perpetuated these traditions there). The difficulty still remains of saying exactly what happened in both places. In the case of Jerusalem it could have been the discovery of the empty tomb or at least the failure to discover the body of Jesus, and perhaps also experiences that were interpreted as encounters with the risen Jesus involving persons, women or others, who were not so markedly adherents of Jesus' group and so less endangered by their being in Jerusalem. The stories of the appearances in Galilee, on the other hand, are very much bound up with commissioning – the great commission of Jesus in Matt. 28.16–20 and the commissioning of Peter in John 21.15–17. And in the tradition of a renewed commission, i.e. a renewed sense of, and motivation for, a missionary task, lies perhaps one explanation for a return to Jerusalem, to resume the task that had taken Jesus and his followers to Jerusalem in the first place, unless, that is, it was a lively expectation of the end and of Jesus' return in glory that brought them back to Jerusalem, perhaps at the next pilgrim festival after Passover, Pentecost. This latter explanation stands, however, in some tension with the tradition in Mark 14.28 and 16.7 parr. which pointed the disciples to Galilee.

If, however, one is to explain the disciples' departure from Jerusalem in the first place, it is easier to suppose that what happened in that city on the first Sunday after Jesus' death occurred after most of the disciples (but not necessarily all), above all those who could most easily be identified as Jesus' followers, had left the city, free to travel again after the end of the sabbath. That raises the question who was still there to witness or experience anything there on that day, let alone what they experienced. For it has to be noted that the discovery of an empty tomb not only did not necessarily mean that its occupant had been raised from the dead; it did not even mean that the raising had occurred on the same day as the finding of the empty tomb. And yet this discovery could subsequently be seen as significant in the light of later resurrection appearances, as providing at least a certain *terminus ante quem* for the event of the raising itself.

(d) The role of the women in the story

It is a persistent and at the same time puzzling feature of the resurrection stories that it was a woman or women who first discovered the empty tomb, and in some cases women first encounter the risen Jesus (Matt. 28.9; John 20.14). This is strange and really quite remarkable. For we must bear in mind both the world in which the Christian movement arose and the purposes which such traditions were meant to serve apart from their stating what had happened. For they were not told to satisfy mere idle curiosity or to serve a purely antiquarian interest. In part the stories of Jesus' resurrection were meant to persuade the outside world of the truth of the Christian faith, written to prove the reality of the resurrection, that the risen Jesus was no phantom (Luke 24.37, 39; John 20.25, 27–28), and to disprove the discreditable alternative explanations of the empty tomb (Matt. 27.62–66; 28.11–15). The stories also, however, served to provide the foundation for the ministry either of the church as a whole (Matt. 28.16–20; John 20.21–23) or of its leading figures (Luke 24.34; John 20.8; 21.15–19). Whether the resurrection stories and traditions are seen as Christian propaganda for the world outside or communal stories that are more concerned with the ordering of the church and in particular with the equipping and authorization of its leaders for their subsequent role, the women are an oddity: they are untrustworthy witnesses in Christian propaganda, as Luke hints with some irony (24.11);[137] and though privileged to have the first glimpse of the risen Lord in two of the Gospels (Matt. 28.9; John 20.11–18), they later received no share of the power and authority that flowed to others from such encounters. As Judith Lieu rightly comments, the tradition of the women's role was

> too resilient to be effaced, but it could be confined, restrained and limited so that the women have a voice, but a voice which declares its own limitations.[138]

It is probably for such reasons that Paul does not mention the women among his lists of witnesses to the resurrection in I Cor. 15.5–8. If the lists that he used were bound up with the authority of the witnesses in the church, as the parallel references to lists headed respectively by Peter (Cephas) and James (vv. 5, 7) may suggest, then the absence of the women would point to their absence of power and authority.[139] Already D. F. Strauss had detected a similar elbowing-out of the female witnesses, in this case above all Mary of Magdala, in John 20:[140] it looks as if 20.2–10 has been inserted into the narrative involving Mary that begins at 20.1;[141] one possible motive was to let the two male disciples discover the empty tomb first and in the case of the Beloved Disciple to come to faith as a result (v. 8). Even that cannot, however, detract from the fact that Mary is here the first to see the risen Jesus, and the tenacity with which the Gospels attest her role in the resurrection stories points to a significance of this woman in the life of the later Christian community, even if it was accompanied by no commensurate authority or rank.[142]

Lüdemann, however, sees in the stories of women finding the empty grave a later, secondary and apologetic development in the traditions, necessitated and motivated by the need to take account of the flight of the male disciples. And, were the women a part of the passion tradition, then presumably, he argues, the early Christians felt the need to tell how they came to learn of Jesus' resurrection. Thus there came into being 'an apologetic legend with the women as recipients of the proclamation of the resurrection at the place where Jesus was buried'.[143] In consequence Lüdemann considers that the story of Mary of Magdala's going (with other women) to the tomb on the day after the sabbath can hardly be historical (153). But despite the account of the male disciples' flight, the Gospels are not deterred from having some of them close at hand to be informed of the women's discovery at the grave,[144] and Lüdemann himself grants that the story of Peter's denying Jesus presupposes that Peter at least had not taken flight immediately (at least away from Jerusalem and its immediate surrounds).[145] In Matthew the women are to tell the disciples to go to Galilee, which presupposes that they have not yet set out, although, as Grass notes,[146] it is not then clear why they then need to set out at all, if Jesus could just as well have also appeared to them in Jerusalem. In Luke they must remain in Jerusalem anyway and there is no question of their departing for Galilee. John 20 (but not 21) presupposes that not only Peter and the Beloved Disciple, but also the rest of the disciples were still within reach on that Easter day. Even the command in Mark 16.7 to tell Peter and the others that Jesus is going before them to Galilee suggests that they are at any rate not yet in Galilee, and the most obvious interpretation is that, as in Matthew, they are still in the vicinity of Jerusalem. The incongruity of all this with the accounts of their flight does not seem to have occurred to the first Christians. Why should it have? That the disciples ran away in Gethsemane does not mean that they ran away to Galilee (a very long run!), but simply that they left the immediate area where the arrest was taking place and where they themselves were in grave danger. According to the story in the Gospels it did not prevent Peter following the arrested Jesus to the palace of the High Priest (or of Annas in the Fourth Gospel) at a distance (Mark 14.54 parr.). In some accounts it did not prevent some of them at least from observing Jesus' crucifixion, again at a distance, again despite the attendant risks (Luke 23.49; John 19.26).[147] Nothing therefore compels us (or the first Christians) to say that the male disciples all immediately made a beeline for Galilee; almost everything in the Gospels' accounts in fact presupposes that they did not.[148] The references in Mark 14.27 and John 16.32 to the 'scattering' of the disciples 'to their own place, their home' (εἰς τὰ ἴδια), to which Lohfink appeals,[149] do not compel us to say that they scattered as far afield as Galilee *immediately* after the arrest of Jesus and the initial scattering of his followers in Gethsemane. If they did in fact leave Jerusalem and its immediate vicinity straight away, this has made next to no impression on the traditions (the major exception being John 21). The foundation of Lüdemann's argument to explain the rise of the tradition of the women at the tomb thus crumbles away and we are left with the likelier explanation that women played the major role in the earliest stages of the events of Easter, namely already 'on the third day', and that the Gospels have retained this tradition despite its shortcomings as evidence. It is far likelier that a prominent role of women, particularly of Mary of Magdala, was later suppressed, than that such a tradition was a later accretion.[150]

What, however, was the role of the woman or women? Did she or they find Jesus' tomb again, but find it empty? Or was it simply a matter of not finding the body, leaving open the question of whether it was findable at all, or whether they looked in the right place? For failure to find the body could then subsequently be explained otherwise in the light of the resurrection appearances: (of course) they did not find the body because it had been raised from the dead (regardless of whether such a disappearance of the body was necessary for 'resurrection'). Yet the woman or women's failure to find the body could in itself be enough to ensure them a valid place in the tradition, as an important link in the chain of events and arguments that led to the rise of belief in Jesus' resurrection. Was it then simply that they looked and did not find, looked immediately after the ending of the sabbath when the return of daylight allowed it, and perhaps also before they too set off for Galilee, and that they thus sealed the importance of the 'third day' in the Christian calendar?

(e) The failure of anyone to produce Jesus' body subsequently

It is also true that it remains a striking and puzzling feature of the rise of the Christian church and of its proclamation of the risen Jesus that the only refutation offered of its claim that Jesus had risen from his grave seems to have been the Jewish counter-claim that the disciples had stolen Jesus' body (Matt. 28.13–15). It seems that the body or remains of Jesus could not be produced to refute the claims of the Christians. That remains true and impressive even if Matthew's story of the placing of a guard at the tomb is a later embellishment, like the even more elaborate account in the Gospel of Peter. At the same time it is perhaps also surprising that there is no trace of any attempt to disprove the Christians' claims by producing just any human remains and claiming them to have been those of Jesus. The argument just does not seem to have been conducted along those lines: there is no evidence that there was ever any opening up of tombs to produce a body or demonstrate the lack of one. Instead of such empirical forms of argument the matter remained one of claim and counter-claim, with the first Christians claiming that Jesus had been raised, and Jews alleging against them that they had stolen the body.

Equally, however, the anomaly of a condemned criminal being allowed to be buried in such a way should give us cause for thought. Generally the Romans may have left the bodies of those crucified to rot on their crosses or to be devoured by wild beasts, as an object-lesson to others, but in Palestine the Romans may normally have respected Jewish scruples about the religious defilement that such corpses brought upon the land (as evidenced by Deut. 21.23), which would be a particularly serious matter on the eve of a major feast (serious both for Jewish susceptibilities and also, consequently, for public order, which would be a matter for concern in the eyes of the Roman authorities). But the form of burial accorded the corpses of such offenders was usually more likely to have been that of being thrown into a common grave, or more precisely a criminals' grave.[151]

At any rate it is only in the later Gospels, particularly in John, that we receive a clear impression of a dignified and honourable burial, so that the earliest accounts may have been of a rather more hurried procedure: Mark mentions neither washing nor anointing of the corpse, which would have been normal marks of respect for the dead person. Is such a fate in fact reflected in Acts 13.29, where 'they', that is presumably the same inhabitants of Jerusalem and their leaders as in 13.27, have taken down Jesus' body from the cross and have laid it in a grave? Something of the same tradition seems to be visible in John 19.31,[152] Gospel of Peter 6.21 and Justin, *Dialogue* 97.1. Is this then the origin of the tradition about the role of Joseph of Arimathea, namely that he was originally no (secret) disciple of Jesus, as later Christian tradition made him out to be, but a member of the Jewish aristocracy who was entrusted by his fellows with the task of disposing of Jesus' body so that it would not defile the land just before Passover?[153] His name crops up persistently in the traditions and is perhaps unlikely to be just a legendary invention. That Joseph was in fact no follower of Jesus, probably not even a sympathizer, would also explain why the women took no part in Jesus' burial, but merely observed it (Mark 15.47).[154] Normally it might be expected that they would have assisted in the burial rites. Such a fate for Jesus' body would at any rate also explain how neither the disciples nor the Jewish authorities could subsequently prove anything either way by investigating graves: the relevant one would have held the remains of others, so that it would not be empty; equally, however, the fact that it was not empty would not disprove the Christians' claims unless Jesus' remains could be identified. That would have been extremely difficult (and thoroughly unpleasant and religiously defiling as well) after any length of time. Yet it was apparently the practice, at least at a later point of time, for the bones of those who had been thus buried, who were not allowed to be buried in their family graves, to be gathered together and placed in an ossuary, and this seems to presuppose, as Raymond Brown notes,[155] that one was able to determine which bones were which. At any rate it was indispensable for Christian claims that Jesus had had a tomb to himself so that its emptiness could be attested, but that stands in uneasy tension with another feature of early Christianity:

(f) The absence of any cult around Jesus' grave

Although cultic veneration of heroes' graves was well-attested in the Graeco-Roman world, we never read of any Christian veneration of that of Jesus.[156] In contrast, that of his brother James was well-known, even if it was not a place of worship: around 180 CE Hegesippus records that James the Righteous had been buried near the Temple in Jerusalem and that his gravestone was still there.[157] But if the subsequent uncertainty as to the exact place of Jesus' burial is anything to go by, no such memory was preserved in his case, even though Jeremias deems such a lapse of memory unthinkable,[158] and Joan E. Taylor, who earlier had expressed considerable scepticism concerning the reliability of the traditional siting of the tomb, now regards it as possibly correct, situated in a larger area called 'Golgotha'. This site, unlike the site of the crucifixion, required no special signs or wonders to authenticate it, she thinks, because it was 'self-evidently' the right one (and Hadrian had perhaps intentionally placed a statue of Jupiter on this site: Jerome, *Ep.* 58.3.5).[159] Betz, on the other hand, remarks that Jesus' grave seems to have remained unknown for 'over 300 years' and no one bothered; in his opinion it was only 'rediscovered' when that became necessary in 326.[160] From this absence of knowledge of where Jesus' grave was, let alone of worship offered at it, scholars like J. D. G. Dunn argue that this indicates that 'the first Christians did not regard the place where Jesus had been laid as having any special significance because no grave was thought to contain Jesus' earthly remains'.[161]

Even so, it is surely surprising that the first Christians did not venerate a spot where, in Dunn's view, nothing less than the beginning of God's new creation had been supposed to have occurred. Was that not in itself reason enough to note and remember and cherish the site, regardless of whether it contained Jesus' remains or not (for we shall see that it is by no means certain that all would have considered their continuing presence to disprove the fact of resurrection; that depends on what one understands by 'resurrection')? There was, after all, by way of contrast, an early interest in the place of Jesus' birth: Justin, in the mid-second century, pointed out that Jesus' birth in a cave (a tradition not found in the canonical New Testament) fulfilled Old Testament prophecy;[162] Origen, in the third century, pre-supposes that inhabitants of Bethlehem could point to a cave where Jesus was born,[163] and it is to be assumed that it was in all probability a place of worship and pilgrimage at this time, just as it was later in Jerome's time.[164] Was it that the early Christians were unsure where the place of Jesus' burial actually was? If that were the case, then it need not follow that their failure to venerate a grave is unintelligible unless that grave were in fact empty. Or even if they could remember where it was, the argument of the last section opens up another possibility: it was in fact unsuited for purposes of veneration and represented the utmost depths of their Lord's degradation and ignominy. However, ignominy as such does not seem to have deterred the early followers of Jesus, and they could moreover have found in this feature of Jesus' passion a fulfilment of Isa. 53.9: 'He was assigned a grave with the wicked, a burial-place among felons' (REB), just as Luke placed on Jesus' lips the fulfilment of Isa. 53.12, 'he was reckoned among transgressors'. It is thus more likely that it was the difficulty of identifying the body or the grave again which would have caused this part of the tradition to have been suppressed; this is of a piece with the care of the Gospels' accounts to record that the women had observed where Jesus' body was laid (particularly Mark 15.47; Luke 23.55).[165] This care may well betray the apologetic concern that mistakes could all too easily have occurred here, that it was here that the Christian tradition and claims were vulnerable.

Thus this piece of evidence from early Christian tradition, the absence of any cult connected with Jesus' grave, is in fact far more ambivalent than Dunn allows, and could equally well point to the scenario outlined in the last section, namely that Jesus' body had been thrown into a common grave, where it would be next to impossible to say after a short while whether his remains were there or not. This would hardly be a site to be venerated in the eyes of the early Christians, even if for us it could underline Jesus' solidarity with the oppressed and downtrodden and the outcasts. For the early Christians it would carry the additional stigma of ambiguity. At any rate, as Carnley drily remarks, 'the pious interest in the alleged site of the Holy Sepulchre in our own day seems to render such an argument [as Dunn's] completely impotent'.[166]

However, apart from the ambivalence of the last two arguments, the other evidence just mentioned does form a strong case for holding that something did indeed happen on that first day of the week, something that initially involved some of Jesus' female followers, and something that loomed so large and ranked as so important in the memory of the early Christians that they held this day of the week to be their Lord's special day and theirs too. The evidence therefore points to something having happened on that day, but it does not tell us what exactly that something was: it may simply have been a fruitless search for a body. Nevertheless, this fruitlessness was later to be seen as immensely fruitful in the formation of Christian tradition, since it opened up the way for the assertion of Jesus' resurrection according to at least one understanding of what 'resurrection' meant and involved.[167]

4

The Nature of Jesus' 'Resurrection'

All the evidence that we have seen so far does not really tell us what sort of event it was that took place on that 'third day'. For already we have seen at several points that there is scope for considerable doubt about the precise nature of the event of Jesus' resurrection or even what it was like to encounter the risen Jesus subsequently. So Dunn, for instance, grants that we do not know what happened. Indeed he is prepared to contrast the very earthy, physical portrayal of Jesus' resultant form in the Gospels, above all in Luke's account, with the 'spiritual' resurrection portrayed by Paul: 'What Luke affirms (Jesus' resurrection body was flesh and bones), Paul denies (the resurrection body is *not* composed of flesh and blood)!'[168] Small wonder, then, that Strauss, after investigating the information that we are given concerning the nature of Jesus' risen body and the nature of his risen existence, found 'the evangelical representation of the corporeality of Jesus after the resurrection to be contradictory'.[169]

At the root of this problem is certainly the absence of any witnesses to the actual event of the resurrection itself, but even so this fuzziness is surprising, for witnesses did exist who claimed to have experienced an encounter with the risen Jesus, as Paul reminds us in I Cor. 15.6: some of them were still alive when he wrote. Even if no one had seen what actually happened in the tomb, there were those who should surely have been able to say what it was like to have met Jesus: was it, for instance, like meeting another fellow human being of flesh and blood, or was it like meeting a being who belonged to a different world or a different order of being? But on that question our sources do not speak with a single voice.

Our basic datum is the faith of the disciples that the Jesus who had died had appeared to them again and was no longer dead. This was a faith of the committed, of believers, for we know of none who claimed to have seen the risen Jesus but remained unbelieving. This is recognized by Acts 10.40–41, for there we are told that God caused Jesus to be seen, not by the whole people, but only by those witnesses chosen by God. Some were perhaps initially unbelieving, as Matthew candidly grants (28.17), but it is never implied that they were able to experience this encounter and remain aloof and unbelieving for long thereafter. However, it was not only those who had already been Jesus' disciples and committed to his cause who experienced these appearances and were convinced by what they had seen: for the witnesses include Paul, the zealous Jewish persecutor of the church,[170] and we should probably also mention here Jesus' own brother, James, who does not seem to have been among his followers during his earthly life.[171] Whatever these experiences of the risen Jesus were, they seem therefore to have been capable of turning the sceptical or the downright hostile into devoted followers. Yet, whatever the experiences were, they were not experiences of the resurrection, the raising of Jesus itself; to infer from the experiences that Jesus had been raised from the dead necessarily involves an inference, an interpretative step beyond the actual experiences themselves and the thing experienced.

(a) 'Resurrection' as interpretation

Now 'resurrection' is, as Dunn rightly remarks, an interpretation of those experiences and an inference from them.[172] That is, Jesus' followers inferred that the only thing which could have given rise to what they had experienced, the only explanation of it, was that God had raised Jesus from the dead. That was, we should note, by no means a self-evident inference. Gerhard Lohfink, for instance, recognizes three possible conceptual frameworks that lay to hand: the concept of the exaltation of one humiliated in suffering and death (cf. Isa. 52.13–15); that of an exceptional individual taken to be with God at the end of his or her life (cf. Gen. 5.24; II Kings 2.1–18); and lastly that of the general resurrection at the end (cf. Isa. 26.19; Dan. 12.2).[173] It was this last category, he argues, that was chosen at first to interpret the phenomena of the visions of Jesus, but it should be noted that, more precisely, 'resurrection' for Jews of that time usually meant one of two things. It could mean a restoration to a still mortal life in this world, in this present age, still subject to eventual death in the fullness of time, in other words a rescue from a death that came earlier than it need have, but a rescue nonetheless which by no means removed the necessity of eventually dying once more; that was the sort of resurrection brought about by prophets like Elijah and Elisha in the Old Testament (I Kings 17.17–24; II Kings 4.18–37) and by Jesus and his followers in the New (Mark 5.35–43 parr.; Luke 7.11–17; John 11.1–14; Acts 9.36–41; 20.9–12).[174] Or it referred to the final, general resurrection at the end of this present age, however that was conceived of, an event ushering in a new age. But to combine elements of both views and to argue that a single individual had finally conquered death, had experienced resurrection in this second sense, while this present age continued on its course, was a novelty without parallel. Rightly, therefore, Gerhard Friedrich concludes, against D. F. Strauss, that the belief in the resurrection cannot simply be explained as a deduction from Jewish apocalyptic beliefs, for 'the concept of the eschatological raising from the dead of an individual is utterly unparalleled and not to be inferred from the tradition'.[175] And even if one argues for the belief in certain circles that Jewish martyrs would immediately rise, as we have seen that Müller does, we have seen that this belief had no direct connection with a general resurrection or the eschatological consummation of all things, nor was it usually linked to appearances of those risen.

Perhaps it is not surprising that the portrayals of what encounters with the risen Jesus were like varied so greatly: Jews of the time differed so much in what they understood by 'resur-rection', if they understood anything by the term at all,[176] that to claim that someone had risen from the dead was compatible with a considerable variety of descriptions of what an encounter with that person would be like. The assumption, the inference that 'Jesus is risen' could therefore in principle lead to all sorts of accounts of the form of the one encountered that this 'resurrec-tion' could lead to, ranging from a crude resurrection of Jesus' former physical body, just as it had been when he died (wounds and all), to an exaltation of him to a state of other-worldly glory like the effulgence of heavenly bodies (cf. Dan. 12.3, even if the resurrection there is still this-worldly). Nonetheless that does not really explain satisfactorily the variation in the New Testament accounts of encounters with the risen Jesus. For it is not being claimed that the disciples simply learnt at second hand that 'Jesus is risen' (although according to some accounts they did hear that from the figures whom the women first found at the empty tomb) and that they then each made, from this second-hand informa-tion, their own varied inferences as to what encounter with that risen Jesus might be like. Were that all, then one might indeed expect very different conceptions of what encounter with a resurrected person might be like to surface. Rather, it is being claimed that they also themselves had certain experiences and inferred from these that 'Jesus is risen'. According to this way of looking at the traditions, 'resurrection' is not a concept which generates a number of different accounts of the result of that rising, but an inference drawn from a series of experiences. 'We have seen Jesus,' the disciples say; 'therefore he must have been raised from the dead.' If we look at things from this perspective, then the only thing which could generate such a variety of different accounts which were all equally valid, and all equally true to what the first Christians had in fact experienced, would be a series of experiences which were indeed equally different in character, ranging from an encounter with what seemed to be just another (unknown and unrecognized) human being to an experience of a blinding light and a heavenly voice. That would suggest that the nature of the risen Jesus was as variable and elusive as that of the mythical Proteus.[177] Or is it indeed the case that the affirmation 'Jesus is risen' alone has spawned a number of different depictions of what that being risen was like?

(b) The priority of Paul's account

However, before we draw such conclusions, it is worth asking whether all of these varied descriptions of encounters with the risen Jesus should be treated as equally valid or have an equal claim to be heard. For quite plainly some are at first sight more valuable than others: some are older than others and some seem to be dependent on others. On the basis of the usual account of the relationship between the Synoptic Gospels, Matthew and Luke had before them Mark 16.1–8 and both follow this account fairly closely, yet with slight, often tendentious and presumably redactional divergences. That Matthew and Luke thereafter, that is, after that point in the narrative which Mark has reached in 16.8, diverge so sharply from one another is to my mind one of the strongest arguments for the correctness of the majority view of Synoptic relationships[178] and at the same time for the correctness of the view that Mark originally ended at 16.8; had anything followed that verse the other Evangelists seem not to have known of it.[179]

As far as we can tell, the only New Testament writer who actually claims himself to have seen the risen Jesus is the apostle Paul, and his account therefore quite obviously deserves to be heard first. He discusses the nature of the resurrection 'body' in I Cor. 15 because some at Corinth have apparently denied that there is any resurrection. It is true that he is therefore, in this context, primarily talking about the nature of the resurrection 'body' of Christians in the latter part of that chapter, but at the same time, since he regards the risen Christ as the 'first-fruits' of the resurrection (v. 20), of 'all' (v. 22) or of 'those who belong to Christ' (v. 23), it is reasonable to assume that what he says about Christians' resurrection might also, in his eyes, apply to Christ's.

All his stress, we discover, is on the discontinuity between the old 'body' and the new, so much so that it comes as rather a surprise that he adds, seemingly as an afterthought, that the new is also, like the mortal and perishable old nature, a 'body'. (We will come later to the problems which this presents.)

Earlier in the chapter, however, he had spoken of Christ's appearance to him as the latest and last of the whole series of Christ's appearances to various people (v. 8). Had we not had the Gospels, we would very naturally have supposed from the way that he recounts the list of resurrection appearances that what he experienced was of the same kind as the experiences of the other witnesses, and that the only difference lay in the fact that his experience occurred at a later time.[180]

Such a conclusion comes as a surprise, particularly to those familiar with Luke's accounts of Jesus' resurrection appearances in his Gospel on the one hand, and with the same author's description of the appearance of the risen Christ to Paul on the road to Damascus in the Book of Acts on the other. For these two experiences seem to be of a wholly different kind: the Jesus of the Emmaus road seems all too human and one could easily mistake him for just another person – the two disciples evidently did just that; in contrast, the Jesus of the Damascus road does not seem to take on any human form, but is manifested in dazzling light and as an unearthly voice from heaven. It may be, however, that Matthew's account of Jesus' appearance in 28.16–20 might be more easily reconciled with the manner of the appearance to Paul;[181] the fact that the 'doubt' of some is mentioned suggests that this is no mere mundane encounter. What they 'see' also induces worship (v. 17).

Persistently, then, Paul describes his experience and that of others as a 'seeing' (and here the preoccupation of Carnley and others with the passive form ὤφθη found in I Cor. 15.5–8 and its parallels in Septuagintal accounts of epiphanies may be misleading if it leads one to suppose that this can just mean 'God made him epiphanous'; one also has to take into account the active form ἑόρακα in I Cor. 9.1).[182] However, what is seen is clearly not just a this-worldly experience in any of the accounts of Paul's conversion experience.[183] One is fully justified, therefore, in describing Paul's experience as in some sense 'visionary',[184] whether or not one wants to go on from there to distinguish 'subjective' (i.e. self-induced?) visions and 'objective' visions (i.e. visions occasioned by some external factor).[185] But because it is our faith which interprets these visions as 'objective', they are ultimately, Marxsen maintains,[186] also 'subjective'. Küng's proposal[187] that here one should compare the calling of Old Testament prophets is particularly suggestive; for Paul himself describes his calling in terms strongly reminiscent of both Deutero-Isaiah and Jeremiah (Gal. 1.15 with Isa. 49.1; Jer. 1.5).[188] However, it is only safe to speak of Paul's experience as 'visionary' *in some sense*, since the analogy with the experiences of the prophets raises the question of the nature of *their* 'visions'. Are these accounts of visions, for instance, sometimes at least to be regarded as the product of a creative imagination that actively uses images to portray an intellectually perceived truth?

K.-H. Ohlig's question is therefore justified, namely whether Paul's own references to his conversion would ever have been understood as a sort of visionary optical perception were it not for our knowledge of the descriptions of the event in the Acts of the Apostles.[189] For in Ohlig's opinion, a prophetic 'seeing' or 'recognition' that the Jesus who had apparently failed was the one whom God had raised would not require Paul's experience to be interpreted as a visionary optical perceiving.[190] Doubtless more was meant, however, than when someone explains something to us and we say 'Oh, I see (what you mean)', but how much more is perhaps a question that is more open than some would allow. Again, we speak of leaders as 'visionary' figures,[191] but how far did the ancient world share this metaphorical way of speaking? I suspect that the answer is 'Very little indeed'. Something more concrete was meant when, for instance, Philo describes Israel as the visionary people, namely those who see God,[192] for this is to be interpreted within a mystical and visionary tradition in which ecstasy played an important part, even if it is an open question whether the language of ecstasy was not sometimes used figuratively.[193] The analogy being claimed in such language lay, at any rate, in experiences seen then as real cases of contact with another world.

One gets the impression, on the other hand, that while any travellers who happened to have been on the road to Emmaus at the same time would also have seen this mysterious stranger, there is considerable doubt as to how much of Paul's experience could be shared by *his* travelling companions: in Acts 9.7 they hear the voice, but see no one; in 22.9 they see the light, but do not hear the voice.[194] One cannot, then, easily imagine Luke setting Peter's or the Emmaus road disciples' experience within the same sequence of events as Paul's, and Luke presumably did not see them as such: for one thing, they are separated, the one from the other, by the ascension of Jesus to heaven, which seems to put an end to the series of experiences of the former, earthly kind. What follows that event must then surely be different.

Still, we have seen that if we are to trust anyone's account of what it was like to encounter the risen Jesus, then it is Paul's word to which we must listen first, as the only writer who is talking of something which he claims to have experienced in person. Furthermore, if we must gauge the likely ages of different traditions, it seems to me doubtful whether a tangible, earthly, this-worldly tradition would be later spiritualized rather than the contrary shift in the tradition, namely for a 'spiritual', visionary account to be given a more concrete form. Both would in theory be possible, but the spiritualizing tendency would be more likely, say, under a strong Platonizing influence which held the physical to be inferior to the immaterial; it is Luke who portrays the other-worldly experience of Paul's conversion, and this same author stresses as no other the starkly physical character of the risen Christ in ch. 24 of his Gospel, in all probability with a strong apologetic motive. That suggests that the movement from the intangible to the tangible and thus to the demonstrable is likelier and at any rate more clearly attested than one in the opposite direction.[195] Does that not then mean that we cannot without good reason assume that *any* claimed 'appearances' of the risen Jesus were different in kind and nature from whatever Paul experienced on the way to Damascus? We would need good grounds for believing that any other appearances were different in nature from what he saw. That would be all the more true if we can also show why other Christian writers may have wanted to describe the experiences differently. In the case of Luke, for instance, we have seen his concern to refute the suggestion that the risen Jesus was just a 'spirit', meaning in this case a 'ghost' (Luke 24.37, 39),[196] presumably to counter the suggestion of some that that was all that he was. We have also seen his tendency to describe events involving the Spirit, like Jesus receiving the Spirit at his baptism or the first disciples receiving it at Pentecost, in surprisingly tangible, sense-perceptible terms.

But of what kind and nature was this 'appearance' to Paul? If we turn again to his account of the nature of the resurrection 'body' in I Cor. 15 we may be left puzzled, because this 'body' is more clearly defined in terms of what it is not than in terms of what it is; it is, namely, none of those things which we normally associate with human bodies: it does not decay, is not weak, and so on (vv. 42–44). What it is asserted to be does not seem to accord with any sort of 'bodies' according to the views of modern physics, even if some ancient physicists may have believed heavenly bodies like the sun and moon to be eternal and unchanging. (But not those sharing the viewpoint of the Jewish apocalyptic tradition, for it believed that all 'bodies', even of that sort, had been created by God and would eventually be destroyed by God.)[197] This sort of 'body', which Paul postulates for the resurrection existence, seems very mysterious and elusive, defined only by the absence of the familiar characteristics of bodily nature. And that Paul should think of the resurrection 'body' in this way should occasion no surprise when one considers what is possibly, in the view of many, a reference to what he experienced on the way to Damascus, in II Cor. 4.6: 'The same God who said, "Out of darkness let light shine", has caused his light to shine within us, to give the light of revelation – the revelation of the glory of God in the face of Jesus Christ' (NEB). If this refers to Paul's conversion, as many think it does, then he is clearly comparing that experience to the creation of the world; nor is that surprising if he considers one who is 'in Christ' to be a 'new creation' (II Cor. 5.17). However, that may be a strong argument for seeing in II Cor. 4.6 a more general reference to the experience of all believers, albeit one that may be coloured by Paul's own experience of the way that God's revelation had once come to him.[198] The experience to which Paul here refers is both mysterious and strongly mystical in tone.

Some may be uncomfortable with this conclusion, for they too feel the need for Luke and John's earthy this-worldly accounts to reassure them that this is, indeed, no ghost, no figment of the imagination or wishful thinking. Yet Pokorný grants that all the witnesses to Jesus' resurrection are

> at the same time witnesses of faith, so that their testimony always was and is exposed to the suspicion that it is a case of wishful thinking or a hallucination (subjective vision), or the historicization of a myth or ideology.[199]

Paul's experience seems too mystical, too other-worldly, too visionary, to provide this assurance.[200] How can we be sure that he got it right and that he did indeed encounter the risen Jesus and did not merely experience some fantasy bred of a too vivid and impressionable imagination? To this the answer may well be that we do not and cannot know for certain. Moreover, we must beware of making our perceived need for certainty a reason for asserting that the experiences were of a more tangible, this-worldly kind. That would be to reshape history according to our own predilections.

(c) A psychological explanation?

It is a frequently held view that Paul's 'conversion' can be explained in purely psychological terms, and to talk of his experience as a 'vision' does nothing to discourage that.[201] That is the line taken recently by Lüdemann, as one of the latest in a long series of proponents of such theories.[202] Paul had been, he argues,[203] a committed and zealous persecutor of the Christian community, and such a violent reaction presupposes that the basic elements of the Christian proclamation had affected him deeply. His encounter with Christians and their preaching and their practice took place not only at a cognitive level, but also at an emotional and unconscious level. His aggressive response points to a blockage in Paul's psyche. It is not too far-fetched to suppose that he had been unconsciously attracted to the basic elements of early Christian preaching and practice. His anxiety at his unconscious yearnings was projected on to the Christians, so that he could attack them all the more ferociously. For fanatics often suppress their doubts about their own values and practice. Here Lüdemann quotes C. G. Jung's view that even before his conversion Paul was unconsciously a Christian, that he had an unconscious 'Christ-complex'. What Paul had unconsciously yearned for had become reality in a human being. That 'Christ-complex' would have involved the Jewish law, and Rom. 7 is to be seen as a retrospective portrayal of that unconscious conflict which had raged in Paul before his conversion.

However, if genuine, [204] Phil 3,4b–11 is equally or even more clearly a retrospective analysis of Paul's pre-Christian experience which portrays little of internal conflict, and only a reversal of values. In this account the pre-Christian Paul, even when seen retrospectively by the Christian Paul, knows nothing of dis-content, but only of achievement of righteousness (3.6), an achievement, however, that has been superseded and called into question by the divine gift of another righteousness (3.9). Such attempts to account for Paul's 'conversion' in psychological terms, which seem to fly in the face of what Paul's writings tell us about him and to stand his statements on their head, seem to me problematic in that those very writings ought to be the starting-point and the basis of our attempts to understand the apostle, for we have little else to use as a basis.[205]

Yet the very fact that such an explanation has been suggested, and not just by Lüdemann, means that we cannot so easily discount *a priori* the possibility that such an explanation may be correct. Disproving it may be extremely difficult if the *prima facie* meaning of Paul's writings may indeed legitimately be turned on its head and so much read between the lines.

(d) Experience of Jesus or experience of spirit?

There is also a certain plausibility in those accounts of the New Testament evidence which interpret the stories of Jesus' appearances in terms of 'spiritual' experiences or, better, experiences of the Spirit, and that again points in the direction of an experience far less like that of an encounter with another human person. This may be compared with the later, Gnostic, Sophia of Jesus Christ, according to which Jesus

> appeared, not in his previous form, but in the invisible spirit. And his likeness resembles a great angel of light.[206]

There are even, for instance, those who think that Paul's mention of the appearance of the risen Jesus to 'more than five hundred brethren' (I Cor. 15.6) is a variant of the same tradition which Luke narrates as the outpouring of the Spirit at Pentecost in Acts 2.1–13: what one branch of the tradition has described in terms of an experience of encounter with Jesus, another has described as the gift of the Spirit.[207] That makes it the more intelligible that the Fourth Gospel should associate the gift of the Spirit with an appearance of the risen Jesus (John 20.22), in marked contrast to Acts, which describes this endowment as only becoming possible after Jesus' ascension into heaven and final departure from the company of his disciples; and again, it is the same Gospel that speaks of the Paraclete, the 'spirit of truth', as 'another Paraclete', that is, besides Jesus himself (14.16). It would also help to explain why Paul can on occasions speak of the risen Jesus in such a way that he seems to identify him, *qua* risen, with the Spirit: this can be seen most clearly in I Cor. 15.45, where Paul describes Jesus, the 'Adam' or human being of the end-time, as having 'become a

life-giving spirit' or having 'become life-giving Spirit'.[208] However, this identification is never complete, for the Spirit had not
died on a cross and thus had not needed to be raised from the
dead; for Paul, the Spirit was indeed God's agent in that raising,
as he presumably implies in Rom. 8.11.

The more one allows the resurrection appearances to be
assimilated to experiences of the Spirit, the more one comes up
against a problem which Grass has articulated more clearly than
most, even if he has not solved it altogether satisfactorily:[209] what
then distinguished what were regarded as appearances of the
risen Jesus from other ecstatic experiences (which were evidently
plentiful in the early church),[210] and why were the former considered to have come to an end at a particular point of time? This
is also a problem as long as one treats Paul's experience as
normative and the all too physical encounters of the Gospels as
secondary; in other words, the problem does not first arise when
one begins to assimilate the resurrection appearances to outpour-
ings of the Spirit, for others claimed later to have seen visions as
well. But is it enough to say, as Grass himself proposes, that the
content of the resurrection appearances was different, namely a
seeing of the exalted Jesus? That might distinguish them from
some subsequent visionary or ecstatic experiences, including
Paul's own experience in II Cor. 12, where he only claims to have
heard 'unspeakable words' (v. 4), but what of other appearances
like the vision of Revelation 1? Or was the tradition of corporeal
appearances by then so firmly established that no one would
dream of reckoning such a vision among the resurrection appearances?[211]

In many cases a call to service was evidently thought to be
involved, particularly when the claim to apostleship rested, at
least in part, on having seen the Lord (I Cor. 9.1), but not
apparently always, as far as we can tell from instances like the
appearance to more than five hundred.[212] (And in such differences Grass sees reason to doubt whether all the appearances are
indeed, as has been claimed, dependent upon one single experience of someone like Peter.)[213] One has to ask, then, whether the

early church had in fact no hard and fast criterion for distinguishing resurrection appearances from other visions. And had
Paul such a criterion if Dunn is correct, as he probably is, in
asserting that Paul distinguished clearly between the initial revelation to himself and all his subsequent spiritual experiences?[214]

A seeing of the exalted Jesus is, on the other hand, unsatisfactory as a criterion. For already by the time that Acts describes
Paul's conversion, it is by no means clear that he saw Jesus rather
than a blinding light; he heard a voice, but that is also on a par
with other ecstatic auditionary experiences (like that of II Cor.
12). Indeed, perhaps Paul's own claim to belong to the ranks of
witnesses to the risen Jesus was a not uncontroversial one, even if
the 'pillar apostles' of Gal. 2.9 (cf. 1.18-19) were prepared to
accept it, and some may well have regarded the series of resurrection experiences as already terminated before Paul's conversion. It may even be that Paul's claim to have seen the risen Jesus
was itself a catalyst that compelled some to say 'Enough is
enough'. For, as we have seen, one would never have thought,
from Acts alone, that Paul's experience belonged to the same
sequence as the earlier resurrection appearances. But if one
regards the formal leave-taking of the ascension story as a later,
peculiarly Lukan, development, the way lay open for late-comers
to claim to belong to the same select circle of witnesses and that
open door was an invitation to abuse and fraught with danger.[215]
That was all the greater, the less one was in fact able clearly and
sharply to distinguish between experiences of the Spirit of Jesus
and experiences of the exalted Jesus himself. Perhaps – and this
would have been fortunate for the apostle Paul – this danger and
the resultant suspicion of such claims was not sufficiently acute at
an earlier stage to undermine his position and his claims; he made
it into the ranks of the divinely accredited witnesses before the
shutters finally went up.

This likening of the stories of encounters of the risen Jesus
to experiences of the Spirit is an approach to the resurrection
stories that has been followed recently by Alistair Kee in his short
study, *From Bad Faith to Good News*, although he makes no use

of the possible identification of the appearance to more than five hundred of I Cor. 15.6 with the account of Pentecost; for, perhaps mesmerized by Luke's way of telling the story, despite all its incongruities, he argues that I Cor. 15.6 'must be a reference to the church *after* Pentecost' (95, my italics). Despite that, he insists that the reason why there was any sequel to Jesus' death was, in a single word, 'Pentecost', an experience of a power from beyond this world which transformed and empowered the disciples; this power was, moreover, 'that same Spirit which the disciples had experienced in the presence of Jesus while he was still alive amongst them on earth' (89). So he is prepared to dismiss the evidence of an empty tomb or encounters with a risen Jesus as unprovable; the main evidence and basis for the Christian faith is rather the sheer fact of the existence of these transformed and empowered disciples. Could and should one then say, as J. M. Robinson has put it in a reformulation of Bultmann's position, that 'Jesus rose, as the revalidation of his word, into the Holy Spirit'?[216]

D. J. Davies, too, sheds light on another way, an exegetically based way, of regarding the relation of Jesus' resurrection and the coming of the Spirit. Basing himself on Luke's account he argues that

> in Luke-Acts . . . the resurrection, as such, is not the phase of triumph one might have expected assuming that Jesus' violent death, overcoming the theme of suffering which is so strong in Luke, would lead to his own form of direct rebounding violence or conquest. . . . It is not the resurrection appearances that power the church, but the coming of the Spirit.

For the encounters with the risen Jesus leave the disciples apprehensive and still 'overcome by death, despite the resurrection appearances'.[217] It is then legitimate to ask whether the resurrection does not as a result become somewhat redundant – but not, of course, for the author of Luke-Acts, inasmuch as the resurrection still plays an important role, for instance in the speeches of Acts, as vindicating Jesus (Acts 2.24–32; 3.15; 10.41; 13.30–37, etc.). The resurrection in itself is not saving, but rather attests that Jesus has been saved and inaugurates that era in which the risen Jesus is savingly present (e.g. 3.16; 13.38) and sends the Spirit (e.g. 2.33).

In a rather similar fashion, too, at least at first sight, Peter Carnley finds the grounds for believing in the Christian faith in Christians' present experience of Jesus, in the church's experience of the spirit of Christ. For Carnley recognizes to the full the difficulty of deciding whether the appearances of the risen Jesus were objective or subjective visions and finds a solution to this problem in another empirical basis for belief in Jesus' resurrection, namely in the experience of Jesus' continuing presence with his community as spirit. Our

> present experience of the Spirit of Christ convinces us that stories of the empty tomb and appearances are 'substantially true'; i.e. they convince us that Jesus was raised from the dead. The occurrence of this past event is the ground of our current experience. . . . if faith is based upon the present perception of the Spirit of Christ, then it may be that the visions were subjective or psychological phenomena which functioned nevertheless as signs of the substantial truth that Jesus had been raised.[218]

What is particularly difficult here, however, is the way in which present experience is supposed to prove the 'substantial truth' (whatever that may mean) of past events, even if they are supposed to be past events with continuing effects. Is Carnley saying that only the resurrection events (whatever they were) can explain present experience? But how do we know that? And quite what present experience of Christ as spirit is meant?[219] With this one may contrast Pannenberg's forthright statement when, having asserted that the resurrection of Jesus is a historical question in so far as it is a question of what did or did not happen at a certain time, he further maintains that only historical arguments can answer this question:

unless we had present experiences of the resurrected Jesus from which we could conclude that he did not remain dead. But obviously we have no such experiences.[220]

For those outside charismatic circles the Spirit can be somewhat elusive, mysterious, hard to define, in short hardly that which is really suited to satisfy the demand for the empirical. And Carnley seems to recognize that when he speaks of the 'ambiguity in the present perception of the presence of the Spirit' and of 'its . . . very elusive and transcendent nature'; therein he sees the reason for the possibility of women and men being able either in faith to recognize its presence or to remain oblivious to it.[221] However, at this point it should be emphasized that I have no wish to deny the reality of religious experience, but only that it is of such a kind as by itself to warrant the deduction 'Jesus is risen'.

Or are we to think here of that spirit of Jesus, the historical Jesus, as Albert Schweitzer saw it, in the sense of the way in which the Jesus of history can still move and influence us today?[222] But Carnley gives the distinct impression that he means considerably more than this. It is, for a start, the Spirit (with a capital S) of *Christ* of which he speaks, not the spirit (lower case s) of Jesus. If one seeks parallels to Schweitzer's 'spirit of Jesus' in Carnley's account it would rather be in his use of the notion, derived from John Knox after considerable pruning, qualification and clarification, of the church's 'memory' of Jesus, the corporate 'memory' retained down the centuries of the sort of person that Jesus was. Yet Carnley insists that the church 'remembers Jesus . . . precisely in order to recognize the *Christus praesens*' (297–8). But in the word 'recognize' there lurks a danger and an ambiguity, for the church does not go through its life being confronted, for instance, with visionary experiences such as Paul had, which raise the question 'Who are you, Lord?' What Carnley means in concrete terms is not quite clear, as we have seen. Is it more a matter of recognizing in the present what the demands of discipleship, of following that Jesus whom the church remembers, are? Is the recognition in fact nearer Schweitzer's conception in that it is a discernment of whither that 'spiritual force' is leading us and how it is shaping our lives? We 'recognize' that this decision or that way of life in fact embodies the spirit of the remembered Jesus. But Carnley will seemingly not be satisfied with that, as is clear from his subsequent critique of Paul van Buren and Josiah Royce, even though his comparing the reality of the Spirit of Christ to a 'team spirit' may come near to such an understanding of 'spirit' here (313). Or are we simply to understand that all that is meant is that a spirit of self-giving love like that of Jesus is observable in the church (334)? Coupled with this, however, is the problem that much of his discussion about 'recognizing' or 'knowing' Jesus or Christ in present experience seems to involve some sort of 'mystical' experience in which we, individually or collectively, can say of the experience, 'This is Jesus/Christ'. For Carnley concentrates on the problem of the identity of Jesus which the church remembers, while the problem is surely that of the nature of the present experience or encounter in which Jesus or Christ is to be recognized; that remains quite vague and elusive, if more is meant than that Jesus' self-giving love is replicated in the Christian community. Schweitzer's talk of the 'spirit' of Jesus, on the other hand, I take to be far less 'mystical' in this sense, and to consist rather in an observable and demonstrable continuity in attitude and conduct, a following of the example and the precedent set by Jesus in the past.

Carnley also claims the authority of Paul as support for his view, but where does Paul appeal to the work of the Spirit of Christ as 'an additional empirically based indication of the fact that Jesus was alive as one who had been raised as a "spiritual body" and exalted to the heavens whence he would return' (250)? Paul did appeal to the experience of the Spirit of Christ, for instance to show that Christians had been adopted as God's children (e.g. Rom. 8.15–16; Gal. 4.6) or that Christians could be confident of their final redemption (e.g. Rom. 8.23; II Cor. 1.22; 5.5), but never to prove the reality of Christ or his resurrection. When in his letters he does need to 'prove' the resurrection of Jesus, as in I Cor. 15, it is to the list of resurrection appearances and the indisputable place of the resurrection of Christ in the early Christian proclamation that he turns, not to the experience of the Spirit in the church. And frankly, while we have no idea how he 'proved' this when speaking to those outside the church, it may be doubted whether he appealed to the experience of the Spirit to prove his point, however impressive this experience may have been otherwise. And that Paul could in some contexts speak of (the exalted) Christ and the Spirit as if they were identical is not the same as expressly using the one to prove the reality of the other.

A further example of an interpretation of the resurrection of Jesus in terms of 'spirit' is to be found in the work of Paul Tillich: in the resurrection is overcome the negativity of the disappearance of the one who was the New Being:

> In an ecstatic experience the concrete picture of Jesus of Nazareth became indissolubly united with the reality of the New Being. He is present wherever the New Being is present. . . . He 'is the Spirit' and we 'know him now' only because he is the Spirit. In this way the concrete individual life of the man Jesus of Nazareth is raised above transitoriness into the eternal presence of God as Spirit.[223]

I would be uneasy with this brief account: does it not *seem* to combine an account of the individual Jesus as 'Spirit' (not as an immortal 'soul', for Tillich rejects that account of Jesus' survival) with an ethical, existential experience of his followers, which recalls Schweitzer's talk of Jesus' 'spirit' moving us today? ('Spirit', we recall, can mean many different things, just as the adjective 'spiritual' can.) The latter notion, however, is not really speaking of the 'survival' or even the 'continued existence' of Jesus, but more of his 'continued influence'. The term 'restitution', which Tillich then uses in speaking of the 'restitution of Jesus as the Christ' or 'to the dignity of the Christ', is, moreover, somewhat unfortunate (as far as I can see, one usually speaks of the restitution of *things*), and I am unsure what more normal word it represents here: is it 'restoration (to the dignity of the

Christ)' or 'reinstatement (as the Christ)', in both cases implying that he was the Christ before? That leaves open the question whether anything more is meant than that his followers can once again regard him and revere him as the Christ; they see that, despite the apparent disavowal of Jesus in his shameful and accursed death, he is nevertheless, paradoxically, God's anointed one.

(e) A transformation of 'resurrection'?

The early Christians were transformed and empowered; they also inferred that Jesus was risen, but not necessarily as a direct inference from their transformation and empowering alone, and attempts to couple the two aspects of their existence with one another as cause and effect do not seem to correspond to the evidence of the New Testament texts and the arguments which they in fact use. The first Christians at any rate used a Jewish belief to explain their experiences, but Kee argues that in being applied to Jesus the Jewish idea of 'resurrection' underwent a transformation, just as Jewish ideas of 'the Messiah' and 'the son of man' had also been drastically revised in being applied to Jesus. That should occasion no surprise if, as Verweyen argues, it is questionable whether 'resurrection', a metaphor stemming from the world-view of Jewish apocalyptic eschatology, is a suitable metaphor for the life of Jesus in God and our own future hope.[224] But is that simply a modern question, or had the first Christians, at least intuitively, also raised it? In that case, what 'resurrection' was in the case of Jesus cannot simply be inferred from Jewish traditions; so 'resurrection' in this instance, Kee argues,

> has nothing to do with an empty tomb and a body getting up and walking about again. It has everything to do with the new life of the Spirit which came at Pentecost (129).

The fact that 'resurrection' may have been reinterpreted, or even certainly has been, does not prevent it from still having something to do with 'an empty tomb and a body getting up and walking about again'; such a judgment depends on the sort of reinterpretation that has taken place. All that Kee's observation has done is to make room for the possibility that we *may* here have to do with a 'resurrection' that does not involve 'an empty tomb and a body getting up and walking about again'; we could then no longer argue that just because, when Jews spoke of 'resurrection', they meant something that involved a tomb being emptied and a body getting up and walking around, therefore, when Jesus' followers spoke of his 'resurrection', they too must also mean that his tomb was empty and his body was walking around. Indeed we could now turn this around and argue that, just as in other respects there was a tendency for at least some Christians to revert later to Jewish positions and Jewish under-standings (e.g. in the case of observance of the Jewish law), so too here there may have been a tendency to reinterpret 'resurrection' back again into a more typically Jewish view of 'resurrection' which did involve Jesus' grave being empty and sightings of his body raised from it and walking about.

In other words a Christian reinterpretation of 'resurrection' does not *compel* us to abandon the empty tomb and appearances of Jesus' risen body; it merely creates room for that, allows for that possibility. In the last analysis the arguments in favour of such a course will be those which Kee advances, based on those problems and inconsistencies of a literal view of the ascension in which we find ourselves ensnared when we so interpret it, and based on the convoluted arguments which Paul advances for a 'spiritual' body in I Cor. 15: 'a lot of blustering words designed to silence the Corinthians', as Kee puts it, harshly but not without at least some justice (136).[225] Apart from these negative arguments, there is surely also the more compelling positive one that, if one goes back to the nature of the experience of Paul and tries to gauge its nature, it is not expressly said to involve an empty tomb, and seems to be visionary and at least in part private to him.

It has often been noted that Paul says nothing in I Cor. 15

about the empty tomb tradition; this raises the question whether he knew of it, or whether it was in fact a later addition to the resurrection traditions. It is true that, somewhat desperately, some scholars have clutched at the words 'and was buried' (v. 3), and have seen this as evidence that Paul must have been aware of the tradition of the empty tomb.[226] Yet it is dangerous to infer from the mention of Jesus' burial an awareness of a subsequent reversal and undoing of that burial. At any rate, as Merklein and others have seen,[227] 'he was buried' is attached to the death of Jesus, not his resurrection, and confirms that the former occurred, just as the appearances then provide support for the assertion of Jesus' resurrection. Indeed one could as easily infer from Paul's argument from the process of nature and from the dissimilarity and discontinuity between the natural body and the resurrection 'body' in I Cor. 15.36–44 that the former body remained sown in the ground, as it were, with the resurrection body as something completely new, a new creation, created out of nothing as in the original creation of all things. So great is the stress upon the newness and the difference of the resurrection existence, as we have seen, that this might seem to a logical corollary. Therefore Lüdemann is right to question whether the Paul who so emphatically declares that flesh and blood shall not inherit the kingdom (I Cor. 15.50) was likely to be interested in the empty tomb.[228] Or, putting it crudely, the emptiness of the tomb could imply that the crucified and buried flesh and blood of Jesus was indeed on its way into the kingdom, and that, Paul maintains, would be improper. The mention of Jesus' burial in the tradition recorded in I Cor. 15.3 has as its likely purpose to confirm the reality of his death, for the function of this rite of passage is to mark and seal the passage of the one buried from one mode of existence to another, and Paul mentions our burial with Christ in Rom. 6.4 in order to underline that reality and with it the reality of Christians' death with Christ to their old life and the consequent completeness of their break with sin: their old nature is done away with (6.6) and it is thus inconceivable that they should remain in sin (6.1).[229]

Another writer to insist, as Kee does, upon the transformation of the concept of 'resurrection' occasioned by the experience of Jesus' 'rising' is Peter Selby in his monograph *Look for the Living*. Indeed, not only the concept of 'resurrection' is changed; the very world-view, that of Jewish eschatology, in which this concept had its place, and within which it was intelligible, is transformed by the impact of the disciples' experiences:

> when Jesus was raised from the dead the first casualty was the idea of resurrection. In proclaiming the resurrection as the resurrection of *Jesus*, the disciples contributed without knowing it to the demise of that world-view in which such a proclamation, in those words, could continue to be understood as they intended it to be.[230]

One would think, then, that in that case Christians should no longer have felt themselves able to speak of 'resurrection' and to expect to be understood. At least, even if the first-century Christians had not yet realized what they had done to this term, one would have thought that by the late twentieth century the penny might have dropped. Selby too continues to use the term, yet, although he comes near to speaking of the abandonment of the historical sense of 'resurrection' in favour of a symbolic interpretation of it, he never expressly says that that is what he is advocating.[231] Elsewhere, indeed, he sets his face against a Bultmannian interpretation of the resurrection as simply the coming to faith of the disciples, alleging that this makes 'faith . . . incredible, for it would ultimately be resting only on itself' (141).

What, then, is the object of their faith, and on what does it rest? And is this object of faith aptly described in terms of 'resurrection' except perhaps in a symbolic or figurative sense, like 'newness of life' (cf. Rom. 6.4)? Selby is here insistent that the characteristics of the life of the Christian community must 'match' the story which it tells of Jesus' resurrection; only so will its claims for the universal significance of what happened to Jesus be credible. Here he seems, like Kee, to find 'resurrection' in the new life of the Christian community. However, he does not say that the life of community should match the story of Jesus, so that Jesus can be said to live on, say as Spirit, and take concrete form in the life of his followers. He says, rather more opaquely, that it should match the story of Jesus' *resurrection*. Still more opaque is the claim that Christians' faith rests not only on this 'matching', but also on what can be verified historically (37, 40–1). This external event acts as a standard by which a Christian community is measured, and to which it needs to be recalled. Selby also talks of a common memory as giving the Christian community reality (37), and a memory is usually a memory of something, but that takes us no further towards saying what that 'something' is. For we have seen that very little can be verified historically above and beyond the disciples' faith: something, a mysterious something, happened to them, but further than that we cannot penetrate.

Need that mysterious something be 'resurrection' in anything but the most figurative of senses? Selby identifies a number of motifs or features of early Christians' 'resurrection faith' which, in his opinion, should still characterize those who share that faith today, but it is not clear why a historically verifiable event of 'resurrection' is a necessary presupposition or basis for any of them. If 'resurrection' meant for the early Christians, for instance, a new justice, a new righteousness for all (the first of Selby's features of 'resurrection faith'), nevertheless the proclamation of that new righteousness as being here now, in the midst of a still unrighteous world, shattered the categories of Jewish expectation, leaving one to ask what need there was still to affirm a *post mortem* establishment of that righteousness in some still future world. So when, for instance, Selby argues that 'resurrection faith' must be 'concerned with a justice that remains discontented unless it includes all', which 'is at once so radical and so impossible a demand as rightly to be called the resurrection of the dead' (171), then surely 'resurrection' is being used in a very different sense from that of Jewish eschatology. And that is precisely as it should be, to judge from Selby's insistence upon the transformation that has taken place in the language of 'resurrection'. But is he saying that the disciples' 'resurrection faith' *was* their concern for this new justice, rather than the far more conventional claim that their concern for this justice arose from their belief in the raising of Jesus and its perceived implications? In the former instance, is the use of the language of 'resurrection' really helpful here? Certainly, when Selby comes to speak of the justification of the ungodly, the entry of the individual into righteousness (174), then terms like 'new creation' would surely be more appropriate; they would at least avoid any suggestion that might lurk in the term 'resurrection' that this was simply a restoration of what had existed before. In other words, in reacting against a 'resurrection faith' that is of purely antiquarian interest, Selby has rightly insisted that one cannot properly speak of a 'resurrection faith' unless the community that holds it bears the hallmarks of those who first held this faith. 'You say that you believe in the resurrection,' he is in effect arguing, 'but how can you say that unless you show these characteristics of the "resurrection faith" of the disciples of Jesus?' But would it not be better to say that the faith and the vision of Jesus lived on in his disciples; that Jesus' cause lived on in this sense, not only despite his death, but all the more because of it, in that he had been prepared to die for this cause and this vision?

If the experiences of the 'resurrection' also produced a sense of 'mission', which is Selby's next motif or feature of 'resurrection faith', then so apparently did, or should, the message of the earthly Jesus as he sent out his disciples as an extension of his own mission. Another of Selby's themes, exaltation, is found at its most paradoxical in the Fourth Gospel, where the language of exaltation is used of Jesus' crucifixion (John 12.32). It may be questioned whether the language of 'resurrection' rather than 'exaltation' was in fact necessary to preserve 'the continuity that exists between the risen and exalted Christ and the Jesus whom [the disciples] had known in his ministry and death' (99); for examples abound in Graeco-Roman and Jewish traditions of human beings who are exalted to heaven. What one could and probably should say here is that 'resurrection' entails the death of the one to be exalted, whereas 'exaltation' may by-pass death. The further theme of 'life', as Selby interprets it in the light of the Fourth Gospel, means that this 'life' was 'life tied to the person of Jesus and to existence in the physical world' (103). Indeed, Selby regards the sense of present fulfilment in the Fourth Gospel, and the sense of eschatological realities already being made present, as being so overwhelming that after Jesus' great cry on the cross of 'It is accomplished!' (John 19.30), Jesus' resurrection becomes redundant: John merely retains the resurrection stories as part of Christian tradition (103, 117). Jesus' resurrection, as the fulfilment of Old Testament promises, was, finally, the realization of Jewish hopes for the future; it offered an answer to the quest of the mystery-cults for the 'destruction of mortality' and to 'the Jewish search for a future under God . . . in a manner that gave meaning to the present experience of the believer' (109). Although Selby immediately goes on to quote a clearly futuristic passage from Moltmann,[232] is there any good reason why that same meaning should not now be found in this world and in a this-worldly future, rather than being entirely dependent upon some existence after death, particularly if one concentrates more upon the destruction of the *fear* of mortality?

Thus the importance for Selby of his argument, a perfectly proper one, for the necessity of 'resurrection faith' has perhaps meant that he has not given sufficient attention to the question of the necessity of belief in the resurrection, of Jesus or of his followers, in any sense approximating to the traditional one, in any sense that would justify the retention of the term 'resurrection', despite the risk that its meaning would be misunderstood. For if Selby is right in saying that the disciples' experience meant the end of the Jewish world-view (that of apocalyptic eschatology, at least), and that meant the end of the framework within which 'resurrection' could be understood, how can we go on talking, in a post-Easter period, of Jesus' 'resurrection', if that event marked the end of the possibility of using the term intelligibly, as though we knew what it meant?

(f) 'Resurrection faith'?

Perhaps the characteristics of 'resurrection faith' which Selby has listed stem not so much from '*resurrection* faith' as from beliefs about the nature of the God who was believed to have raised Jesus and about the nature of the Jesus whom they believed had been raised. Their belief in the resurrection of Jesus may have enabled them to see certain things about God or about Jesus more clearly, or may at least have confirmed their earlier perceptions, gained during their time with Jesus during his ministry, that God and Jesus were like that. That God and Jesus were, and are, like that, and the implications for discipleship which follow from their nature, may then be valid without our needing to talk of 'resurrection' or to look back to a historical event over and above the disciples' coming to faith.

Something like that is, in the last analysis, also Lüdemann's conclusion: all that Easter finally revealed was already there before Easter, for Jesus' teaching and story already contained within themselves all the characteristics of the oldest 'resurrection faith', so that the early witnesses said the same as Jesus had said, though in part in different terms. In this respect his conclusion is also similar to Marxsen's, when he affirms that 'what comes today [is] the same thing that Jesus of Nazareth brought'.[233] For integral to this oldest 'resurrection faith' were the experience of the forgiveness of sins,[234] of the overcoming of death in the living of life, this-worldly life present now in the Christian community as spirit, and lastly a belief in eternity which is as such an '*Endglaube*', in which time and eternity become one in such a way that the heart gazes into eternity.[235] Aspects of this definition of the content of the 'resurrection faith' are highly problematic, but what concerns me here, as in Selby's account, is more the question what is meant by labelling this faith 'resurrection faith'. Is the content of this faith somehow bound up with the resurrection of Jesus or the resurrection of his followers? Is it directed towards 'resurrection'? Or is the designation more a temporal one, the faith that one has after Easter?

For in all this, it seems to me, the problems of the much-used phrase 'resurrection faith' have not been fully recognized.[236] There is, for a start, its basic ambiguity: does it mean a faith that Jesus is risen or that we will be raised, or does it mean that sort of faith which the (supposed) resurrection of Jesus engendered in his followers? These two definitions imply very different criteria for determining their truth: if 'resurrection faith' is 'faith that' something has happened or that something is the case, then one must ask whether that 'something' is indeed the case as far as we can ascertain.[237] If, on the other hand, it is the faith engendered by the belief that Jesus has been raised from the dead, then one needs to show, first, that the disciples had this faith and secondly, if possible, that this faith did indeed arise from, and was bound up with, their belief in the raising of Jesus. But unless greater clarity can be achieved in the use of the phrase 'resurrection faith' (it may simply serve to sound orthodox while covering up a major reinterpretation of what has traditionally been assumed to be part and parcel of the Christian faith), then there would be a strong case for avoiding it altogether.

I have the same misgivings about Maurice Wiles' attempts to find a new definition of 'resurrection', corresponding to different ways of giving meaning to the term 'incarnation'. He suggests three possibilities:[238]

1. The term expresses the 'continuity of Jesus' living identity through death' (although, as we shall see, albeit briefly, this 'continuity' and 'identity' must be considered philosophically problematic);

2. 'Resurrection' may be used 'to indicate the positive and distinctive nature of the aftermath of the life and death of Jesus without intending to imply any particular understanding of how that creative aftermath came about' (this seems to me to come near to Marxsen's position, namely that Jesus' cause lives on);

3. '"Resurrection" may be used with less specific attention to the figure of Jesus, as a general term either for continued personal identity through death or for that potentiality in human life as a whole for the emergence of new life out of old – or, of course, for

both' (here, he recognizes, Jesus may be a 'focal example of either or both of these senses of "resurrection"', but his experience is then no different in kind from what belongs to wider human experience).

Now when we write about 'resurrection', at least the inverted commas may signal that the word may not be used in its traditional or expected sense. When talking about it, on the other hand, there is the danger that, unless we are very clever with our tone of voice or gesticulations to emphasize the figurative or unconventional use of the word, the distinction may be lost on our hearers. Is there not a very great danger in a term that can mean so many different things to its hearers? True, its very elasticity may serve to hold together the proponents of a wide range of different beliefs and theologies and to give the impression that some views, which are quite drastic reinterpretations of Christian tradition, are in fact of one piece with more conventional interpretations of that tradition. But at least some hearers, if they realize what is being masked by this verbal elasticity, will want to question the right of the others to belong to the same fold: 'resurrection' in this sense, they will say, is a fraud, an impostor.

So are we here simply talking about 'resurrection faith' in the second sense which I have just mentioned, namely that faith which Jesus' followers had in the period following what they called the 'resurrection' of Jesus? Is what is meant by 'resurrection faith' in fact that faith which characterized them then, from Easter onwards, a faith whose content was determined not so much by the event of 'resurrection' as by the nature and message of the one whom they believed now to be risen? In other words: Jesus' life and work and teaching and the manner of his death were now constitutive of their existence, and that in a new way; for they believed that his authority, his claim to speak for God, his lordship over themselves and their world had been reconfirmed in a most signal and decisive way. If that is the case, however, then we should not let ourselves be mesmerized by the potentially misleading word 'resurrection' or the ambiguous phrase 'resurrection faith', and be prepared to move beyond this 'resurrection' to expound the nature of Christian existence in a way that is independent of this term.

The outcome of this first part of the book is therefore, I confess, a somewhat disquieting one. For the result of a historical investigation into the traditions of Jesus' resurrection seems to yield little that is of much use for Christian faith. In that respect I am in agreement with Sarah Coakley's conclusion that 'the available evidence for Jesus' bodily Resurrection is such that the historical route [Pannenberg] proposes ends only in unsatisfactorily uncertain conclusions, which cannot hope *per se* to convince the sceptic'.[239] Indeed, I would go further: *any* historical route is likely to prove just as unsatisfactory and its conclusions are unlikely to convince the sceptic, even if they do not stand alone, but are reinforced by other arguments, of whatever kind. And to seek refuge in 'mystery', as Coakley does, is a dangerous move on her part, for it lies open to precisely the same criticism as she levels against Pannenberg, namely that, if we cannot know what 'resurrection of the dead' means, then we cannot know whether it has occurred, for it lacks all 'noetic content' (109–10). At any rate the results of historical investigation prove highly elusive; what happened indeed remains ultimately inscrutable, 'mysterious' in the sense that we cannot attain to any clear, definite perception of it. For while something may well have happened in Jerusalem on the first Sunday after Jesus' death, that 'something' may be little more than the women's failure to find Jesus' body. Something may also have happened to various disciples, both in Galilee and probably also in or near Jerusalem, and also to the persecutor Paul, something which led them to believe that they had seen the risen Jesus. But again this 'something' proves highly elusive. Even if one is not persuaded by the various psychological explanations offered for it, they cannot be ruled out, and may therefore mean that the cause of the disciples' experiences lies in their own (possibly disturbed) psyche and not in the miraculous action of God. (Or at least the miraculous action of

God becomes superfluous to explain the rise of this belief.) Indeed, however unconvincing they may seem, these psychological explanations have a built-in advantage over against more supernatural explanations of the resurrection, in that it is very difficult to 'explain' an event that is allegedly without any real analogy or parallel in any of the usual ways in which one offers explanations of historical events.[240] The supernatural 'explanation' may in fact be little more than a denial that any of the other non-supernatural explanations is really satisfactory or convincing. Or, if the psychological explanations of Lüdemann seem less than convincing, then there is, as an alternative, Müller's account based upon expectations of the vindication of martyr figures by their exaltation to heaven, backed up by visions as the 'visual articulation' of a process of reflection upon Jesus' death.[241] At any rate, as Broer points out, there are parallels of visions of dead persons and exalted ones appearing, and neither reason nor historical criticism has the means of distinguishing between those visions which God has caused or sent and those whose cause lies elsewhere.[242]

Similarly, it cannot be ruled out that the manner of Jesus' burial made it impossible to discover the body again and that this gave rise to the tradition of the empty tomb. It therefore seems to me to be beside the point when Wilckens in his critique of Lüdemann points to how the first Christians understood and proclaimed the resurrection of Jesus, and complains that Lüdemann's explanation has nothing to do with 'historical exegesis'.[243] It has at least, on the other hand, a great deal to do with historical criticism, with that radical questioning and search after causal explanations which Ernst Troeltsch rightly saw to be fundamental to that discipline.[244] And in the case of the traditions of Jesus' resurrection these methods lead, in my opinion, to a high degree of uncertainty as to exactly what happened, regardless of how the early Christians may have seen it and proclaimed it. The logical conclusion of such an investigation seems therefore to be, apparently, a regrettable and thoroughly unsatisfactory 'Don't know', a historical agnosticism that seems to undermine any profession of faith, unless one somehow manages to anchor it independently of any historical occurrences. That was very clearly seen by Antony Flew in a debate on the resurrection of Jesus: he sets a question-mark against all arguments about what happened by stating that 'we have not got enough evidence of what actually happened in that undated year of the Easter events'.[245] If I were to level one criticism at Gerd Lüdemann's study it would be this: he displays in his thoroughgoing historical criticism a dogmatism that is not in keeping with the agnosticism which the nature of the evidence demands. That becomes particularly clear in Lüdemann's retort to Ulrich Luz's balanced and sympathetic review-article: Luz had granted that the resurrection of Jesus itself cannot be apprehended historically and denied that the issue of faith or unbelief was to be settled according to the emptiness or otherwise of Jesus' tomb.[246] To that Lüdemann asks why, if Jesus' resurrection is not to be apprehended historically, one cannot state plainly that Jesus corpse just rotted away; why, he asks, does Luz talk about a postulate of the principle of analogy instead of the fact of Jesus' decomposition?[247] In so murky a piece of history one can, however, speak only of possibilities, even if some are admittedly much more probable than others; decomposition of Jesus' corpse is certainly more probable than, say, the hypothesis that he was not really dead, but the latter suggestion remains a possible one. Whether the decomposition is also more probable than a divine intervention depends in large measure, as we shall see, on one's view of God and God's relationship to the world and the natural order. But it is to be emphasized that there are several possibilities that remain in the running, so that the dictum of Sherlock Holmes which Richard Swinburne cites, 'When you have eliminated the impossible, whatever remains, *however improbable*, must be the truth', is of little help.[248] Rather one should say that, when the impossible has been eliminated, the truth is to be found among the remaining possibilities, and some of them will be less probable than others. As far as the resurrection of Jesus itself is concerned, a decisive historical judgment is to my mind episte-

mologically improper and impossible; a 'reverent agnosticism', as
Robert Morgan rather deprecatingly calls it, is not only a 'safe
policy', but also the surest and the most soberly scientific and
scholarly.[249] What would be, in my view, quite improper is to use
the historical impasse as an excuse to give the resurrection stories
the benefit of the doubt, so to speak, or to jump from the recognition that, in the nature of things, they cannot be proved false,
at least *in toto*, to the assumption that they can be treated as in
some measure true. That particular move is an intellectually
illegitimate one.

The resultant uncertainty is very far removed from the
triumphalistic view which, equally dogmatically, uses the 'fact' of
Jesus' resurrection to 'prove' all sorts of things – the existence of
God, the power of God to work 'miracles' and to intervene in
nature and in history, the divinity of Christ and so forth. Those
who maintain that Christian faith stands or falls with the doctrine
of the resurrection are indeed correct in the sense that much of
traditional Christianity can, in the last resort, appeal to this 'act
of God' as its principal and conclusive argument, and must
indeed resort to it, for it otherwise finds itself on decidedly shaky
ground.[250] But if that ground which is its last resort itself turns
out to be more than a little unsteady, then that in turn raises the
question how Christian faith can appropriately come to terms
with this shift in perspective, with this realization of the nature
of the evidence for Jesus' resurrection. For it is, in my opinion,
illegitimate to try to circumvent this epistemological gap or to
spring over it as if it were not there; at the start of this study we
saw some of the various ways in which this has been attempted,
like the redefinition of 'history' and 'historical', which seem at
first more sophisticated and intellectually respectable than a bald
assertion that, because the early church said so, therefore it
must be so. But if the resurrection of Jesus indeed impinges on
history in such a way as to be vulnerable to historical criticism,
then the nature of this history and of the results of the historical
investigation of it is such that little can be said about it that is
not hedged about with a veritable thicket of caveats and qualifi-

cations. The second part of this book is therefore concerned with the implications of this apparent 'dead end' for our understanding of Christian faith and of God, with a coming to terms with the loss of what had previously been thought to be the firm basis for so many traditional assertions about God, Jesus and the world.

Part II: Coming to Terms

5

Handling the New Testament Texts

The fate of Christ and that of his followers are closely inter-twined; what he experienced dictates what they can be expected to experience. That much is implicit in Paul's calling the risen Christ 'the first-fruits of those that have fallen asleep [in death]' (I Cor. 15.20). Hence our dilemma with regard to what actually happened in the case of Jesus is not merely a matter of anti-quarian interest; it spills over into the question of our own destinies and with it are bound up our own hopes and expecta-tions. If we raise questions about what actually happened to the one regarded as the 'first-fruits' of the future harvest of the resurrected dead, then obviously predictions about the nature of that future harvest become perilous in the extreme; its very existence may be threatened.

However, before we embark on that question, it is worth making two interrelated remarks about how we shall proceed in this second part of the present study. The first point is that we shall see in the next chapter that the Christian church, in formu-lating its credal position with regard to the resurrection, went beyond what Paul seems to say on this subject. And despite its appeal to Paul for support, it is far from clear that it has a better claim to that support than those adversaries whom it sought to refute when it invoked Paul's teaching.

The second point is that particularly in the subsequent chapters, I will again and again have to stress that the argument which I am advancing goes beyond anything that any of the New Testament writers actually say, however much I may take them as a starting-point. Indeed they may at many points contradict

my arguments. However, in treating them in this way I am not
doing something that I see as intrinsically any more reprehensible
than what the early Fathers of the church did when they built
up their tradition about the resurrection using or reusing the
building-blocks which Paul had provided, or rather using only
some of them and fitting them together rather differently from
the apostle himself. It is, moreover, something which in the view
of Gordon Kaufman has always belonged to the task of Christian
theology in so far as it has sought critically and constructively to
work out 'more adequate ways to conceptualize God'. For,

> All such constructive efforts . . . involved moving in some way
> beyond what was given in the Bible, either by drawing on
> extra-biblical materials or through new creative insights.
> Hence, however much theologians have understood their work
> to be essentially hermeneutical in character, it has, in fact,
> always involved much more than this.[251]

And, it may be added, it is far better to realize this and to
acknowledge it to oneself and to one's readers, than simply to do
it quietly and in secret, or perhaps even to fail to see what one is
in fact doing.

For it is as if the utterances of the New Testament writers are
pointers, each pointing in the direction of something which they
cannot adequately describe; if they *do* all ultimately point in the
same direction, it is as yet far from clear that they in fact do so,
and it therefore follows that ultimate agreement and cohesion
cannot be assumed. Now there was a time when 'trajectory' was
a very fashionable word in New Testament scholarship:[252] there
were various 'trajectories' within early Christianity, that is, various different movements, different religious traditions, amongst
the earliest Christians, each with their different characteristics.
One could, however, use the term in another context as well,
hermeneutically rather than historically: there is a sense in which,
when a writer writes and publishes a work, that piece of writing
is launched on a course, a history, which the writer can no longer
control or predict, as it is read and interpreted by successive

generations of readers who come under its influence.[253] At this point the imagery of the 'trajectory' breaks down, however, both in its application to church history on the larger scale, and in its hermeneutical use here of the effects that a text may have upon its subsequent readers. For the 'trajectory' of an object is usually determinable from the moment that it is despatched, and it follows a single course without deviating unless it strikes something. (Robinson recognized that his 'trajectories' were not pre-determined either, however much the use of the term in physics might suggest that.)[254] But what the New Testament texts do and what becomes of them is by no means to be determined in advance, nor is their course pursued surely and steadily towards a single goal.[255] No one can predict how an utterance, an idea expressed in the New Testament, may be taken up in the future or what effects it may have, nor do these interpretations and applications always lie along a single line; very often, looking back upon the history of the exegesis of a passage or verse or upon the influence and impact of an idea, one can see that that history has divided into several different strands or branches.[256] The words and the ideas of the New Testament are therefore potentially both open and polyvalent.

Paul's words were therefore 'open' to the Fathers' use of them as they built up their orthodox teaching on the resurrection, but they were also 'open', perhaps even more 'open', to the Gnostics to use them in support of their teachings, as we shall see in the next chapter. What I am attempting to do is to take Paul's ideas, and also certain ideas contained in the Fourth Gospel, and to ask whether they might also be 'open' to, in the sense of 'suggestive of', yet another line of argument, and might point in another direction as well. What then arises as a result of these reflections is not a 'biblical' theology in the sense of a theology that records and re-expresses what is already stated in the biblical text, for it clearly and explicitly follows through what in my judgment is the thrust of certain biblical ideas and takes them far beyond what their writers ever envisaged, and it also equally clearly disregards or rejects other ideas which they held.[257] If it can be called 'biblical' at all, it may be only in the sense that it has taken these particular biblical insights as a starting-point and, in interaction and dialogue with them, has attempted to weave a new and contemporary expression of Christian faith, a redefinition of what a Christian can and cannot believe today.

It will be clear from this that I do not regard the biblical writers as having said the last word on this particular subject, and that presupposes certain assumptions about the nature of the revelation of truth through the documents of the New Testament, if indeed one wants to use the perilous term 'revelation' at all. In a sense, what I am doing with the New Testament is similar to what the Fourth Gospel declares legitimate with regard to the teaching of Jesus himself: Jesus is made to declare that he had much to tell the disciples, but they were unable to bear it; so, when the spirit of truth comes, it will guide them in all truth (John 16.13).[258] Doubtless the Fourth Evangelist saw that as a legitimation of his way of proclaiming the message of Jesus, yet it is always a way that is fraught with danger and open to the charge of arbitrariness.[259] It is a way that the Christian church has consequently viewed with suspicion, at least since in the strife with the Montanist movement this principle and the accompanying promise of the Paraclete became a matter of contention.[260] But much depends on the way that is chosen; the way that I wish to tread is not a flight into the uncontrolled irrational, into that which is above and beyond all criticism – rather, as Gordon Kaufman says of the element of 'mystery' in his own theological work, it by no means involves a letting down of 'the bars of a thoroughly critical employment of our faculties; on the contrary, we are alerting ourselves to the necessity here to employ our critical faculties to their utmost'.[261] The 'going beyond' the New Testament that I am advocating here is likewise not an uncritical flight of fancy, but rather stems precisely from a critical approach to the New Testament, from a *Sachkritik* that cannot rest content with the answers which the New Testament gives us, for it sees that the New Testament is not internally consistent, nor can it be shown to correspond to what we know of the world. Nor is it a path that leads us away from the earthly Jesus to a heavenly Christ to whom we somehow have a privileged access; rather, it is a path that forces us to hold even closer to that earthly, suffering Jesus.

At first sight this might seem to imply that we today know better than the New Testament writers, and that at first seems a most audacious and presumptuous claim. However, whether we know 'better' or not, we at least know things differently, and it is inevitable that we do; we cannot turn the clock back or shut our eyes to all that has happened in the past two millennia, even if not all of it can count as 'progress'. The New Testament writers belonged to their own time and not ours, and saw things in terms of their own time. For whatever else the documents of the New Testament may be, they are human products, human responses to what human beings perceived to be divine action and move-ment in historical events in which they had themselves partici-pated or of which they had heard from others. They were human attempts to respond adequately to what they had seen and heard and experienced. As human, and therefore fallible, attempts they should not be regarded as the only possible adequate responses, even for their own day and age, let alone for later periods. Theologians today should, however, pay careful attention to their responses; for in the first place it is only through their responses, including their interpretation of events around them, that theo-logians have access to that to which they are responding; and that to which they are responding is also something to which *Christian* theology today must in its turn also respond if it is to be called Christian. For our Christian theological strivings are an attempt to believe in, and to live before, God in a way that is in accord with what we believe is discernible of God in the person of Jesus of Nazareth. And of him we learn first of all through the witness of his first followers, through a witness that is both response and interpretation. It is true that even Christian theologians will also (or should also) learn from the subsequent experience of men and women, both of faith (of all sorts) and without it, in the past and in the present. But if they are properly *Christian* theologians, their starting-point and primary orientation-point, though not necessarily in an exclusive sense, is going to be the life of that man of the first century to whom witness is borne by the New Testament writers, the significance of whom is the common focus of all their varied writings.

Their witness is not in itself that primary point of orientation; their witness points beyond itself to Jesus, seeking to express, for the different communities for which its various writings were composed, what it means to believe in that Jesus. We can and should learn from these attempts to express Christian faith in a first-century setting, but we cannot expect to be able to transpose first-century faith over two millennia ready-made into another soil or expect it to flourish there with the same vigour as it once did. If the witness of these first Christians *is* still relevant today, then that to which they bore witness had a relevance and a potential significance beyond anything they could imagine or grasp, for they could not imagine their world lasting as long as ours has, nor could they imagine a universe as vast as we now know ours to be. Had they lived twenty centuries later they too would have had to have said things otherwise, as we must.[262] But still it is legitimate to take Jesus as our ultimate point of reference and orientation: to try to understand him in our vaster world and to understand it through him and in the light that he sheds upon our human life in it.

However, this necessity to refashion theology for another age and for a world that has become far vaster is, to my mind, a good reason for resisting the idea that truth is somehow encapsulated in those first-century writings. Rather, what their writers wrote were but gropings after a truth greater than they could comprehend or express and greater, too, than we can grasp or formulate. It is the task of succeeding ages to sift out what the first-century writers have sought to express, and to try to make better sense in the light of the insights of a different age of what they were trying to say.

It is from that perspective on things that I would seek to justify what may otherwise seem at times to be a high-handed and wilful handling of the New Testament text in this present study. For while I think that one can still responsibly handle the texts in such a way, I am also acutely aware of the perils of using texts in such a context without paying due heed to their original meaning. When one is handling texts which are viewed by many as authoritative, or even definitive for what one should believe or do, there lies a great danger: when one places side by side statements about what the texts say and what one believes, there is the risk that it will be assumed that one has found what one believes in the text, that one believes it because that is what the text says. Yet particularly if one hearkens to those literary critics who seem to be saying that the meaning of a text is in the eye of the reader or in the ear of the hearer, there is a sense in which the text does indeed say that to me, if reading it, interacting with it, has led me to believe this. For according to some extremer versions of 'reader-response criticism', 'the meaning' of a text is what a reader makes of it.[263] The trouble with this claim is that many of those hearing what a reader makes of a text which they hold to be authoritative will assume that the reader's views also carry the weight of the authority of those texts. Yet for them that authority is linked to such assumptions as that this text was written by authoritative (e.g. 'apostolic') authors or that its authors were placed historically in a particular proximity to the founding events of the Christian church. What the text says is authoritative because that is what these authoritative writers are believed to say. If, however, it is the authority of the writers which makes the text authoritative, then the meaning of the text which can claim that authority cannot be divorced from the meaning intended by the authoritative author and still remain authoritative. (Unless, of course, one holds to so thorough-going a theory of inspiration that the really authoritative author of all the texts is God; then one could claim that what one understood by the text was what *God* meant by these words, regardless of what the human author may have intended. But, since there would then be different competing human interpretations of the text, including that of the original author, one would also have to appeal to the divine inspiration of the particular reader to guarantee that that reader's understanding was also God's. And that path leads directly to an arrogant and authoritarian fundamentalism of a most pernicious kind.) So it is perilous to give the impression that because, say, a particular text means something to me as its reader, then that meaning which it has for me has the same authority as it would have had if Paul or another New Testament writer had actually meant it to say that. That would be to give my reactions or response to the text a quite spurious claim to authority and significance. For it is difficult to see what weight then attaches to the meaning that I have found in this text which would not equally attach itself to whatever meaning I find in non-biblical texts. It is significant, not because I found it 'in' the biblical texts, but because it makes sense, philosophically, theologically and existentially: because it 'rings bells' as I and others seek to find meaning in this world and in human existence in it. That my starting-point lies in the biblical texts is of consequence only because unsolved problems, 'loose ends' of the account given in those texts, have provided the spur to these more speculative answers to these problems.

Consequently it is perhaps better to give up the claim that what I am offering is a 'reading' of the given texts; their role here is not that of a text, let alone an authoritative text, which I am expounding, but of a conversation-partner many of whose remarks I do not find particularly illuminating or relevant for the discussion in hand, but who sometimes throws out hints or suggestions which I find extremely productive or thought-provoking; these hints and suggestions then fuel further reflection. There the analogy with a conversation-partner ends, however, for in a conversation one would then be able to say something like, 'Now that's a very interesting idea; say one took that a bit further, couldn't one then say . . .?', and the conversation-partner would then be able to assent or to say that she or he hadn't actually meant it that way or wouldn't want to be interpreted in that way. At this point, alas, the written text remains silent and Paul or John or the writer in question in reality has no chance of such a right of reply.

For that reason, therefore, in what follows I have tried to signal as clearly as possible the extent to which I believe that my ideas are based upon those actually held by the ancient authors as well the points at which they either merely run parallel to, or pass beyond, or even run counter to, those of the New Testament writers whom I cite. Only thus can I avoid investing with a spurious halo of canon-approved sanctity the products of my own imagination and my own wrestlings and searchings for a credible and tenable belief.

In this second part of this book I acknowledge first of all the status of assertions of the resurrection of Jesus as an integral part of the Christian tradition, enshrined from the very first in its credal statements, to which the earliest Christian documents bear witness. But it must also be noted that this tradition very rapidly went beyond, even ran counter to, the intention of at least one New Testament writer, Paul, for it was arguably those rejected by the orthodoxy of the following centuries who were in fact nearer to him in their understanding of resurrection. Orthodoxy insisted upon the corporeality of the resurrection in a form foreign to Paul's thought, but that thought is by no means readily intelligible today (or apparently in earlier times). That prompts the question how far the 'body', in whatever sense the term is used, is in fact indispensable for Christian faith, and whether another of our earliest witnesses, the author of Mark's Gospel, while paying lip-service to the tradition of the resurrection, may not in fact be saying that the whole idea of it was so ineffable that the less one said about it the better; indeed, by virtue of his writing an account of Jesus' earthly ministry in the first place, it could be argued, as we shall see, that he and his successors were implicitly pointing Christian faith elsewhere for its basis and its orientation. Can the message of the New Testament then be reinterpreted as speaking solely of a faith for this life and world alone? That is certainly a message that goes beyond anything that the evangelists or other New Testament writers actually say; for it also goes beyond Paul, even contradicts him; but it is nevertheless a message that has surprisingly many

points of contact in his writings and above all in the Fourth
Gospel.

Similarly, the question must be raised what sort of doctrine of
God is implied, first in the traditional view or views of Jesus'
resurrection, and secondly once one questions whether anything
in fact happened at Easter above and beyond what went on in the
minds of the followers of Jesus. Jesus' revision of contemporary
Jewish views of God and of the divine nature was daring enough,
but questioning traditional views of the resurrection goes beyond
anything that Jesus ever said and challenges us to rethink our
perception of God. All such reformulations and rethinkings have
cast themselves loose from what has traditionally been seen as the
bedrock, the firm foundation of all Christian thinking about God
as the one who raised Jesus from the dead. From that supposedly
historical, empirical fact one could, it was held, go on to make
assertions both about God and about our human destiny beyond
the grave. But neither of these sets of assertions would be
possible in the light of this questioning, at least on the same basis
as has hitherto been the case. However, is that a sufficient reason
to reject this questioning and to revert to some version of the
status quo ante? Does it not, should it not, provoke fresh thought
about God and human existence? To leave that firm foundation
is a step into the unknown, into uncertainty. On the other hand,
the impetus for this step comes from the recognition that the
supposedly firm foundation is more than a little uncertain, and
that security which it is thought to provide is in fact illusory.

6

Resurrection – Enshrined in the Christian Creeds

(a) The earliest creeds

From earliest times it was a basic tenet of Christian belief that God had raised Jesus from the dead. That Christ had been raised from the dead on the third day was part of the Christian faith that Paul himself had inherited and passed on to the Corinthian church (I Cor. 15.4), and this statement of faith is echoed time and again in his letters in various forms.[264] One is right to speak of 'earliest times' here, for in all probability this statement gives the content of the Christian faith which Paul himself had received, a content, therefore, which may well go back to the time of Paul's conversion, most probably in the first half of the 30s.[265]

In favour of the general assumption that Paul is here quoting a traditional formulation are:

- the terms which Paul uses to introduce these verses ('receive' and 'hand on/down' as technical terms for the transmission of tradition; cf. 11.23).
- the accumulation of (for Paul) untypical expressions like 'according to the scriptures' (he usually uses a phrase like 'as it is written'); 'on the third day'; 'he appeared'; 'the twelve'.
- the fact that the references to Christ's death and burial in this context are superfluous, for it is the resurrection of Christ which is significant for Paul's argument, unless one sees in the death and burial a reminder to the Corinthians of their own

continuing mortality. (But then the fact that this death was for our sins is still not so relevant.)

- the parallel structure of the two verses which is often regarded as a characteristic of early Christian credal or liturgical formulations: this is especially clear in vv. 3b and 4b:

  3b: Christ died   for our sins   according to the scriptures

  4b: he was raised   on the third day   according to the scriptures.

Whether one should go further and see a parallelism in the statements 'and (that) he was buried' (4a) and 'and (that) he appeared' (5a) is less clear; 'he was buried' is a self-contained statement; 'he appeared', on the other hand, must really be regarded as incomplete in itself: it calls for further information to be supplied, namely to whom he appeared.[266] However, both the burial and the appearances may play a similar role with regard to the preceding statements, namely, as we have already seen, a confirmatory one: the burial attests and seals the death, the appearances confirm the assertion of Jesus' resurrection.[267]

If, however, this passage is traditional, how much of it is traditional and does it all belong to the same tradition? There are a number of signs that we are not dealing with a unitary tradition: for one thing there is the fact that anything added to 'he appeared' destroys the parallelism with 'he was buried' and the more that is added, the more it is destroyed. But more important, the structure changes in v.6: up to this point we have a number of statements introduced by 'that' (the repetition of this conjunction need not in itself be an argument for a multiplicity of traditions),[268] but in v. 5b the structure changes and there begins a listing of appearances introduced by 'then' (εἶτα or ἔπειτα),[269] ending with a 'finally' in v. 8; this last reference is surely to be regarded as Paul's own addition to the sequence, for it is unlikely that a formula included this appearance to Paul, especially framed in this self-deprecatory way, and especially not a formula that was part of what Paul himself had received.[270] Again the latter part of v. 6, with the reference to the fact that most of the five hundred were still alive, is likely to be Paul's own assertion.[271] On the other hand the mention of 'all the apostles' at the end of v. 7 looks like a traditional element, since it seems to overlook the fact that one apostle was still lacking from that circle, the one who is mentioned in the following verse, even if it is going too far to view the following verses (8–10) as a polemical excursus provoked by v. 7.[272]

To the question of the unity of the traditions is linked that of their purpose, both in Paul's argument and in their original context. And if one sees signs of the diversity of the traditions used, then that opens up the possibility that, at least in their original contexts, the traditions served different purposes. That is in keeping with their contents: the statements of vv. 3 and 4 offer an interpretation of Christ's death and resurrection, stressing in the case of his death that this death was salvific, and in the case of both the death and resurrection that they were according to scripture. God purposed it so and the purpose of that death was to deal with our sins. (That Christ's resurrection had a saving purpose as well is mentioned in another passage which is probably a traditional credal formula too, Rom. 4.25: Jesus was 'delivered up for our misdeeds and raised for our justification'.) That this is true of 'Christ' in I Cor. 15.3–4 may also be significant: the first Christians needed to explain how one whom they believed to be God's anointed, his Christ, could and should have suffered such a fate, for that ran counter to all Jewish expectations about the coming Messiah. The seeming unseemliness of his fate was, moreover, contradicted by the resurrection which could be regarded as God's acknowledgment of his righteous one.[273]

The function of the list or lists of appearances seems to be a different one: while the statements of vv. 3 and 4 and the appearances may have a common apologetic function, the interpretative element of vv. 3 and 4 ('for our sins, 'according to the scriptures') is lacking in the list(s) of appearances. Moreover, their form, as I mentioned earlier in connection with Paul's failure to mention

the appearance to Mary of Magdala or the women, may suggest
that they served as much to establish the credentials of certain
human servants of the risen one. As Albertz recognized, what are
relevant here are events that are the foundations of the church.[274]
Indeed there are other reasons to doubt whether the lists were
complete and exhaustive or were even meant to be: the appearance to the two disciples on the way to Emmaus is not mentioned
(contrast Mark 16.12). The parallelism of vv. 5 and 7 may
suggest that we have two alternative, perhaps even competing
listings, headed respectively by the authoritative figures of Peter
and of James, stemming from two different circles. That these
two play such an important role in Paul's listing is all the more
striking because a separate appearance to Peter is only elsewhere
obliquely referred to in the New Testament (Luke 24.34)[275] and
that to James appears only in the New Testament apocrypha, in
the fragmentary Gospel of the Hebrews.[276] However, that is
insufficient reason to doubt the tradition, for, as we have seen, it
seems that James and other members of Jesus' family did not
believe in him during his ministry (Mark 3.21 and also John 7.5),
but James clearly played a leading role in the early church in
Jerusalem (cf. above all Gal. 1.19; 2.9). But this argument, like so
many here, is a two-edged one: did James' position, to be secure,
demand that he too had to have had such an experience in order
to compete with the claims of Peter and the others? At any rate
Paul gives no hint that he had any cause to doubt James' claim,
however much it might have been convenient to do so at certain
points in his career (cf. Gal. 2.12!).

If the authorization of leaders of the early Christian community played a decisive role in shaping these lists of resurrection appearances, Paul shows little interest in *this* function of the
appearances in this passage, although I Cor. 9.1 clearly shows
that he was aware of the potential significance and evidential
value of such an experience in his own case. Confronted by some
who deny that there is a resurrection, he wishes to show that that
was Christ's experience and that because he is the representative
human being of God's eschatological new creation, his experi-

ence is also normative for those who are his. Paul insists that those who deny the resurrection are not repudiating some optional extra of the Christian faith or some little peculiarity of his own version of the Christian message, but something that is integral to the Christian faith, his and theirs and that of all Christians, and that it has been so from the start. That he has added the appearance to the more than five hundred to his citations of tradition is in itself significant: as far as we know, there was no authoritative body of five hundred, for whose status this collective experience was formative.[277] It is therefore unlikely that this item ever had the function of bestowing authority upon the recipients of this revelation. Paul's appeal to their experience is different: they function as witnesses, witnesses to the reality of that resurrection which some in Corinth seemingly deny.[278] As Dodd puts it,[279] 'there can hardly be any purpose in mentioning the fact that most of the 500 are still alive, unless Paul is saying, in effect, "the witnesses are there to be questioned"'. And whatever those who denied the resurrection did believe, and for whatever reasons they denied the resurrection,[280] Paul, as might be expected of a former Pharisee, considers that the very credibility of the gospel depends on this tenet and that without it Christians have no future and no hope and that without a future and a hope the Christian faith is futile and worthless. For some that verdict of the apostle's is decisive, but we shall see cause to call that in question.

(b) A credal inheritance misunderstood?

Our own resurrection, as well as that of Christ, is also enshrined in the major Christian creeds of a later period: in the Nicene Creed, as well as its echoing the statement of Christ's resurrection in I Cor. 15.4, 'we look for (look forward to, προσδοκῶμεν) the resurrection of the dead'; and, with greater precision, the Apostles' Creed affirms belief in the resurrection of the *flesh* (*resurrectio carnis*) or, as some modern versions have it, the resurrection of the body.[281] One could hardly expect resurrection to be accorded a lesser place, given both the pivotal nature of the event of Jesus' resurrection for the rise of the Christian church and the emphasis with which this tenet of Pharisaic Judaism was reaffirmed by the first Christians (cf. Acts 23.6).

And yet in their affirmation of the 'resurrection of the flesh' rather than of the body, let alone of a body, the beliefs of many early Christian, from Ignatius, *Smyrn.* 3.1 on, rested uneasily upon the supposed New Testament foundations of their beliefs. J. N. D. Kelly plausibly argues that they were led to this formulation of these beliefs by their desire robustly to combat Gnostic denials of the resurrection, choosing this phrase in preference to the New Testament's 'resurrection of the dead', which is still retained in the Nicene Creed.[282] He also notes, however, how easy it was for their opponents to point to Paul's words in I Cor. 15.50, that '*flesh* and blood' would not inherit God's kingdom. It might indeed seem perverse to insist, as Tertullian did, that 'flesh and blood, with their proper qualities' would rise again,[283] but that only those also possessing the Spirit would inherit the kingdom. Was this not rather a case of choosing the wrong ground upon which to take one's stand, and a case too of a re-Judaizing of Christianity?[284]

In fact it may well be that at this point Kelly underestimates the extent to which the heretical opponents of the church were more faithful and scrupulous exegetes of Paul than their catholic protagonists. For, as we noted earlier, Paul's characterization of the resurrection body in I Cor. 15.35ff. is more notable for the absence of those qualities which we normally associate with bodies than for any positive description of the nature of the spiritual body or for any justification of why this resurrection existence should be described as bodily at all. In line with this, the Gnostic Ophites could appeal to I Cor. 15.50 to prove that the resurrection body was formed of soul and spirit.[285] It is small wonder, then, that Gnostics also appealed to Paul's distinction of different sorts of 'flesh' in 15.39 and of different 'bodies' in 15.44 in support of their views. It is understandable, too, that Paul had argued in this way, since, if my reading of the situation is correct, the apostle is here concerned to convince those who deny the resurrection that they cannot and should not be satisfied with whatever spiritual state they have in this world at present;[286] for in his eyes our present state does not satisfy his conception of, and expectations for, the full completion of God's purposes for humanity. If we do not share his assumptions, which are only too easily intelligible in a former Pharisaic Jew, then perhaps we may look more kindly on those in Corinth whom he rebukes. And perhaps Paul would have looked more kindly on them, too, had not his upbringing made the resurrection of the body a shibboleth for him. For despite the scorn of Epiphanius, one is also left with considerable sympathy for those Valentinian Gnostics whom that church father derides as 'saying something mysterious and ridiculous, that it is not this body which rises, but another rises from it, which they call spiritual'.[287] It is the more remarkable, and the more embarrassing, because we can see that their view has a very clear and a very obvious basis in Paul's statements. They were trying to be faithful to the apostle's teaching, and were succeeding, or succeeding better, at least, than their critics. For the apostle, too, was content to recognize the 'mystery' in what he was proposing (15.51), but did not consider it a matter for ridicule. *Pace* Epiphanius, the view of these Valentinians would not have been, in this respect at least, a denial of the resurrection of the dead, but an affirmation of it in a thoroughly Pauline form.

Thus the apostle left behind for the church a more than somewhat ambiguous legacy on the matter of resurrection. Or at least it is the orthodox and catholic appropriation of that legacy which renders it ambiguous, if that appropriation is in the least valid as an exegesis of what Paul was saying. For without that later credal development one might readily have agreed that, if one could speak of the resurrection of the flesh at all, for Paul it could only be by insisting that this 'flesh' was something very different from the 'flesh' in which we now live, indeed 'flesh' without those qualities which characterize and are of the essence of 'flesh' – weakness, mortality and so on: whatever the 'flesh' would be in which we were to be resurrected, for him it could not be anything like what we know and experience as 'flesh' now in our this-worldly existence. And so, for reasons of clarity also, it would be better not to speak of what was raised or was to be raised as 'flesh' at all, quite apart from the obvious tendency of the term to have very negative connotations in Pauline usage. Now much of what has just been said about 'flesh' also applies to 'body'. If all that we can say about the resurrection 'body' is that it is not like the body in which we now live, would it not be better to avoid the term altogether? For otherwise we are in danger of taking a familiar term and stripping it of all its usual meaning, and simply replacing that meaning which has been removed with no new definition apart from that negative one of a denial of all of the term's normal connotations. Such a radical *via negativa* is hardly helpful to understanding.

So while the resurrection may be enshrined in the creeds of the Christian church, in some formulations of the belief there is found a concept of resurrection which is markedly different from that of Paul, despite whatever appeal may be made to his authority in its support. One perhaps possible line of interpretation of Paul's views, but hardly the most probable or obvious one exegetically, has become the official one. But we have seen that it may be being charitable to describe this line of interpretation as 'possible'; frankly it seems to do grave violence to what the apostle says, and to represent a reversion to a form of expectation that owes more to some of the cruder expressions of resurrection faith in Judaism. If our 'flesh' is to be raised, then this suggests the same sort of belief as seems to be expressed in a writing like II Maccabees: there a certain Razis, preferring suicide to capture by Nicanor, the Seleucid governor of Judaea, fell rather inexpertly upon his sword and, having failed to kill himself thus, then threw himself from a wall; finally, after surviving all this, he tore his entrails from his (at last) dying body and 'took them with both hands and hurled them at the crowd, calling upon the Lord of life and spirit to give them back to him again' (14.46). If that is what orthodox belief in the resurrection entails, then perhaps, it might be thought, one is indeed better off without it! But, we may ask, is not a belief in the resurrection of the body, even in this seemingly crude and grotesque form, something that is nevertheless philosophically and theologically both desirable and indeed necessary? For whatever one thinks of such depictions, they, and the insistence upon the resurrection of the flesh, do have the great merit that the continuity between the deceased and the resurrected is at least relatively unproblematic – although there remains the problem of continuity and the bearer of continuity over any gap in time between the death of the person and his and her eventual resurrection: who or what is the 'I' that exists between my death and my resurrection? But as soon as one says that the form of the resurrected life is different from that of this life the problems begin to multiply, as we shall see in the next chapter. For not only is the continuity between the old bodily existence and the new problematic, but the continuity of the old *with* the new raises a whole set of further problems.

7

Bodily Resurrection – A Theological and Philosophical Necessity?

The problem, we saw, with an account of appearances of the risen Christ such as I gave in the first part of this book, namely as perhaps nothing more than inward and private visions, which would be a possible result of taking Paul's experience as normative, is that they are then all too easily dismissed as illusions and delusions, the products of disordered minds or over-active imaginations. And even if one describes the visions, more flatteringly, as the 'visual articulation' of a process of reflection on Jesus' death, it is still quite possible to say that the reflection was a piece of wishful thinking and that its 'visual articulation' has no more value than the questionable processes of thought to which it gives expression. Certainly internal phenomena like the inner experiences of Paul are by their nature such that they are not open to public scrutiny. The most that one can hope to do is to ask questions like: were the circumstances under which it is claimed that such an appearance took place of such a nature that one might expect a person to have such an experience? (So, for instance, Peter's hunger in Acts 10.10 might be regarded as a physical state in which a trance might be more easily induced. In the case of Paul, however, there is considerable uncertainty as to his state of mind as he travelled to Damascus, let alone as to his physical condition, so that theories based on such considerations are precarious in the extreme.) Or was the character of the person claiming to have had such an experience of a nature to engender confidence in his or her claims? That question need not involve just the matter of the honesty of Paul or the other disciples; we have no reason to suggest that these early Christians deliberately lied – and received their reward of persecution and in some cases martyrdom. There is, however, also the question of how susceptible they were temperamentally to such experiences. Paul, for example, although he plays down the importance of these experiences, does refer to a heavenly ascent that is probably something different from, and subsequent to, his conversion experience, though not necessarily different in kind from what he experienced on the way to Damascus (II Cor. 12.2–4);[288] there too he mentions (presumably other) 'visions and revelations (plural) of the Lord' (v.1; cf. v.7); he also tells us elsewhere of his speaking in tongues (I Cor. 14.18). So one might fairly say that he shows a certain tendency to ecstatic experiences.

How far does that take us? Whatever Paul experienced convinced him of the continued existence and the divine vindication of Jesus. Studies of the circumstances and nature of that experience cannot, however, ultimately answer the question whether or not Jesus does in fact still exist or has been vindicated by God. The story is told, for instance, about one eminent New Testament professor that a friend of his attended a *séance* during which the apostle Paul announced through the medium that the professor's latest book on him had expounded his thought correctly, a confirmation of scholarship granted (fortunately or unfortunately?) to few. We may mock the experience and the gullibility of the professor's friend if he or she believed the medium's message, but that would leave unresolved and indeed untouched the question whether that professor's book had indeed correctly expounded Paul's thought; that question one would attempt to answer on another basis. Only if this experience were the sole grounds for thinking that, would it become questionable whether it were true. Similarly, the point can reasonably be made that it is unlikely, perhaps even impossible, that any such studies of the circumstances of experiences like Paul's, or even of Paul himself, will ever settle, or even begin to settle, the question whether Jesus still exists and has been vindicated by God. If such experiences are our sole evidence, then we may have to grant that a verdict of 'Not proven' is, in the nature of things, the best that we may hope for.

Or if we view the visions as in some way the culmination or product of a process of reflection, then surely we have to scrutinize that process of reflection and to ask how valid it is. In themselves the visions are no guarantee of its correctness. But once we start to examine the ways of thinking in the first century we may well find that it is a process of reflection whose steps we can in no way follow today. The ways, for instance, in which the Old Testament scriptures were interpreted and applied then are often very different from ours and indeed often seem to break many of the rules of what we consider responsible and acceptable exegesis, so that it is unlikely that today we could endorse for ourselves the scriptural arguments which the first Christians used in their reflections. In other words, we may well find that we cannot come to the same conviction as theirs by the same route. If we come to the same conclusion at all, e.g. that Jesus was after all, despite the manner of his death, God's anointed one, then it may well be by another route and wholly independently of those visions which sealed the validity of this process of reflection for the disciples of Jesus. In short, visions are a singularly unsatisfactory part of the story, for they seem to prove nothing, except perhaps for those who claim to have seen them for themselves.

(a) Bodily resurrection – theologically appropriate?

It is, then, perhaps hardly surprising that Christian apologists often insist on sticking to the sort of account which we find in Luke and John with all its inconsistencies, tensions and unanswered questions. For with such concrete and quite literally tangible experiences we at least seem to have some evidence which is less liable to evaporate under examination or to recede into an inward and private sphere of the mind that is inaccessible to us. Yet, attractive as these accounts therefore seem, their very attractiveness should make us cautious: they may exist precisely because they were equally attractive to minds like those of Luke and John. For we saw earlier how Luke at least was given to describing other-worldly phenomena in bodily terms, and how in the case of the resurrection stories he shows an apologetic concern to prove that the risen Jesus is no mere ghost. So the attractiveness of such stories is not an adequate reason for our accepting them, since we have seen that historical enquiry cannot and should not be employed to deliver, made to measure, the results which faith or theology demands of it. That would be a prostituting and enslaving of the discipline which distorts its very nature and has no part in any respectable intellectual tradition. By its very nature it cannot and will not prove such things to be true, and we cannot and must not demand that it do so.

Indeed, the sort of proof which these apologists demand does not meet with much approval in the New Testament, at least in the Fourth Gospel. For the writer of that Gospel tells the story of Thomas, who was not present at the original appearance of the risen Jesus to the other disciples. On hearing their news he was sceptical, and refused to believe their report until he had seen and felt for himself. Eight days later Jesus appeared again and challenged Thomas to see and touch. That was enough – we are not told that Thomas actually needed to feel the nail-marks or the wound inflicted by the spear in Jesus' side; he immediately confessed Jesus as Lord and God. Jesus then addressed him again:

> Have you believed because you have seen me? Blessed are those who have not seen and yet believe (John 20.29, RSV).

Implicit here is the idea that Christian faith should not need, or be dependent upon, such tangible proofs, however insistent the Fourth Evangelist may be that such proofs were indeed available, perhaps like the this-worldly realism of Luke, as a counter to any sort of docetic notions.[289] It is true that the evangelist is thinking of, and writing for, an age when experiences such as the apostles enjoyed were no longer accessible or possible. Jesus was no longer walking amongst them in visible form. But the Fourth Evangelist does not just say that believing without such experiences is the best that one can now manage or expect, a second best to which we are reduced by our living in a later age. Rather, a blessing is pronounced as if those who by virtue of their circumstances or by deliberate choice come to faith without relying on such aids and props to faith are in fact in a better position than those who have to have such aids and props, and who might be tempted to rely on them.[290]

This is relevant here, for the apologetic quest for proof in tangible, concrete experiences is like an attempt to apply Thomas's test by proxy. We cannot see with our own eyes any longer, nor can we place our own hands on Jesus' risen body, but we seek to be assured that at least some of Jesus' followers did in fact do so, or could have done so had they felt the need for it. We want to know that Jesus was indeed there, perceptible by normal human senses. But in John's eyes that is an improper demand, or at least for him it is a sign of human weakness and fallible frailty. But one might then respond by saying, 'All right, this *is* a sign of human weakness. Our faith is evidently not as robust and independent of such aids as John would like. But isn't it better that we should believe, however inadequately, and even if for the wrong reasons, rather than that we should fail to believe at all?'

Such a position is plausible, and, if we try to answer it on John's terms, we may have to grant the point: after all, Thomas's faith, even his demand for proof, is not rejected or repulsed. He is merely told that it would have been better had he not demanded faith on those terms. John consoles those who cannot have it on Thomas's terms with the thought that, so far from being disadvantaged, they are actually better off as they are; their faith is the better and the stronger for their not having had the confirmation that Thomas had or could have had, even if that may seem like making a virtue out of a necessity.

If, however, we go beyond the world-view of the Fourth Gospel, we see that there are very compelling reasons for not seeking to make Thomas's demand our own, by proxy as it were. It is, as we have seen, asking for that which is, by the nature of things, impossible and improper; historical enquiry cannot and

will not supply us with answers of this sort. So, although faith
and theology may seem to demand this, historical criticism says
that it is impossible, and refuses to grant this request. What then
are we to do if we are not to bend and subvert historical enquiry
in order to fulfil our wishes? The answer, I suggest, may lie in
questioning whether faith and theology really need, or should
have, that sort of basis which they seek in the stories of Jesus'
resurrection.

There is, too, the further point well made by Selby, that to
treat the resurrection story as one's secure possession may in
itself be an obstacle in the way of searching for, and discovering
the reality of, the life of Christ and the life of what Selby calls
'resurrection'.[291] If the critique above took its starting-point from
the story of Thomas in the Fourth Gospel, Selby's criticism (and
indeed the title of his book recalls the reply of the two shining
figures at the tomb in Luke's account: 'Why do you seek the
living among the dead?', Luke 24.5) is just. Poking around in an
empty tomb (to make sure that it is empty and to assure oneself
how and why it is empty) is a distraction; one should rather be
looking around in the present, looking for the signs of life and
of the one who is life. Perhaps one can only avoid being thus
distracted if one realizes that this life can exist and be credible
regardless of the question whether Jesus' grave was emptied of its
occupant or not. The prospect is otherwise grim, for we have
seen the reasons why uncertainty must remain as to the question
of the emptiness of that grave. The alternatives for us are to
appropriate (to use a term which Selby deems most fitting) a faith
and a life that exist independently of such grave-searching, or
to live on in the make-believe that such searching can yield
worthwhile results, overshadowed by the ever-near threat of
the realization of the futility of this and the resulting disillusion-
ment.

The first Christians did not need Jesus' resurrection in any
literal sense to tell them of God's love and readiness to forgive,
or to impress upon them God's concern for righteousness and
justice. The Old Testament and the earthly Jesus had told them

of that already, unmistakably and clearly, and had called them to service of their God, their fellow human-beings, and the world which that God had brought into being. It is true that Jesus' resurrection would have been proof of God's power even to conquer death, but as this part of this book will try to make clear, I wonder whether this is a lesson that we either ought to, or need to, learn. Is it not rather something that we need to unlearn? For so much of the incoherence in our notions of God stems from a view of a divine power, an omnipotence, which is but a magnified version of the capricious power of an oriental potentate whose *fiat* all obey. The tension between divine sovereignty and predestination on the one hand, and human freedom and responsibility on the other, as well as the whole tormenting problem of evil and suffering in a world supposedly created by an all-powerful yet somehow infinitely loving God and the resultant acute problems of theodicy, are all nurtured by such a view of God as omnipotent and are, in the last analysis, the result of opting for that model of the way God is. As a result, to pose the question whether Jesus' God in fact either wished or was able to raise Jesus from the dead, to perform that ultimate stunt of the all-powerful miracle-worker which finally authenticates God as indeed the all-powerful miracle-worker, may be a truly liberating experience. For it may leave us with a God who is unambiguously on and at our side, who suffers with us in all our pain and indeed in our helplessness and frustration too, without our constantly being tempted to reproach this loving God of Jesus for not intervening in this predicament or that, for not supplying us with the easy solution to it which an omnipotent God could by definition supply if that God really wanted to.

If, then, the inscrutability and mystery and unprovability of the resurrection stories forces us to reappraise our faith and to find a new basis for, and ways of speaking about, what we believe and why we live as we do, this may be of considerable worth. Some will call the resultant faith emasculated, but I suspect they will be those who pride themselves on a 'strong' faith like some sort of virility symbol, or as a form of self-assertion. I do not

think that faith should be like that. A faith such as I have just
described may be vulnerable in that it cannot produce proofs of
its rightness, but such a faith is surely fully appropriate when it
is faith in a God whom, if the Judaeo-Christian tradition teaches
us anything of that God's nature, we should shrink from regarding as invulnerable.

(b) Bodily resurrection – philosophically necessary, philosophically tenable?

It must be asked whether any idea of human survival after death
is tenable without our retaining some sort of notion of the
survival or reconstitution of the human body. In his essay on
'The Concept of a Person', A. J. Ayer refers at one point to the
difficulty of the idea of a 'person' surviving the destruction of
that individual's body. This is the more significant in that there
is still a tendency in much human thinking to cling to the dualistic notion of the immortality of an immaterial human 'soul' that
survives the dissolution of the material body. So in raising this
question Ayer challenges something that many still consider a
realistic option, as we shall see. The long-dominant tradition of
Platonic thought dies hard! We can perhaps imagine, Ayer says,
that a person has certain experiences after death, but in saying
that a person has those experiences, 'we are making a tacit
reference to the body which is supposed to have been forsaken'.
Here he is criticizing not so much the dualistic tradition just
mentioned, as P. F. Strawson's more sophisticated suggestion
that memories alone could 'secure one's continued existence as a
person', for Ayer believes that 'personal identity depends upon
the identity of the body'.[292] And certainly it is hard for us to
think of ourselves without our bodies or really to imagine a disembodied existence in which we would be ourselves and in which
we could recognize ourselves and others as being who we and
they once were. One only has to think of the proliferation of very
physical and corporeal features in all attempts to depict a future
existence or survival after death, even if it be only in a wraith-like

formation of ectoplasm in the views of some more recent spiritu-
alists, or in the twittering ghosts of Homer's *Nekuia*, quite apart
from the often blatantly this-worldly representations of the after-
life and the world of the dead in myths of all sorts. Is not all this,
then, a very cogent argument for retaining the idea of a bodily
existence in the after-life? In short, could there ever be a non-
corporeal after-life? And it is not only positivist philosophers
who would answer that last question in the negative, but also
systematic theologians.[293] For must not survival after death
involve the body, and does it not therefore demand bodily
resurrection?[294]

The question remains: which body, the same or a transformed
or a different one, a completely new one? For we have already
seen more than once the problems presented by the accounts of
Jesus' resurrection appearances and the strangeness of the non-
recognition that is more than once depicted there. Kai Nielsen,
for instance, assumes that the resurrected body is 'an energized
physical body essentially like that of our present body except that
it will be a better one, though better along familiar lines, and
differing only from our present bodies in that it cannot ever wear
out or become de-energized'.[295] Yet the identity of the crucified
with the risen Jesus, which should be preserved by the corporeality of the resurrection existence, was seemingly not apparent to
all, despite the implication of John 20.25–27 that the risen Jesus
bore in his resurrected body the all too tangible scars of the
terrible ordeal which he had just endured – a fairly distinctive
feature, one would think! Interesting and instructive here is the
example which John Muddiman gives, even though I think that
it undermines his argument more than he realizes:[296] having
rightly argued that a corporeal after-life is philosophically and
theologically more satisfactory than a disembodied one, he tells of
an uncle who had lost his arm at the age of sixteen; he was still
aware of the loss, but his whole character 'had been critically
formed by his disability'. The loss was, in other words,
character-forming. Muddiman then poses the question, 'In the
resurrection, how many arms will he have?', which, like so many

other 'foolish questions', in fact gets to the heart of the matter.
For, if the arm were restored, would the character of the mature
personality not be decisively altered? That is a problem which
also lurks in the views of resurrection contained in the accounts
of martyrdom in II Maccabees that I have already mentioned in
the previous chapter, for there the martyrs seemingly expect the
resurrection to restore to them what they have just lost in their
sufferings and death as martyrs.[297] The resurrected Christ is
portrayed, on the other hand, as still bearing the scars of his
sufferings. What Muddiman's example makes clearer is that a
wound or disability borne for a longer time (say one's entire adult
life or even one's entire life if one was born disabled) is so much
part of the person concerned that it is hard to conceive of that
person apart from, without, that disability. In that respect his
example is a far more serious problem than the future state of the
martyrs, whose mutilations only occurred immediately before
their deaths. Without such a disability such a person would no
longer be the same.[298]

Here it must be freely admitted that the sort of resurrection
which most easily, adequately and fully satisfies the needs for a
bodily resurrection as the basis of personal survival after death is
indeed a very crudely literalistic one: it is the very same body,
warts and all, which is to be raised, as indeed we saw asserted by
a variety of voices in the previous chapter. That is naturally
rather an uncomfortable view to swallow if the body has decomposed or has been cremated, mangled or mutilated. And it
certainly does not seem to be what Paul had in mind, whatever
his orthodox interpreters have said, as we also saw in the last
chapter.

Paul's own account of the nature of resurrection bodies, too,
presents considerable problems and is no real improvement on
the more (naively?) materialistic conceptions just considered, for
his 'spiritual body', the dissimilarity of which to the physical
body in this world is stressed, would presumably be similar to
notions like that of 'subtle bodies' or, in Flew's more exotic
language, 'astral bodies', i.e. non-material bodies of some sort, as

postulated by some philosophers and theologians. His 'spiritual body' is therefore exposed to the same problems at least, especially the question of the basis of any continuity between the physical, material body that has died and the supposed non-material body in which the person is supposed to live on after death.[299] Furthermore, the notion of a 'spiritual body' is open to the charge of incomprehensibility, that it is a combination of mutually incompatible terms very much like 'a square circle'. As I have already suggested, what is clearest about this notion is what it does *not* mean: it does not mean a body like the ones we experience in this life and in this world. Paul's chief concern in I Cor. 15 is to stress the unlikeness of the body of the new age to the body of Adamic humanity, and that leaves fully unexplained what it then *is* like.

There are other voices which plead that that we should look elsewhere for a solution of these problems. For Paul Tillich the physical account of the resurrection leads to

> the absurd question . . . as to what happened to the molecules which comprise the corpse of Jesus of Nazareth. Then absurdity becomes compounded into blasphemy.[300]

Thus he rejects this and other solutions, opting instead for what he calls the 'restitution' of Jesus as the Christ. So, too, Samuel Vollenweider suggests, for instance, that it would be better to look on the σῶμα that is raised not primarily as the physical body, but as the 'deposit of all the historical experiences of a corporeal living being', and therefore sees in the resurrection of Jesus the preservation of the past, i.e. of Jesus' earthly existence.[301] One must be clear, however, that this is a *re*-interpretation of the New Testament witness, for there can be no question that the New Testament writers meant something less sophisticated than this when they talked of a (resurrected) σῶμα. 'Bodily resurrection' here is being treated symbolically, in a way that goes far beyond the intentions of the New Testament writers themselves. In itself that is in no way invalid, as I have already argued in defence of my own way of handling the witness

of the New Testament, as long as the gap between the reinterpretation and that which is being reinterpreted is clearly recognized, and one sees how far 'beyond' the text one has gone.

Amongst philosophers, on the other hand, there are those who,
despairing of finding any intelligibility or coherence of thought
in the idea of the survival beyond death of a body, be it either
material or non-material, speak of the immortality of the 'soul'.
John Hick, for instance, pleads unrepentantly for the retention of
a dualist view of the human person, so that the idea of a disembodied consciousness, and indeed a disembodied consciousness that survives death and the dissolution of the body, can be
preserved intact.[302] His conception is of the continuance and
indeed perfecting of the conscious personality, but he also
wishes to retain a further 'period of embodiment', 'a further psy-
cho-physical existence which is probably located in another
space', though only for a limited period of time, another period
of mortal existence or further periods of mortal existence in the
plural, culminating in 'a last life beyond which there is no further
embodiment but instead entry into the common Vision of
God'.[303] But in such speculations Hick takes a step far beyond
any evidence that we possess. Essentially this is a reassertion of a
form of reincarnation, probably bereft of the memory of any
previous existence prior to our present one, and postulating the
existence of future ones on the basis of a form of reasoning that
gives the impression of being very arbitrary: such a scenario may
be logically possible, but then so are a great many other scenarios
if possibility is to be the chief criterion. And I suspect, too, that
talk of a human soul is philosophically no less problematic than
that way of speaking about the 'mind', which Gilbert Ryle so
contemptuously described as 'the dogma of the Ghost in the
Machine'.[304]

Other philosophers imply by their talk of the 'soul' something
far less like that Platonic dualism which seems to have so much
in common with Orphic and Pythagorean traditions. D. Z.
Phillips, for instance, interprets statements about the 'soul' as
statements about the kind of life that a person is living here and

now,[305] and regards questions about the 'immortality of the soul', correspondingly, not as 'questions concerning the extent of a man's life, and in particular concerning whether that life can be extended beyond the grave, but [as] questions concerning the kind of life a man is living' (49); 'the immortality of the soul refers to the state an individual is in in relation to the unchanging reality of God' (55), and that state exists here and now.

> For the believer, his death, like his life, is to be in God. For him, this is the life eternal which death cannot touch; the immortality which finally places the soul beyond the reach of the snares and temptations of this mortal life (60).

(Much of this echoes, doubtless deliberately, what the Jesus of the Fourth Gospel has to say about 'eternal life' as something which the believer already has, here and now: e.g. John 3.15–16, 36; 5.24; 6.40, 47, 54). One has to ask, as we asked of the phrase 'resurrection faith', whether it might not make for greater clarity to drop both 'immortality' and 'soul' as potentially confusing words, if this is what one means by them.

At any rate, the upshot of the quick glance at the philosophical problems of the idea of the survival after death, in either bodily or disembodied form, is, like the conclusions reached in investigating the historical problems surrounding the resurrection of Jesus, a somewhat negative one: it is hard to be other than agnostic about the survival of the human person after death and about the nature of any such survival. It is very hard, perhaps impossible, to conceptualize how this could be or what. That is true of our expectations for ourselves; it is true also of the accounts of the resurrection appearances of Jesus, as the discrepancies in those accounts show. Nor can one resolve the problem by turning to the biblical witness: the notions of survival after death to be found in the Old Testament are vague and elusive, and it is only in the latest writings, or at least in some of them, that any clearer concept and hope emerges. It is then offset by the sombre words of Eccles. 12.7: '. . . before the dust returns to the earth as it began and the spirit returns to God who gave it'

(REB). The New Testament, on the other hand, clearly presupposes a life after death and sees that as undergirded by the
resurrection of Jesus. Yet, as we have seen, the way in which this
is expressed and conceptualized is puzzling in the extreme, and
the concrete form which life after death, at least that of Jesus (but
see Luke 23.43), is supposed to take is variously portrayed. With
this is linked the variation in the anthropologies presupposed in
the New Testament writings, which are the deposit of the
flowing together of varying anthropological traditions, not all
of which are compatible with one another or capable of being
welded together into a single, homogeneous picture.

At this point, however, we must turn, more specifically, to two
New Testament witnesses. One of them, Paul, seems to stress a
bodily resurrection, but for other reasons than an interest in
personal continuity, and in a way that hardly helps with this
philosophical and theological problem; the other, Mark, gives
an account which is so mystifyingly open-ended that we are
uncertain where he is pointing us!

(c) Bodily resurrection in Mark?

Here we must first turn to a witness whose account we have
hitherto somewhat neglected, namely Mark, whose Gospel is in
all probability the earliest of the synoptic Gospels (but still a considerably later witness to the resurrection than Paul and above all
the traditions which Paul quotes). That Mark's witness is highly
problematic is clear from two facts: first, whereas the text of
Mark in a series of textual witnesses, including the majuscules
Sinaiticus and Vaticanus, which are particularly significant for
textual criticism, ends at 16.8, other witnesses add to this text
either the so-called shorter ending or the longer ending consist-
ing of 16.9–20 or both, and this phenomenon in itself indicates a
widespread feeling that a text of Mark which ended at 16.8 was
somehow incomplete and unsatisfactory. To that may be added
the second fact, which we have already noted, that on the
assumption that Matthew and Luke had before them a text of

Mark as one of their sources, these two Gospels also felt the need to add something further, but each added something very different (e.g. in Luke resurrection scenes that are explicitly and deliberately confined to Jerusalem and its immediate vicinity, in Matthew a climactic conclusion on a mountain in Galilee). Fellow-evangelists and copyists alike seem therefore to have felt the need to complete in various ways that text of Mark which they had before them. It seems to me doubtful whether Mark himself ever added anything after 16.8, although this hypothesis is still favoured by some scholars.[306] Hypotheses of accidental loss or intentional pruning lack conviction. An accidental loss is, of course, always theoretically possible, but it must have occurred very early on and have affected the sole original from which the entire manuscript tradition of this Gospel stems. For none of the attempts to supply an ending are convincing claimants to be Markan compositions, and certainly in the case of Matthew and Luke one can detect the theological proclivities of both authors at work in the sections that follow the equivalent of Mark 16.8.[307] A deliberate deletion is also theoretically possible, but this explanation can really carry conviction only if one could show why it should have been deleted. What did Mark say that was so appalling that it was excised, and why cut him off at precisely that point? Or there is the even more far-reaching question that John Fenton asks, following J. M. Creed, namely what ending could have followed on from 16.8, 'without hiatus, contradiction or redundancy'.[308] The point is well made by Matthew and Luke who, in order to describe a sequel to Mark 16.1–8, are forced to modify v. 8: Matthew mingles fear (presumably in the sense of awe in the presence of the divine) with joy and makes no mention of the women's silence; Luke omits both the fear and the silence.

We should therefore reckon with the possibility, perhaps even the probability, that Mark's text ended at 16.8.[309] The problems with this ending are twofold, both stylistic and also with regard to the content and meaning of the rather abrupt conclusion. Stylistically it is unusual, to say the least, for a work to end with the words 'for they were afraid', where the last word is in fact the conjunction γάρ, 'for', which is never found as the first word of a sentence and therefore must follow the verb, the only other word in this two-word sentence. It is true that one can point to examples of sentences ending with this conjunction, and the Septuagint contains the close parallel of Sarah's denial that she had laughed at the idea of her bearing a child, 'for she was afraid' (Gen. 18.15 LXX: ἐφοβήθη γάρ).[310] One can also appeal stylistically to the literary device of a 'suspended ending', an *aposiōpēsis*:[311]

> a sudden lapse into silence often adds to the forcefulness . . . [Demosthenes'] silence [in the cited example from *De corona* 3] is almost more effective than anything anyone could have said.[312]

One can appeal to various literary examples of such 'suspended endings', from Homer on, which have a considerable dramatic effect, an effect which may be heightened by predictions of an outcome that lies outwith the narrative of the work itself. Such artfulness is not foreign to the Bible, either, for Genesis ends with Joseph's foretelling of God's coming to the aid of his people and taking them into the promised land (50.24), and Magness can also point to the Book of Jonah which leaves a whole series of questions unanswered. But what then was the ending which Mark left readers to supply for themselves?

Here we have a twofold prediction to help us, the repetition of which in itself points to its significance for the author: in 14.28 Jesus foretells that after he has been raised he will go before the disciples to Galilee, and this prophecy is taken up again by the 'young man' at the tomb in 16.7: the women are to tell the disciples and Peter that Jesus is going before them to Galilee; there they will see him as he had already told them. When we ask about Mark's understanding and his composition of this account, then it is in the last analysis of secondary importance whether 16.7 is a redactional insertion into the traditions which Mark has received.[313] If that were so, then it only serves to underline the

importance of the content of this verse for him and for his understanding of the material. And if Paulsen is right in supposing that
v. 8b is also a redactional insertion in the pre-Markan tradition,[314]
then this half-verse too should provide an important clue to
Mark's intentions. We need not concern ourselves at this level of
questioning with the nature of this material before Mark edited
it.[315] What concerns us here is how Mark understood the story
which he was telling.

Now it is clear from 14.28, as well as from the earlier passion
predictions of 8.31, 9.31 and 10.34 and the young man's statement in 16.6, that Mark had no wish to deny the resurrection of
Jesus, even though he tells of no appearances of the risen Jesus:
all these passages point towards it and prepare the reader for it.[316]
But the Gospel closes with the account of the empty tomb and
the young man's declaration that Jesus was not there, as he
points to the spot where Jesus had lain. He is risen. He is not
here; he is on his way to Galilee, he tells them. And there Mark's
story ends with the awestruck amazement of the women, nothing
more.

Is this conclusion the product of the writer's literary and
narrative skill? Is it so obvious that Mark has not spelt out the
conclusion for such artistic reasons as scholars like Magness have
suggested – quite sophisticated artistic reasons, one might conclude? Others have certainly thought otherwise: Bousset and
Bultmann, for instance, saw here an explanation why the tradition of the empty tomb had been so long unknown (for they
assume that this tradition arose only later): it remained unknown
because the women said nothing![317] Wilckens, on the other hand,
holds that Mark ends thus because the passion narrative
originally ended in this way, with no accounts of resurrection
appearances; these, he thinks, arose later and it was the narrative
of the discovery of the empty grave that came first.[318] (But if
something more than the discovery of the empty tomb did in fact
happen, is it really plausible that no accounts at all were available,
not only when Mark's Gospel was written, but also even earlier,
as the passion narrative was formed? Has one not, by such an

explanation, simply pushed the problem a stage further back in the formation of the tradition?)

One consequence of this ending is, at any rate, that, in contrast to Matthew's account, where the risen Jesus then appears to the women (28.9), Mark implicitly seems, at first sight, to make the women a further case of failure on the part of Jesus' disciples.[319] The differences between them and the male disciples earlier in the Gospel have to be noted: time and again the male disciples' lack of understanding has been castigated by the Markan Jesus; then they fail him by reason of sheer cowardice and flee from Gethsemane, and, in the case of Peter, deny him in the house of the High Priest. The 'fear' of the women might be similar – and yet telling the other disciples would not endanger their lives, as staying with Jesus in Gethsemane or confessing him amidst the followers of the High Priest would. It seems rather that their fear is to be interpreted with the aid of the reference earlier in the verse to their trembling and amazement (*ekstasis*): this 'fear' is not a fear of their fellow human beings and what they might do to them, but the all too justifiable fear of mortals confronted with an ineffable and incomprehensible mystery, as it is elsewhere in Mark's Gospel.[320] So is their fear a sign of misunderstanding,[321] or is it not rather a sign that they have understood only too well the significance of what they have witnessed, however indirectly?[322]

Leslie Houlden refers at this point to Mark's 'sort of agnosticism',[323] which is in keeping with the whole thrust of his Gospel as a call to 'sheer trust'.[324] Certainly this Gospel, if 16.8 is its true ending, is more mysterious than the others, less overtly miraculous and supernatural, what Vermes calls 'a simple insinuation of a happy ending'.[325] To some extent Francis Watson's explanation here is similar: the reticence of the Markan narrator is his response to the 'mystery of the divine act'.[326] Before one accepts such an explanation, however, it must be asked whether it is in keeping with what we know otherwise of the narrative strategy of Mark: we have no account of Jesus' birth to compare with it (but cf. 6.3), yet we do have an account of Jesus' transfiguration

(9.2–8), where there is at least a voice from heaven, but also a
command to secrecy (9.9). Even the angel or angels of Matthew
and John[327] are lacking in Mark, at least explicitly; there is only
the mysterious 'young man' (νεανισκός), who has been variously
identified: as the same 'young man' who fled naked after Jesus'
arrest (14.51); as an Essene;[328] or even as Jesus himself, at least
symbolically.[329] If his white garment is meant to indicate that he
is a heavenly messenger, as most commentators suppose, the way
he is introduced, the restraint and the reticence shown here, are
nonetheless striking. A sort of demythologizing seems to be going
on! The reticence of the women, too, is all the more surprising,
because Mark 9.9, where Jesus, after his transfiguration, commands his disciples to keep silent about what they have just seen,
at least till the son of man had risen from the dead, would rather
suggest that this was precisely the moment when one could start
speaking openly again.[330] Or had the habit of silence and secrecy
as the correct response to the disclosure of the wonder of Jesus
become so engrained, above all in the narrator, that he forgot that
now was in fact the moment to break silence? (One should not
always demand too great a sophistication, too thorough a consistency, on the part of the narrator, although it would be ironic
indeed if the story whose commands to silence had so often been
ignored were to end with a command to speak out which is
answered with silence!)[331]

If one resists the tendency to interpret the women's reaction as
a failure, on the other hand, then one can see this description of
their 'profound emotion' as serving 'to bring out the overwhelming and sheerly supernatural character of that to which it was the
response'; this in turn may show that 'Mark may well have
felt that the actual events of the resurrection and the risen
appearances did not lend themselves to narration in a book'.[332] Or
was it rather that he also considered that they would be a distraction to his readers? For Houlden, in the unpublished paper
mentioned before, makes a further important suggestion when he
comments that in itself

to write a Gospel was to shift weight and attention away from the risen Lord . . . and towards the past Lord of miracles and parables and aphorisms and of death.[333]

Even in the case of Matthew, Houlden feels, the evangelist's main concern is not the resurrection as such, but the resurrected Jesus' validation of his earlier teaching – that is, to invest the contents of the preceding Gospel with an eternal authority here and now.[334] And he argues that

> in their various ways, all the evangelists placed the real heart of what made Christianity salvific elsewhere than in the resurrection.[335]

In other words, if Houlden is correct, the evangelists deliberately or instinctively pointed their readers away from a preoccupation with the risenness of Jesus in itself and back to the man Jesus who had encountered and challenged his followers while on earth. Gabriel Josipovici refers here to the various strategies employed by the evangelists 'to avoid the trap into which the apocryphal gospels fall, of returning us to the world of fairy-tale from which the Passion had freed us'.[336] That is correct, at least with the following qualifications: 1. it need not be implied that the evangelists deliberately sought to avoid this trap, as if they clearly saw and recognized it for what it is; if they indeed avoided it, it may be more a matter of their intuition as to what was appropriate or of their theological instinct. For 2. it also needs to be asked how far they did in fact avoid it; we have seen how many elements of the stories of the encounters of the disciples with the risen Jesus bear disturbing marks of 'fairy-tale' elements (recognition and non-recognition, this-worldly or other-worldly traits). At any rate the mysterious ending of Mark is the most successful in avoiding such features. (Yet not entirely, for the stone has been rolled away when the women arrive.)

It may well also be significant that, as Norman Perrin notes, Mark's threefold predictions of Jesus' sufferings are more varied than the stereotyped references to Jesus' resurrection, mentioned

above, which in each case follow them.[337] In the variations in the
references to Jesus' sufferings Perrin sees evidence of Mark's
theological interest in this theme. After rather surprisingly maintaining that the repeated, stereotyped references to the resurrection also show their importance to Mark, he more consistently
sees in their lack of variation a sign that Mark is not interested in
the details of the resurrection. It may be doubted, however, that
what Mark is interested in is 'the immediate state of Jesus
after the resurrection'; of that there is no mention here. More
plausible is his interest in the parousia which Perrin infers from
Mark 13 and 14.62. But the connection between the empty tomb
and that still future event is less than clear here, unless seeing
Jesus in Galilee (16.7) refers to it. So how is that prediction
realistically to be understood? Did Mark know of resurrection
appearances in Galilee and interpret them as fulfilment of the
predictions of the parousia?[338] Or did he not know of such
appearances? But then he surely knew that the disciples had not
remained in Jerusalem waiting to see Jesus, or not all of them, at
least. It is easier to assume that he knew of these sightings in
Galilee, but did not identify them with the parousia.[339] His
silence about them is therefore more likely a sign of disinterest in
them, perhaps even of mistrust in them.[340] And the later history
of Christianity can be considered to underline the wisdom of this
mistrust and its attendant interpretative strategy of deflecting
attention back to the earthly, suffering Jesus, for otherwise all
sorts of teaching could be and were only too easily set upon the
lips of the risen Jesus, with no control whatsoever over their content. This was, for instance, a preferred literary form of a whole
range of writings which today have their place amongst that
motley collection of writings which we call the New Testament
apocrypha, or in the Nag Hammadi library.

It is in keeping with this that Andreas Lindemann sees here
Mark's fending off of a *theologia gloriæ* which regards Jesus'
suffering and crucifixion merely as a staging post *en route* to
glory.[341] In this he draws upon an insight of Dietrich-Alex
Koch's in his study of the miracle stories in Mark's Gospel: 'the

more pronounced the elements of epiphany and revelation are [in these stories], the more substantial are the counterweights which Mark sets against them in his account'.[342] So massive is the revelatory epiphany which is now announced, one could say, that Mark must counter it with this equally massive and perplexing anticlimax. It is in that sense a continuation of the motif of the 'messianic secret' in Mark, but its effect is to turn the reader back to the earthly, suffering Jesus, for that is the Jesus whom Mark above all presents in his Gospel. He therefore avoids closing with a different Jesus who would distract from this suffering one.

If, however, we turn our attention away from the resurrection and in the direction of the earthly Jesus, then we go beyond the evangelists' intentions, and deliberately so, for the evangelists undoubtedly believed that the resurrection event, however they conceived of it, had actually taken place – and not just in the minds of the disciples. They merely wished to focus attention elsewhere. In effect such a going beyond the evangelists is the solution which Perrin offers to the interpretation of Mark's resurrection narrative:

> For me to say 'Jesus is risen' in Markan terms means to say that I experience Jesus as ultimacy in the historicality of my every-day, and that that experience transforms my every-dayness as Mark expected the coming of the Son of man to transform the world.[343]

But the 'in Markan terms' here is perhaps misleading, as the reference to Mark's expectation of the coming of the son of man shows. If Perrin expected the coming of the son of man, he undoubtedly saw that coming in very different terms from the mythological, eschatological world-view of the first-century writer. It is better, then, to see in Perrin's restatement a development, a projection of Mark's concerns, or some of them, into the context of a very different world-view. That, I have argued, is a fully legitimate procedure, as long as it is made clear how one is proceeding, and the restatement is not surreptitiously invested with all the authority of the endorsement of it by a New Testament writer. It is no more authoritative, say, than the writings of a literary, art or music critic; his or her authority stems, not from the greatness of the work being interpreted, but from the way in which the interpretation being offered makes sense, rings bells, for the reader, both as an interpretation of the work and in relation to the reader's own experience. Mark's ending may undoubtedly be enigmatic, but that does not entitle me to claim his authority for my own existential interpretation of the enigma.

(d) Bodily resurrection in Paul

Paul does little to meet a need for greater conceptual clarity, as we have seen, since all the stress in his discussion in I Corinthians 15 lies upon the discontinuity and the difference between our present earthly existence and the future, spiritual one. He simply seems to assume that the future existence will also be a bodily one, and his assumption of this is, in all probability, a legacy from his Pharisaic past. Questions of continuity and of the identity of the one raised with the one who had died were not his concern, as far as we can judge from his extant writings.[344]

Yet it would not be anachronistic to expect him to provide some answer to this sort of question or to address these issues, for it was a concern that exercised at least some Jewish writers of the period. The best example of this is to be dated slightly later than Paul's life-time and is found in the Syriac Apocalypse of Baruch (II Baruch); there we find an account of a two-stage process of resurrection. In 49.2 a similar question to that of I Cor. 15.35 is posed: 'In which shape will the living live in your day?' The alternatives are then put thus:

Will they . . . take again this present form . . .? Or will you . . . change these things which have been in the world, as also the world itself? (49.3)

Back comes the answer that the earth will

give back the dead, . . . not changing anything in their form.

. . . as it has received them so it will give them back. . . . as I have delivered them to it so it will raise them' (50.2).

Why? It is because 'it will be necessary to show those who live [i.e. are still alive at the time of the end and of the final resurrection] that the dead are living again, and those who went away have come back. And . . . when they have recognized each other', then the rest of the events of the end will unfold (50.3–4). Once the dead have been restored just as they were and have been recognized as such, a transformation takes place: the forms of the guilty will be changed for the worse so that they may suffer torment (51.2), and the righteous will be transformed in glorification (51.3), into the splendour of angels and equal to the stars (51.5, 10).[345] The process has been made more complicated precisely because the writer realizes the need to ensure the identity and the recognizability of those raised. Those with one arm will presumably be raised with one arm, even if the second stage may involve the restoration of a second, now glorious, arm. (That still, however, leaves untouched the question of the identity and continuity of the personality if one thereby removes a disability which has made a person what he or she is.)

Even if it is difficult to present a credible and coherent concept of a life beyond the grave without retaining corporeality, at least in a surrogate form, it is doubtful whether Paul is of any help to us here, at least if we confine ourselves to what he actually says. (We might seize on the phrase 'spiritual body' and read into it our own definition of it, as the church Fathers did, but then we could hardly claim Paul's backing for our redefinition.) For, to ensure continuity and recognizability, the 'body' that survives death needs to be identifiable as the same body that it was before, and Paul's imagery from sowing seeds and his other arguments make it plain that he envisages the resurrection body as being something other than, and indeed qualitatively different from, the mortal body which we now have (cf. esp. I Cor. 15.37, 40, 44). That this analogy of the seed is indeed a guide to Paul's view of the resurrection body is reinforced by Vollenweider's observation

that Paul's insistence on the 'dying' of the seed is a striking one
and is in conflict not only with modern molecular genetics, but
also with (at least many) ancient views of transformation and
entelechy.[346] Paul has not then been led into a misleading
description of the resurrection state by a seductive analogy, but
rather the reverse: his convictions about the resurrection have
dictated his (rather unusual) portrayal of the natural process.
Again, it is quite intelligible that he should argue thus, the
purpose of his argument being what I have argued it to be: he
apparently wishes to shake the Corinthians out of their complacent assumption that in their present abundant spiritual
endowment they already enjoyed a heavenly existence in all its
fullness (cf. I Cor. 4.8 again). Death still awaits them too, and
they must wait till it has been conquered (15.26). But the point
to be made here is that, if we wish to use the idea of resurrection
to satisfy this real theological and philosophical need, in order to
present a coherent and tenable view of an after-life, then Paul's
notion of the resurrection will not meet that need, for it lacks that
vital ingredient, the continuity between the old nature and the
new. II Baruch does satisfy that need far better, even if not
perfectly, but then II Baruch unfortunately did not make it into
anyone's canon!

After a careful examination of I Cor. 15 and even more of II
Cor. 5.1–10, Hans Grass in fact comes to the conclusion that
Paul's arguments presuppose that the old corporeal existence is
no longer required in order to gain the new, and thus the tomb of
Jesus need not be emptied (nor ours for that matter). Paul thinks
of the otherness of the new in so radical a fashion that, while he
presupposes a continuity of the person who bears the old body
and who will bear the new, there is no continuity between the old
and the new corporeality.[347] And if the eternal dwelling not made
with hands which is in heaven (II Cor. 5.1) is our heavenly body,
then its independence of the earthly tent-like dwelling which
is our mortal body and which will be dismantled is clear. This
verdict of Grass's is convincing as an interpretation of these texts,
even if the analogies which he draws to Gnostic thought are less

so, and the idea of our 'bearing' a body conflicts with other anthropological passages in Paul where our bodies seem rather to be ourselves in our corporeality.[348]

But one might legitimately ask whether Paul's conception of a 'spiritual body' is not so problematic, as we have seen, that one might do better to leave out the reference to the 'body' part of it entirely, on the grounds that the bodiliness of the resurrection existence was a relic of Paul's Pharisaic past, and that all that he meant, and all that he could say about this existence, was in fact that it was not at all like earthly existence as we know it. Would it not therefore be better to say that we rise, we live on after death, as 'spirits' (and that concept too has its Jewish precedents, either as the ultimate destiny of the individual or as an interim stage before these spirits are again united with a body). ·

Correspondingly, some who question the literal and most obvious interpretation of the stories of the empty tomb and of Jesus' bodily resurrection protest that they nevertheless do not deny the resurrection; rather they still uphold, and subscribe to, a belief in a 'spiritual resurrection'.[349] Yet many of the problems that beset us in grappling with Paul's comments in I Corinthians 15, and beset his patristic exponents too, even if they were unaware of the liberties that they were taking with his words, surface again here: just as we may ask 'What on earth (or in heaven!) is a "spiritual body"?', we can equally properly ask 'What is a "spiritual resurrection"?' And in what sense is it a 'resurrection' except in the most diluted sense of the word, as something roughly equivalent to a non-physical revival or rein-vigoration, of the sort that we may also get from a holiday or a good read? For the first century, however, 'resurrection' usually meant that something was raised up to life again and that some-thing was a body.

One must recognize that the expression 'spiritual resurrection' is remarkably ambiguous and elusive. The word 'spiritual' in particular is a widely used one, and one could say that it is over-used or even abused.[350] Is it, in the present context, simply the equivalent of 'figurative, metaphorical'? In other words, to claim that Jesus has risen, or that we have risen, spiritually is much the same as putting 'risen' in inverted commas: he or we have not 'risen' in any normal or literal sense of the term, but, playing on words, we use the image of 'resurrection' to speak either of, for example, Jesus' continued influence through his followers, or of the quality of life which we experience, inspired and motivated by his life and his teaching. 'Resurrection' is just a vivid way of expressing the power and the vitality of these experiences, a metaphor for the dynamic movement that sprang out of the seeming 'death' of the Jesus-movement along with the very real and physical death of its leader.

Although they do not use the term 'resurrection' in this figurative way, one could see how it might be applied to the reinterpretations of the meaning of the Easter-event by scholars like Bultmann and Marxsen. For the former, we have already seen, argued that:

> The event of Easter, insofar as it can be referred to as a historical event alongside of the cross, is nothing other than the emergence of faith in the risen one, in which the proclamation [of the message of Christ] has its origin.[351]

And we also saw that Marxsen argues in similar fashion that Easter means 'that the cause of Jesus continues' or, quoting a German hymn, 'Still he comes today': what Jesus offers today and the faith which we have in him today are no different in kind from what the earthly Jesus offered and the faith which his disciples had in him before his death.[352] Yet neither Bultmann nor Marxsen, wisely, say that in this the disciples had 'risen' spiritually or even that Jesus had 'risen' spiritually. What happened on that day was the emergence or re-emergence of faith and thus of the proclamation of the Christian message. Their avoidance of the language of 'resurrection' to describe this at least prevents the issues from being obscured by its use.

It is not just that, as J. D. G. Dunn puts it in criticizing the views of these two scholars, the New Testament bears witness to something having happened to Jesus and not only to the disciples; one could after all say things like 'Jesus rose into the kerygma', i.e. Jesus 'rose again' as the disciples resumed their preaching of his message. It is rather that, if this is all that one wishes to affirm, the language of 'resurrection' is an encumbrance, except as a cloak to cover the fact that, from the viewpoint of orthodoxy, one is doctrinally naked. For, as Dunn continues,

> If 'the resurrection of Jesus' does not mean that something happened to Jesus himself, then the character of Christian faith becomes so radically different from what it has been understood to be from the beginning that it has actually become something else – not simply a difference in degree, but a difference in kind.[353]

For Dunn, it is implied, this an adequate reason to say that something, and something more than just still being proclaimed and followed, did happen to Jesus on that Easter Day. However, it has been the argument of this study that we have no means of knowing precisely what happened to Jesus himself, and we saw that Dunn had himself granted that in an earlier work;[354] and if we have no means of knowing that, we must ask whether we can confidently assert nonetheless that something (at least the sort of 'something' implied by talk of 'resurrection')[355] happened to Jesus. Whether the character of Christian faith thereby becomes different is a secondary question. What must first be resolved is whether there is any possibility of a coherent and realistic Christian faith on any other terms at all. But the recognition of the shift that must take place if there is no alternative is an important one for the sake of both honesty and clarity, and it is inevitably obscured if the term 'resurrection' is employed figuratively.

One must recognize that the phrase 'spiritual resurrection' could be used in a different sense, and one that has more hope of remaining in touch with traditional Christian belief. All that might be meant by it is that Jesus rose as spirit, i.e. being a spirit was his resurrection mode of existence. That might find support in I Cor. 15.45: Christ, 'the last Adam became a life-giving spirit'. Does that mean, then, that we too will survive death in the form of spirits?[356] But what is this existence as spirit? Does it differ from survival as 'soul'? Despite Paul's insistence on the idea of a 'spiritual body', existence as a spirit would seem to most to be contrasted with existence in bodily form, an alternative to it, at least in any manner that we know of as bodily existence. It would seem to most to be confusing and perverse to say that 'spiritual body' is just another way of saying 'spirit'. Yet, if existence as spirit is something other than continued existence in the body as we know it, what becomes of the problems of continuity and identity which were raised in the last section? Do we just have to assert, as confidently as we dare, yet ultimately in blind faith, which to the outsider will seem little better than mere credulity or fantasy, that despite all our present experience of personal identity and what constitutes it, the possession of bodies is not a *sine qua non* for that sense of identity, and that it is conceivable that one could retain such a sense of identity in a disembodied existence? That is a possible position, even if a daring one, but one surely needs some good reason for adopting it.

Or is the 'spiritual resurrection' envisaged here a reference, not so much to Jesus' or our own survival as spirits, as to the influence of the Spirit of God and of Jesus on people's lives ever since? This comes near to the first possibility, the metaphorical usage, in practical terms, but differs from it in that 'spiritual' is not just being used in the weaker sense of 'figurative'; rather it refers to the Spirit of God and of Jesus active in the world, how-ever elusive by its very nature that Spirit remains – indeed some may ask whether instead of referring to 'the influence of the Spirit of God and of Jesus on people's lives' above one could not just speak of 'the influence of God and of Jesus on people's lives' without substantially altering what one wished to say. But it is plain that, if one is prepared at all to speak of the activity and influence of a divine spirit as a reality in this world, however con-ceived, then something more is being said by the word 'spiritual' than merely that the word 'resurrection' which it qualifies is being used figuratively. However, it is the term 'resurrection' in this usage that still remains problematic: why use it at all? Does its presence serve any useful purpose at all except to keep up a pretence of orthodox respectability (if that can be called 'useful')? I find this clinging to the word 'resurrection' rather perplexing, particularly in works that are certainly not aiming to be orthodox. The otherwise admirable study by Hugh Dawes, *Freeing the Faith*, which certainly does not eschew treading on the corns of the traditional, describes 'resurrection' thus:

> Wherever light is able to shine through in life, whenever goodness and practical kindness win against uncaring or cruelty, resurrection is at work.

For 'resurrection' is, he goes on, 'really *just life*' (62, his italics), as Jesus' resurrection is 'the living growth and enlargement of the ideas and the lifestyle [Jesus] communicated through human beings unable to allow these to be lost' (67). Would it not be better simply to speak here, say, of the presence of the Spirit, unless, of course, one then also goes on to speak of a future raising of our bodies by the Spirit as in Rom 8.11? Otherwise the only 'raising' by the Spirit which we could experience would refer to the stirrings and promptings of the Spirit which we encounter in our daily lives or the influence of the spirit of Jesus constraining us to follow a similar course to his in the world.

Again and again, then, we have seen, negatively, arguments which render resurrection (or any other alternatives) as a matter of personal survival after death questionable and, positively, various ways of speaking of 'resurrection' and so reinterpreting it that it does not refer to Jesus' personal survival after death or ours. For, from one point of view, the only logically satisfactory way to speak of individual survival seems to be in terms of a resurrection of that body which we now have, yet that does not square with the New Testament (Paul), nor is it a form of belief in the resurrection which has found much favour, even among the most conservative scholars today; and rightly so, since it may seem to solve the problem of continuity and identity, but only at the cost of raising a whole range of other problems. It would therefore be a matter of some relief, sparing us much intellectual embarrassment and bewilderment, were we to discover that indeed 'resurrection' was not about personal survival after death at all. A further step beyond this would be to discard all talk of 'resurrection' as potentially misleading and simply to speak, say, of 'life'.

8

A Faith for This Life Alone?

The problem with the sort of seemingly agnostic view of an elusive risen Jesus that has emerged in this study is that for very many Christians their own personal hopes, their beliefs about their own lives, their whole system of values, are built around that bed-rock of Christian faith which they locate in the bodily resurrection of Jesus. With some justification, for they can surely appeal to the clear teaching of the apostle Paul in I Cor. 15:

> . . . if Christ was not raised, then our gospel is null and void, and so is your faith; . . . if Christ was not raised, your faith has nothing in it and you are still in your old state of sin. It follows also that those who have died within Christ's fellowship are utterly lost. If it is for this life only that Christ has given us hope, we of all people are most to be pitied.
>
> (vv. 14, 17–19, NEB modified)

Seemingly this settles the matter, at least as far as Paul is concerned, and it will settle the matter, too, for those for whom Paul has spoken the last and definitive word on the subject.

(a) A belittling of this life?

But has the apostle given us a clear and binding answer on this matter? Before we assent too readily to that, we need to note the implications of what Paul is saying. For what he says surely implies that a Christian life is worthless, not worth living, if there is no continuation of that life beyond the grave in a resurrection with Christ. But would *we* be prepared to say that of Paul himself? Is it really the case that all that he did, all that he struggled to bring about, all that he has left behind in the shape of his churches and his writings, for us above all his writings, are simply pointless if he did not in fact survive his death to live on in another world? Or what of Jesus himself? Have his ministry and his teaching no value or point or worth unless he rose bodily from the dead? If we only had Mark's Gospel, ending at 16.8 after a promise of Jesus' return, and nothing more, would we write off Jesus' life and his death as worthless and pointless unless he indeed still existed to return alive once more?

Here it seems to me that Paul's logic simply cannot hold water today. His rhetoric has led him astray here. For by implication it utterly devalues Jesus' existence and ministry and all that he achieved during his life on earth, and it devalues Christians' lives on earth as well, including Paul's own life. Jesus' teaching was about how God wanted people to conduct their lives in this world; the way of living for which he called in God's name was not just a preparation for a future life to come, it was a way of life *now* that pleased God because it was an appropriate way of life that manifested God's rule in this world and manifested it here and now. Jesus' demands were not a blind test of obedience in which simply any test was imposed like some ordeal on his hearers; he did not ask his followers to undertake anything at all, whatever it might be, in order to prove their obedience and therefore their worthiness to enter into a future heavenly realm. The radical obedience and the way of life for which he calls reflect the nature of the God whom one is to obey and serve; it is a way of human living that is in harmony with our creator's nature and purposes and which is therefore for the ultimate benefit of humanity itself. Its goal and aim is righteousness and salvation and peace in the fullest sense of the word. Jesus' message does not therefore create the same sort of acute ethical problems as the story of God's demanding that Abraham offer his son Isaac as a sacrifice (Gen. 22), although at times the radical discipleship which Jesus demanded of his followers did run counter to what was reckoned to be a matter of simple human decency and piety at the time (e.g. Matt. 8.21–22 par., which seems to disregard ordinary respect for one's parents and for the dead);[357] while such demands as this may seem destructive of what makes for a loving and caring human society, there is more in his teaching that promoted such qualities of this-worldly obedience as would be regenerative of human society. Moreover, when such demands were placed upon his followers, it was not because human society and its responsibilities were unimportant, but because ministering to this world and its need for the rule of God meant that, for some at least, this task took on a higher and overwhelming priority.

Such teaching as that of Paul in I Cor. 15 also, however, devalues and disregards much that is of worth in other human lives than that of Jesus: countless individuals have lived valuable and admirable lives, regardless of whether their services to humanity and to the God in whose image humanity is made have been performed in the name of Christ or not. Are we really to say that what they were and did was ultimately utterly pointless and worthless unless they also went on to enter another existence beyond the grave and to receive God's reward there? Did they really receive no satisfaction themselves from what they were doing, and is the benefit which others derived from their lives of no account?[358] Paul may argue as he does due to the rhetorical needs of the situation in which he found himself and with which he was confronted in the Corinthian church, but is this argument in any way adequate or valid outside that situation?

It may even be that, as I mentioned just above, we should challenge the validity of this statement with regard to Paul's own life too, though many hold him to have exercised a most malign influence over the history of Christian thought and even the history of humanity in general. For at least for some, the apostle's insights expressed in his writings have been a source of inspiration and of liberation. One need only consider the examples of Paul's influence, exercised through his Letter to the Romans alone, which F. F. Bruce cites in his article on 'The Epistles of Paul' in the revised edition of *Peake's Commentary on the Bible*:

the conversions of Augustine, Luther and Wesley, and the impetus to his thought given to Karl Barth in commenting on Romans.[359] Whatever happened to Paul after his death, that letter has survived him, to the enrichment (as well as, in places, the puzzlement!) of many. And whatever the setbacks that Paul suffered in his missionary work, many of his converts undoubtedly felt a great debt of gratitude to the apostle for what he had brought to their lives. His continued influence after his death is surely a witness to that.[360]

(b) Life now?

Now, while much that Paul says may seem to reinforce this, in my view thoroughly flawed, argument from I Cor. 15, there are some features of his thought that may point us in another direction and may perhaps open up a line of reflection that is more profitable for us to follow now, faced as we are by the predicament of the inevitable uncertainty as to what happened to Jesus after his death and what will happen to us after ours. We have to grant, however, that, not just in I Cor. 15 but elsewhere, too, particularly in that same letter, Paul warns against too high an estimate of what Christians already have in this world. For this was probably a tendency of the Corinthian Christians of which he was critical; in all probability, emboldened by their experience of startling and spectacular spiritual gifts, they were inclined to claim more for their present existence in this world than Paul felt to be warranted. With a measure of exasperated irony he bursts out, in a passage to which I have already referred:

> Already you are filled! Already you have become rich! Without us you have become kings! And would that you did reign, so that we might share the rule with you!
>
> (I Cor. 4.8, RSV)

The whole thrust of his argument in the second part of I Cor. 15 is also to the effect that the Corinthians were deluding themselves if they believed that their present, earthly existence could be their final state; first the final enemy, death, must be defeated (v. 26), and they must not confuse their natural existence in the image of the earthly man, Adam, with the nature of the existence that will be theirs in the image of the heavenly Adam of the end-time, Christ (esp. vv. 44–50).[361] Yet while Paul does use the language of life and death, particularly in Romans 6, in a way that suggests that life is only attainable by passing through death, even if it is death 'with Christ', whether that death with Christ takes place on Golgotha or in baptism or (as seems to me most likely) in both,[362] he does at times also use the language of 'life' and 'death' rather differently.

In the first place, although he seems to wish to reserve the language of 'resurrection' for a future existence, perhaps because the idea of a resurrection now was something of which he could not conceive (and in that case we can perhaps sympathize with him), even if his later followers, who were responsible for writing the letters to the Colossians and Ephesians, could,[363] he shows none of the same restraint with regard to the 'life' which is the outflowing here and now of Christians' sharing in the resurrection of Christ. Dealing with the view that being saved through grace meant that one was free to go on sinning, thus giving grace more scope (!), he argued that this is impossible, not only because Christians share in Christ's death to, and therefore break with, sin, but also because the purpose of their sharing in Christ's resurrection is that they might 'walk in newness of life' (Rom. 6.4). Not only does the word 'walk' suggest that he is referring to their present existence and conduct in this world, but the whole thrust of his argument here demands that he address the issue of Christians' conduct here and now, in order to rebut the suggestion that his message means that Christians may persist in sin to give grace more scope (6.1). So, although he may be critical of the Corinthians for their exaggeratedly 'realized eschatology', he does not eschew all anticipations of the end, the eschaton, in the present. In particular, the gift of the Spirit to Christians is a foretaste, an anticipation, a 'pledge' or 'down-payment' for the future age here and now (II Cor. 1.22; 5.5), a 'first-fruits' of what is to come (Rom. 8.23), just as Christ's resurrection was in his eyes the 'first-fruits' of a still future resurrection (I Cor. 15.20). Thus it is characteristic of Paul's thought that for him Christians live as ones already having, but at the same time not yet having, the future state, and Christian existence is marked for him by this tension between these two poles of the already fulfilled and the not yet fulfilled.

If Paul preserves this tension in all its sharpness, other Christian writers, perhaps even some of his own followers, the authors of Colossians and Ephesians, were perhaps not so successful in maintaining it. The Fourth Gospel, for example, although in its present form it clings on to vestiges of traditional and more Jewish views of what 'resurrection' involved, is at the same time the prime witness to another view of 'resurrection', a reinterpretation of that belief as of so much else in Jewish and Christian tradition. For this Gospel is a prime witness to a 'realized eschatology' in which things and experiences traditionally expected to be granted only at the eschaton, at that culmination of human history which God was expected to inaugurate in the near or still distant future, were already experienced in the present. So, for the Fourth Gospel, 'judgment' is not just a matter of some still future *dies iræ*, but takes place with the coming into this world of Jesus, the light of the world (John 3.19). 'Eternal life' is, correspondingly, not a future gift, but something that those believing in Christ already have (3.36). As Marxsen puts it, 'Jesus lived and gave a resurrection into new life even before his crucifixion.'[364] So too 'resurrection' seems to be a present reality: not only does Jesus declare 'I am the resurrection and the life' in response to, and implicit qualification and correction of, Martha's (traditional) belief in Lazarus' future resurrection at the end of time (11.25), but he also continues:

> He who believes in me, though he die, yet shall he live, and whoever lives and believes in me shall never die (11.25b–26a).

This is ambiguous: if 25b and 26a are contrasted, it could mean that some, like Lazarus, may die and will in the future come to life again, but others will not die at all but will continue to live; or it could be that vv. 25b and 26a are not expressing two different possibilities, but rather that 26a is explaining 25b. The latter, the more likely explanation, would have been easier if the future 'will live' could be taken as a promise that is as much for the present as for the future, even if it is framed in language that reflects the traditional expectations of the way that life will be attained only after one's death;[365] otherwise the tenses of the two statements present problems, for the one who according to 26a never really dies, but remains alive, does not therefore, strictly speaking, need to come to life. It would then be possible to interpret these verses as saying that, even if one 'dies' in one sense (our normal sense), one nevertheless 'lives', for the one who lives and believes in Jesus never really dies in the true (theological) sense of the term. The 'life' that such a person already has cannot be touched by death, and this makes death an irrelevant non-event.[366] One finds an equivalent to this, from the standpoint of a philosophy of religion, when D. Z. Phillips suggests as an interpretation of the notion of 'overcoming death' that this can mean no more and no less than that one has lived in such a way in this life that this present life is not rendered pointless by death.[367] Or, alternatively, one can say that 'belief in the resurrection' is not really concerned with solving the problem of death and affirm instead that 'God is the "beyond" in the midst of our life': not, however, 'beyond' our perceptive faculties in the sense of being in another world, to be encountered in another life.[368]

It is true, then, that the statements in the Fourth Gospel which seem to talk of a still future resurrection in traditional terms seem redundant (thereby leading Rudolf Bultmann to consider them to be secondary additions by a later ecclesiastical redactor).[369] Equally, however, this way of rendering them apparently redundant can be seen as merely taking a (quite legitimate) step further the tension in Paul's thought between life now, through the Spirit, and the (fullness of) life still to be granted in the future when we are raised from the dead and our bodies are redeemed (cf., e.g., Rom 8.10 and 11). One could argue that the residue of

Jewish beliefs is now jettisoned and that that emancipation from those outmoded categories to which Paul to a certain extent already bears witness is taken a stage further, so that these futuristic eschatological categories cease to play any significant role in the Fourth Evangelist's thought.[370] Certainly, if the language of having eternal life now is taken with full seriousness, then the future can have little to add to what we already have. From there it is but a short step to abandoning this dimension entirely and operating only with an eschatology, a fulfilment of expectations for the end, that is wholly realized or realizable within this world and our life in it. But that is a step beyond the Fourth Gospel, at least in the form in which we now have it, perhaps even a step beyond the assertions of the evangelist before any later editors added to it; for even in the uncompromisingly this-worldly interpretation of Luise Schottroff, in which both the individual eschatology of Gnosticism and that of apocalyptic traditions are reinterpreted so that the saving event occurs in the present, the evangelist would answer the question whether there was a life after death in the affirmative.[371]

John does nevertheless describe the resurrection appearances of Jesus, in very tangible terms, with a concreteness second only to Luke's apologetics. Equally that may simply be because that was what the Fourth Evangelist found in his traditions (and there have been those who think that the crucifixion of Jesus is another example of his conservatism with regards to the traditions of Jesus' story and question whether it really plays a significant role in his thought). At any rate, if we treat the stories of the physical appearance of Jesus in the same heavily apologetic way as Luke uses them, we perhaps run the risk of missing the point of the story of Jesus' implicit rebuke to Thomas in John 20.29, as noted in the previous chapter: 'Jesus said to [Thomas]: "Have you believed because you saw me? Blessed are those who have not seen me and (yet) have believed."' Thomas is seemingly rebuked, not just for wanting to touch Jesus (20.25) in order to satisfy himself that this really is the Jesus who died, but even for wanting to see Jesus. The story, we saw, does not say that his desire to touch Jesus was ever fulfilled; seeing was enough for him, but in a sense it was already too much for Jesus.

What is also interesting is that John 20.29 uses the past tense: Jesus commends 'those who have not seen me and (yet) have believed'. This may be just another example of this writer's anachronistic use of tenses;[372] the Evangelist may just be looking back on the generation(s) of believers who since Jesus' resurrection had come to faith in him without the privilege of a resurrection appearance. But earlier in the chapter we read of the 'Beloved Disciple' entering the empty tomb, seeing what was there and who was not there, and believing (20.8); earlier in the Gospel, too, we read on a number of occasions about people believing in Jesus, people who were not yet in a position to see the risen Jesus. Sometimes they were granted evidence of Jesus' powers, but even the need for this is implicitly rebuked, either because it shows an inadequate and superficial grasp of who Jesus is (1.50) or because those in question demand signs and wonders (4.48; cf. 6.30). At best the faith which there was before may have been a fragile faith, liable to be shattered and broken by adversity (cf. 16.31–32), yet, while it lasted, it was faith. The implied rebuke to Thomas is surely related to the criticism of those demanding signs during Jesus' lifetime; both betray a like attitude on the part of those reluctant to believe.

Is not, then, the Fourth Evangelist saying that what was to be seen in the life of Jesus before his death should have been enough to evoke faith, enough to base faith on it? He speaks to 'the situation of those who are dependent upon the witness of the first eyewitnesses alone'.[373] It is because the earthly life of Jesus should be enough to evoke faith that the writer of the Fourth Gospel tells the story which he or she tells (cf. 20.31); this is no account of resurrection appearances alone, but seems to tell of the life of one who was of flesh and blood like ourselves. So do these rebukes uttered by Jesus in this account not then mean that we should neither demand nor expect either the miracles of the earthly Jesus or the manifestation of the heavenly, risen Jesus? And is not our demand for tangible and substantial evidence of

Jesus' survival beyond the grave and of his vindication by God a symptom of the same failure to see what faith should see in the earthly life of Jesus of Nazareth? It is true, however, that it seems easier to see why it is reprehensible to demand or expect this of the Johannine Jesus, for the Fourth Evangelist presents us with an account of the earthly Jesus which is at times hard to distinguish from an account of, and witness to, the heavenly and exalted Lord. It is at times hard to recognize him as a being of flesh and blood like ourselves, despite the obviously human Jesus portrayed in the first three Gospels. And yet common to all four Gospels is the admission that, however impressive Jesus' words and deeds may seem from their accounts of them, however apparently irresistible is the conclusion that he was indeed one sent by God, Jesus' contemporaries mostly did not see it that way, as the Gospels themselves show. Those who heard his words and saw his deeds could interpret his signs and wonders differently, as evidence of collusion with the prince of darkness (Mark 3.20–30 parr.); they treat his insight, his teaching, his claims, his signs, as evidence of demonic possession (John 7.20; 8.48–52; 10.20–21).

Others, however, will object that this step further, beyond Paul and John, in which the future dimension is discarded entirely, is a step in the wrong direction which dissolves a tension that is integral to Paul's thought (and may be held to be integral and essential to all Christian theology), a step which is, moreover, condemned by that follower of Paul who wrote II Tim. 2.18; for there a certain Hymenaeus and Philetus are condemned for saying that the resurrection has already taken place. So Ernst Käsemann observes that John

> affirms what the enthusiasts of Corinth and the heretics of II Tim.2.18 had proclaimed, namely that the reality of the general resurrection of the dead is already present now.

He observes earlier,

> It is quite disturbing that the Evangelist, at the very centre of

his proclamation, is dominated by a heritage of enthusiasm against which Paul had already struggled violently in his day and which in the post-apostolic age was branded as heretical.[374]

If one doubts whether the Corinthians who apparently said that 'There *is* no resurrection of the dead' were really saying 'There is a resurrection of the dead but not in the future, for it has already happened', then Paul did not struggle violently against such a position.[375] And does one need to regard the writer of II Timothy as being *the* definitive interpreter of the Pauline heritage? What if one sets over against his view that other line of Pauline interpretation that is represented by Col. 2.12; 3.1 and Eph.2.6, which also speak of our resurrection as already accomplished (even if not in quite the same way as John, for he apparently sets his affirmations on the lips of the earthly Jesus, and even if the deutero-Pauline authors still preserve elements of a future expectation, above all in Col. 3.4)?[376] Then John's statements may not appear 'disturbing' so much as encouraging and challenging us to think through the possible implications of such a proclamation of the Christian message.

(c) Death now and death to come

The Fourth Gospel may only take us a certain distance along the hermeneutical road that we must travel. For it is one thing to say that we now live so fully that physical death is only a seeming death, and that those who believe, although they may experience death, yet live on, and go on living that life which they already have beyond that point in time which is their physical death. It is quite another to say that physical death indeed marks a real end, and to ask whether we in fact have any evidence that those who die believing actually go on living after their physical death in *any* sense of the term 'live'. This is a different stance, a different standpoint that is provoked by the outlook of the age in which we live, in which many are reluctant to grant that it is evident that there is some sort of post-mortal existence, however insubstantial. (It must be noted, however, for how many even in the Graeco-Roman world death meant, to all intents and purposes, annihilation, the end of the existence of the human individual, if one is to judge by the testimony of countless epitaphs.)[377] Nevertheless, the shift of perspective that John encouraged, in pointing us to what Jesus offers here and now already, in this world, may at least provide us with a starting-point for further reflection if we find ourselves unable to assert with any confidence either exactly what happened to Jesus after his death or what will happen to us after ours.

It may also be helpful to turn back again to Paul at this point: we saw earlier that Paul speaks of entry into life through death 'with Christ', even if that 'death' was something through which we have already passed, but we now need to note another, highly paradoxical way of speaking; not only does Paul speak of 'life *through* death', but he also speaks of 'life *in* death'. This is particularly prominent in II Corinthians, where Paul speaks of

> constantly carrying about in our body the putting to death (νέκρωσις) of Jesus, in order that Jesus' life might be revealed in our body. For we who are alive are constantly being delivered up to death for Jesus' sake, in order that Jesus' life might be revealed in our mortal flesh (4.10–11).

In this passage Samuel Vollenweider draws attention to the 'daring claim to resurrection life already in the present',[378] a claim which echoes the reference to walking in newness of life in Rom. 6.4 which was mentioned earlier, though the resurrection life is manifested, not in leaving death behind or escaping from it, but precisely in the bearing of it. Of his apostolic ministry the apostle affirms that 'we are dying and, look, we are alive' (II Cor. 6.9); this remark is found amidst a series of paradoxical antitheses in 6.8–10 which are somewhat reminiscent of those in I Cor. 7.29–31. Such paradoxes were beloved of popular philosophy of the time, but this particular paradox is stated by Paul with a sharpness unparalleled in extant Graeco-Roman literature of the period. I have suggested elsewhere that parallels are not easily found, because to conclude that true life was to be found in death might seem to encourage martyrdom or suicide as its logical consequence;[379] it may be no accident, then, that a pseudonymous Cynic letter feels able at least to attribute to Socrates, who did in fact die a martyr's death, the view that:

> The philosopher has nothing other than to die, since he disdains the demands of the body and is not enslaved by the pleasures of the body; and this is nothing other than the separation of the soul from the body, and death is nothing other again than the separation of the soul from the body.[380]

Paul, however, is not speaking primarily of his own martyrdom, even when that perhaps threatened him and seemed very near (I Cor. 15.31–33; II Cor. 1.8), for it was of decisive importance for him and for his understanding of his own existence that he was caught up in, involved in Christ's death, and he could even say that he had died with Christ on the cross and therefore like Christ lived to and for God (Gal. 2.19; cf. Rom. 6.10).[381] That was determinative for him – not what in fact happened to his own physical body.

If we seek the basis of the *substance* of Paul's thought and in particular the paradox of his language of life in death, however, as opposed to its literary form, we should in fact perhaps look to the early Christian tradition of Jesus' teaching rather than to that of the Cynics: while Paul's turn of phrase may owe much to the rhetoric employed by contemporary moral philosophers, the ideas expressed here are close to those sayings of Jesus which speak of losing one's life and gaining it and *vice versa* (Matt. 10.39; 16.25–26; Mark 8.35–36; Luke 9.24–25; 17.33; John 12.25); even if the gaining or losing of life were originally meant to be something that lay in the future, these sayings are sometimes also formulated in the present tense (cf. John 12.25a; also 12.24 and Mark 8.36) and the futures of the remaining ones could easily have been interpreted as logical ones: the one who loses his life now will, in so doing, gain it and gain it now. This motif is no trivial one, for not only is it central to the call and challenge of Jesus and Paul, but in the eyes of John Hick it is of the essence of salvation in the major world religions, 'the transformation of human existence from self-centredness to a new orientation centred in the divine Reality'.[382]

Phillips picks up this talk of 'dying to self' and uses it as a riposte to the preoccupation with survival after death: such a death to self means that one renounces the claim on the future; one's own life is no longer a necessity. Those preoccupied with a life beyond the grave do not see that 'by reducing the status of death to the status of sleep', he continues,

> we hope to wake to a new and better life. But then the lesson religious believers see in death is lost, since death no longer reveals the fact there is to be no compensation, but is seen as an additional fact for which compensation must be sought.[383]

One who seeks such compensation, in short, has not in fact died to self, but is still self-seeking and self-assertive. And Gordon Kaufman levels a somewhat similar charge against the triumphalism of Christian belief in resurrection: if eternal blessedness is the reward of the faithful, and eternal torment the fate of those who are not, then what at first sight appears to be an ethic of self-sacrifice 'turns out on closer inspection to be rather an expression of prudential self-interest'.[384]

This aspect of Paul's thought, if followed through, can also be a healthy safeguard against the sort of 'enthusiasm' which so alarmed Käsemann and caused him to shy away from the thought of the Fourth Gospel. It is also a healthy safeguard against that sort of 'docetism' for which he censured that Gospel's christology and which may also mark its anthropology. For not only the Christ who strides triumphantly through this world, laying down his life in the full confidence that he had the power to resume it again (John 10.17–18), but also the believer who lives confident that death cannot touch him, seem to have floated up above the trials and the testings and the frustrations that are characteristic of human life on this earth. Once one sees that the life which Christ offers is only offered and appropriated through

taking up one's cross in obedience to the suffering and loving son
of man, and realizes that we truly live only by bearing about in
our bodies the putting to death of Jesus, then a very different
view of a Christian's life emerges. So far from being placed
beyond the reach of death, one is daily exposed to it and daily
courts it if the call of Jesus and his God demands it. No form of
existence could be more thoroughly 'earthed' in this world and its
sufferings; no form could be further from the pseudo-humanity
which Käsemann so much dreads.

My concern is, in short, to move beyond 'resurrection' and a
faith bewitched by that concept to a faith that is thoroughly this-
worldly, both for the sake of this world and also in the conviction
that the traditions concerning the resurrection of Jesus justify
nothing else than a thoroughgoing agnosticism concerning what
may or may not have happened on that 'third day' and that the
concept of individual survival after death is anyway riddled with
incoherence. In doing this I am conscious that I am not only
moving beyond anything that Paul or the Fourth Evangelist ever
said, but moving beyond anything that Jesus himself ever said.
For it seems to me undeniable that, however much he concerned
himself with the realization of God's kingly reign in this world,
he also expected a still-future realization of that kingly power in
all its fullness.[385] But just as he was a part of his own world and
time and shared the assumptions and many aspects of the then
prevalent world-view and mistakenly expected an imminent end
of the world as we know it, so too he shared the widespread belief
in another world that was still to be revealed. Yet as Karl
Lehmann notes,[386] it is a striking feature of the resurrection
narratives that they are distinguished from other accounts in the
Graeco-Roman world which might otherwise seem to be similar
in kind by the fact that the Gospels offer us no information here
about that hidden world. The risen Jesus assures his disciples
that he is risen and comforts them in their grief and gives them
his commission to serve him in this world. About the world to
come, the world into which he has briefly entered and from
which he has for a short time returned, he tells them nothing. His

interest is still very much with *this* world and with what is to be done in it.

In that respect such an interpretative step would not be fully out of tune with Jesus' own priorities. It is, interestingly, an interpretative step which many less conservative Jews have apparently taken with regard to their own traditions, if E. Segal is right in summing up the thought of most liberal Jews as follows:

> Discussions of the afterlife are almost entirely absent from non-Orthodox twentieth-century religious discourse, which has focused on the absolute commitment to this world as the setting for the encounter with the divine, the covenant between God and Israel, and the obligation to serve humanity.[387]

In that, they may have in a very real sense reverted to the earlier, traditional beliefs of Israel before the belief in resurrection arose, at least in some Jewish circles, relatively late in the history of that people.[388] And, although B. C. Ollenburger argues for the presence, alongside 'traditional' or 'orthodox' views of death, of a faith in a creator God who is mightier than the power of death, he initially questioned the limiting of 'resurrection' to the fate of the individual and proposed widening the concept out to the 'enduring group'.[389] But that group's 'endurance' by no means necessitates another world beyond this one, and indeed is more often thought of in terms of continued this-worldly existence (despite the apparent destruction of the group).

Segal's colleague, T. Penelhum, in the same volume is critical of those who interpret Christianity similarly, although he recognizes the grave philosophical difficulties of the various ways of thinking about post-mortem existence.[390] However, in view of the uncertainties attaching to the tradition of Jesus' resurrection, and the correspondingly questionable status of any belief in resurrection or some other form of post-mortal existence once one is deprived of this warrant, one has to ask whether Christianity too might not be better advised to follow liberal Judaism down a similar, reinterpretative path.

The wisdom of a life-style based on the conviction that this life is (simply) a preparation for another life beyond death and the grave seems open to question. For the basis of that conviction is hedged about with altogether too many 'ifs' and 'buts' to seem reasonable. And if such a conviction serves to distract from the living of this life and from meeting its responsibilities and challenges, then this conviction is not worth the price and is to be regarded as a dangerous delusion. The alternative to belief in another life is not, however, what Paul scathingly dismisses as 'Let us eat and drink, for tomorrow we die' (I Cor. 15.32). We have seen that Paul's message for this life (and also that of John too, though his language is rather different) is in fact an ethically and spiritually stringent and challenging one: we are to die to ourselves and find our life precisely in this death within this world. Here and now we will meet our God and live for our God.

9

The God Of Jesus – and Beyond

It is inevitable in dealing with the question of Jesus' resurrection that one should have to deal with the *question of God* – implicitly or explicitly. For the assumptions that one makes about God, and particularly about God in relation to our world, will inevitably colour, perhaps even determine, our treatment of the theme of resurrection. If we believe that God is so related to the natural world as to be able at will to perform miracles in the sense of suspending or altering the normal regularities of the natural world, then the resurrection of Jesus will present few problems: it may seem, rather, simply to confirm this view of God with a supreme proof of its rightness. If, on the other hand, God is seen as somehow immanent in these very regularities, if their existence is in itself a cogent argument for the divine, then an event like the raising of Jesus from the dead, so unusual and so irregular in the world as we have hitherto known it, fits far less comfortably into this world-view and God-view. To that extent Francis Watson's plea that his own defence of the 'traditional' view of the 'materiality' of the resurrection of Jesus respects traditional views of God's relation to the world and is of a piece with the doctrines of creation and incarnation, in a way that 'revisionist' accounts of the resurrection are not, misses the point:[391] quite apart from the question whether or not one accepts, or should accept, the 'traditional' views of creation and incarnation, there are several ways of construing God's relation to the material world, and it is by no means clear that a 'traditional' view of Jesus' resurrection, however much one reverently shrouds it in mystery (which can all too easily become a convenient way of fudging the issues and

avoiding awkward questions), in fact corresponds to a theologically and philosophically acceptable or coherent view of that
relation. Naturally, if one holds a 'non-realist' view of God,[392]
then quite obviously such a God is not going to be able 'really' to
raise one dead.

Conversely, however, belief in the resurrection of Jesus and
the way in which one visualizes this will play a major role in
shaping the way in which one thinks of God. If one believes that
God raised the dead body of Jesus to new life, then that obviously
presupposes a certain kind of relationship between God and the
created order, a relationship in which the miraculous, as traditionally interpreted, can occur and has occurred, as well as
anticipating the relationship of this world which we experience
today to a future world of which Jesus' resurrection is the first-
fruits and foretaste. God is, accordingly, one who can and will
intervene in the world in this way. If, on the other hand, the
resurrection is simply a matter of, say, 'objective visions', in
which the physical remains of Jesus are unaffected, then does this
mean that we are speaking of a God who can interact with us as
spirit with spirit, but no more? And if even 'objective visions'
become rather elusive entities and we have to confess that we
cannot be sure whether they were not, after all, merely 'subjective visions' and no more, then the experiences of the first
disciples may tell us more about human nature than about God's
nature, and will not even serve as an argument for the existence
of God. Nevertheless, having to let go of this datum may prove a
liberating experience for theology, in that it may set it free to pose
the question of God, and how God is to be conceived of, in a new
way, unfettered by the tradition of God's unique intervention in
the Easter events. Instead one is free to formulate a view of God
that is based on everyday religious experience instead of taking as
its starting-point that which is quite unique and hitherto utterly
abnormal, at least in this present world (and leaving aside the
entirely hypothetical possibility of eschatological verification in
another, future one).

And if the concept of 'resurrection' emerged in the Judaeo-

Christian tradition in a context of *theodicy*, that is, as an answer
to the ethical problem of the sufferings of the righteous and the
apparent triumph of the ungodly, then it is hardly surprising that
one's decisions about the resurrection of Jesus also have such a
dimension, in more than one respect. There is the question that
exercised the suffering Jews of the second century BCE to which
the Book of Daniel provides an answer, the question how an
all-powerful God could so ignore the demands of justice and fail
to right the wrongs being perpetrated upon the faithful in the
present age. But there are also other questions involving the
morality and also the competence of God, for instance the one
mentioned before which James Mackey posed to Ian McDonald:
if, for instance, resurrection leads to a better world, why did God
ever fashion the present, evidently less good world (even if God
supposedly considered it 'very good': Gen. 1.31)? Why did our
creator not give us the higher world to start with? For the
doctrine of the resurrection and the whole tradition of Jewish and
Christian eschatology to which it belongs immediately excludes
G. W. Leibniz's solution to the problem of theodicy, namely his
contention that God *must* have created the best of all possible
worlds. That is immediately repudiated if in fact Jesus' resurrection is the gateway to a better world.[393] And why did God make
us (and all creatures capable of feeling pain) endure this world of
'futility' (Eccles. 1.2 *et passim*; Rom. 8.20) rather than giving us a
better one to start with? But if there is, on the other hand, no
resurrection of Jesus or ourselves, and no better world, has God
then left us in the lurch and consigned us to such a world of
futility? Could not God have done better? Are we stuck with that
verdict of 'very good' even if it grates on our nerves and sticks in
our throats, and we find ourselves asking how anyone could ever
suppose that? It would be hardly fair to blame humanity for all
that we find less than perfect in this world, even if humanity has
played a major part in making it so much less than perfect. And
H. Verweyen argues, rightly, that 'resurrection' is no answer,
even a belated one, to the suffering of the world; it will not do
simply to say that God was present incognito in those sufferings:

the tears of mangled children are too high a price to pay for any subsequent heavenly harmony.[394]

It should therefore come as no surprise that I earlier posed the question whether traditional views of God as omnipotent and the like might not have to be revised if we found that the evidence for Jesus' resurrection was by no means conclusive or was so ambivalent as to prohibit our saying exactly what happened apart from the fact of the rise of faith in Jesus' resurrection on the part of the previously demoralized disciples.

(a) God in the preaching of Jesus

That traditional views of God should have to be revised should come as no surprise. That would be no novelty in the Judaeo-Christian tradition. For fundamental to the understanding of Jesus' teaching and ministry and of the resistance which he thereby encountered was a new vision of God and of the ways and will of God which many of his contemporaries found profoundly disturbing and threatening. God and the kingly reign of God formed the centre of his message, and of course this was no new god, but the God of Israel, whom Jesus' fellow-Jews thought that they knew. But therein lay the challenge. Jesus spoke of God in a way that was implicitly subversive of much that his fellows believed and held dear. They thought that they knew what God was like; Jesus challenged them to rethink their understanding of God and God's ways.

In the role of a teacher of wisdom, an aspect of Jesus' teaching which modern scholarship has particularly emphasized and in some cases one-sidedly over-emphasized, Jesus belonged to the tradition of those wisdom teachers whose teaching in many respects ran counter to normal views and values. He was prepared to turn the common-sense rules of ordinary behaviour and expediency into their opposites,[395] and this characteristic has led to his being likened to those peripatetic critics of Graeco-Roman society, the Cynics, at least of the more radical variety.[396] Gerd Theissen argues that Jesus showed a persistent independence of traditional norms of behaviour, either radicalizing them (e.g. Matt. 5.27–28) or relativizing them, whether by his 'easy contact' with those who did not keep those norms or by assessing them differently from the society of his day (e.g. Matt. 21.31).[397] Such a radical critique of social and religious norms of the day is thoroughly fitting for one who was perceived to be, and quite probably also perceived himself to be, in the tradition of Israel's prophets as much as in that of the teachers of wisdom. Challenges to prevailing understandings of God were no novelty in Israel's history. And just as Jesus' practical teaching was unconventional in the radicality with which he applied the rule and the consequent claims of God to human conduct, so too he did not feel himself constrained by the normal expectations about God held by his Jewish contemporaries. For more menacing still in their eyes than his ethical teaching was his stance in relation to God's covenant relation to Israel. If the Baptist had already warned that God could raise up children of Abraham from the very stones (implicitly so as to replace those who prided themselves on being Abraham's children by rather more conventional means) (Matt. 3.9 par.), so too Jesus spoke of many coming from east and west and taking their place at table in God's kingdom with Abraham and the other patriarchs (and so implicitly threatening to replace those who thought that they had their seats there booked) (8.11 par.). It seems to me likely that a parable such as that of the Wicked Tenants (Mark 12.1–12 parr.) was indeed originally directed against the leaders of Israel who had forfeited their claim to occupancy of God's vineyard through their persistent rejection of God's servants sent to them – and indeed, although many doubt that this goes back to Jesus himself, their rejection of the one who stood in a yet closer relation to God than those servants who had been sent before to God's wayward people.

Jesus proclaimed the God of Israel, but now in a new way. That is already implied if the law and the prophets, which had hitherto been the source of knowledge of Israel's God, had been valid only for the time before God's kingly rule began (Luke 16.16–17 par.). Although the centre of Jesus' message was God's kingly rule, the novelty of his message did not lie in this kingship as such, for the kingship of God over creation and the natural world and the whole human world was a regular theme of the law and the prophets. Israel did not need to be told that God was king; that is a lesson which the Psalter hammers home time and again. Correspondingly the behaviour of kings plays relatively little part in Jesus' teaching (Matt. 18.23–34 is one exception, and Matthew's version of the Parable of the Great Feast, 22.1–14, may be another): the assertion that God was king was as such not particularly illuminating for Jesus, and the ways of earthly kings could even be more than a little misleading, both for understanding the ways of God and as a yardstick for human behaviour (Mark 10.42–44 par.); to see what Jesus thought of kings one need only look at his scathing reference to Herod Antipas as a fox (Luke 13.32). If even human parenthood was an inadequate model for Jesus' understanding of God, how much more the worldly institution of kingship! Yet the parables of Jesus do use the powerful of this world as analogies to what one should expect of God, e.g. powerful, if absentee, landowners (Mark 12.1–12 parr.) and the like, even if not for the most part kings as such: if the mighty of this world do this, then how much more God . . .

One can argue about God *a minore ad maius*. But in the landowner of the Parable of the Vineyard Workers (Matt. 20.1–16) one finds a powerful figure whose conduct is, to say the least, surprising by usual standards: the sovereignty of this person is a sovereignty in goodness and generosity. Still, even that may not burst the bounds of what was conceivable in the ancient world, however aggrieved those who had worked longest may have felt: being a benefactor was part of the business of being powerful in those days, and who is to say that benefactions had to follow precise rules and standards? Something of the same surprising, unpredictable generosity shows itself, too, in the behaviour of the Prodigal Son's only modestly well-to-do father (Luke 15.11–32). The continuity of Jesus' talk of God with the traditions of Israel is plain, and not only when he speaks of God's kingly rule: the images which he otherwise uses are often ones which the Old Testament had already employed to speak of God, e.g. as a vineyard-owner (Isa. 5.1ff) or shepherd (Ps. 23 with Matt. 18.12–14 par.). What Israel already knew is taken up and redefined.

Yet despite so much that was familiar, much was strikingly different, different too from the Baptist's proclamation of God's coming, however much there was which bound the proclamation of John and Jesus together. That showed itself quite plainly in the very different life-styles of the two men and their movements, ways of life which they each evidently considered appropriate as their God drew near (cf. Luke 7.31–35 par.): the one evidently considered self-denial and asceticism, world-denial and penitence necessary; the other held joy and celebration to be more suitable. Such a difference in behaviour of necessity reflects a different perception of the God who called them to these respective ways of life, particularly since it is doubtful whether Jesus regarded his contemporaries as any less sinful than they were in John's eyes.

Above all Jesus' relationship to God was characterized by an attitude of trust (a fact which makes his cry of dereliction, Mark 15.34 par., all the more striking and shocking), and this trust was something that he invited his followers to share; such a trust, however, could not have come easily to many of them, confronted as they were by the uncertainties of life on or near or even below the none too generous subsistence level of those days, and wholly without any safety-net of social welfare, in a land occupied by an unsympathetic and exploitative imperial power. But trust was not something one easily or naturally showed towards the rulers of this world, be they the imperial power or its cronies. In other words, in this respect too, Jesus' God was quite evidently different from other rulers.

On the other hand, while many of Jesus' fellows wished to replace their earthly rulers with a theocracy and correspondingly made much of the will of the divine ruler disclosed in his statutes, a scrupulous observance of the Jewish law often does not seem to have come as high on Jesus' scale of priorities as many of the religious leaders of his day would have liked. This can only have been highly disturbing and disconcerting in the eyes of his more religiously minded contemporaries. His social and religious (and in that society of necessity also political) programme must have been different from theirs. Above all his message was an inclusive one, which gathered in and included those generally considered 'sinners' by his contemporaries, rather than seeking to exclude those who sully the people of God by their presence within it. That also presupposes a different interpretation of the will of God and how to realize it here on earth, even if there was so much in Jesus' teaching that showed the continuity of his message with the faith of Israel. That is underlined by Mark, for instance, when he links with the twofold command to love (12.28–34) a fuller quotation of the Shema (Deut. 6.4–5): the continuity is plain, even if the priorities that are set here may be unusual. Furthermore, along with words and deeds that seem to betray an attitude of relative indifference with regard to the requirements of the law, Jesus' teaching at the same time often seems to have contained, in a most paradoxical fashion, statements that reveal a thoroughly radical interpretation and application of the Jewish law, a readiness to treat its demands with an unusual seriousness and lack of compromise. To this radically phrased demand for obedience corresponds, however, an equally radically conceived proclamation of God's readiness to forgive. Jesus' God is recognizably the God of Israel, but seen in a new way, with a radical seriousness and yet at the same time a radical trust and optimism.

(b) An omnipotent God?

Jesus' proclamation of God called for a revision of the then current view or views about God among his contemporaries. But does that mean that all the revising that has to be done has already been done in the message that Jesus proclaimed? Or does it merely mean that humankind and its thinking about God and understanding of God was launched upon a path, a trajectory, a line of developing thought which would in turn take Jesus' followers on to new insights, which would in turn involve a revision of Jesus' own understanding of God, framed as it was in the context of the concepts of his own day and traditions? Is it not fully legitimate to press on, beyond Jesus' own message, to new insights and ways of thinking about God, making use of categories and ways of thought that have been developed since the first century, and in particular in often ancient religious traditions of which Jesus and his world had no inkling? After all, what Jesus called in question and revised was then believed to be God's own self-revelation of the divine nature and purposes, invested with all the authority which that understanding of the status of Israel's beliefs entails. In going beyond Jesus' actual statements are we intrinsically doing more than he himself did? It may be granted that he was careful to maintain a continuity with the traditions of Israel, so that it was recognizably the same God of whom he spoke, even in the midst of his revising and questioning. That may at least mean that we, in our revision of Jesus' teaching, may also need to demonstrate the continuity of what we say with what Jesus said and did.

So we can ask, for instance, whether that radicality and seriousness with which Jesus proclaimed his God demand that we too insist on the omnipotence of God. Here we must carefully distinguish what Jesus in fact said and thought from what we today can or must say and think, for I do not believe that these two things must necessarily coincide, at least not if we treat the humanity of Jesus with full seriousness. And we would be fully justified in making the distinction if we found that elements in Jesus' teaching in fact pointed in another direction, even if he himself did not follow this other 'line of development' to its logical conclusion. It would not be surprising if Jesus had thought, like all his Jewish contemporaries, that God was all-powerful and had never questioned that principle. Indeed it would probably be anachronistic to expect that he would have been able so to free himself from the framework of this way of thinking about God.

This way of thinking of God has, I think, a twofold root, at least in Christian theology today. In the ancient world, on the one hand, it stemmed from analogical thinking about God based on the conception of the powers of ancient rulers: God was like earthly rulers, only more so, a king of kings and lord of lords; great as their powers were, his were greater, less limited. 'In Judaism, Christianity, and Islam God has usually been conceived in terms of monarchical and imperial models, as a sort of king or emperor; and sometimes God is depicted as a virtual despot who rules by arbitrary fiat.'[398] This sort of model for God's nature and God's relation to the world remained very much in force as the doctrines of God's omnipotence and omniscience were formulated in mediaeval theological and philosophical thought. Moreover the earthly rulers who provided the model and the analogy in Israel's world were no (relatively) innocuous constitutional monarchs, but oriental potentates whose power was often immense and capricious, as the behaviour of Herod Antipas and his father, Herod the Great, amply demonstrated in Jesus' time. Nor were the rulers of the Middle Ages any better suited as analogies to the divine nature. Further, as feminist theologians have insisted, with some justification, this omnipotent ruler is a very masculine construction.

Even so, in the recurring theme of God's kingly rule, Jesus himself seems, we saw, to have endorsed the validity of this way of thinking and speaking about God. It is in this and in the fact of his own masculinity that the problems which many feminists have with the Christian religious tradition lie. At the same time, however, in the fact that the figure of a king appears relatively rarely in Jesus' parables, where one might expect this to be one of the most obvious ways to speak parabolically of the one whose kingly rule is near, we may see a hint that aspects of God's nature are so unlike that of earthly kings that this image is better to be avoided, in order to avoid misunderstanding. In general, should one not say that that form of argument which Jesus uses apropos of human conduct in the ranks of his disciples in contrast to the ways of conduct of the mighty (e.g. Mark 10.42–44 par. once more) also suggests that such a human analogy would not be appropriate for God either? Yet much of Jesus' teaching and conduct might at first sight seem to suggest that indeed such ways of thinking and speaking about God were fitting. Thus Jürgen Becker concludes that 'where God works, his work is always irresistible'.[399] But if that were the case, why is Jesus' ability to do God's works, and thus by implication God's ability to work through him, able to be thwarted by human faithlessness (Mark 6.5–6)? Correspondingly, the correlation between Jesus' ability to heal and human faith or trust is a recurrent theme of the Gospels.

The all-powerfulness of God seems to be enshrined in the Old Testament and correspondingly in early Christian piety. Precisely for that reason Wolfgang Schoberth rejects the possibility of discarding belief in God's 'almightiness': that belief is indispensable for the biblical tradition.[400] It is true that the Greek word παντοκράτωρ, which corresponds more exactly to 'almighty' than any term in the Hebrew scriptures, was seemingly coined relatively late and in Greek-speaking Judaism, and appears in the Septuagint almost exclusively as a translation of $s^e ba'ot$ and $šadday$. It is no coincidence, Reinhard Feldmeier argues, that the term arose and was predominantly used in a situation where righteous Jews found themselves helpless before oppressive rulers, and therefore not in the first instance in the context of philosophical or theological speculations; their Lord, they asserted, was superior, all-powerful, and in that faith they called on their God for help. Similarly the term occurs most frequently in the New Testament in the Book of Revelation (nine out of the ten occurrences), where again the righteous are confronted by an unjust, oppressive and seemingly irresistible world-power. In both Hellenistic Judaism and the New Testament, therefore, 'God is invoked as the almighty, as the ruler of this world, is indeed obligated to exercise power against the oppressing political power.'[401] In such a context, however, the tendency is almost inevitable that the power of God will be construed as similar to the political power of the oppressor but quantitatively vastly superior. One power is opposed by another overwhelmingly greater power. The critique of the whole concept of worldly power that comes to expression in Mark 10.42–45 parr. finds no place here.

Less frequently this divine predicate or the similar παν-ηγεμών occurs in a philosophical context, for instance in the works of Philo as a Jewish counterpart to the Stoic 'ruling principle' (τὸ ἡγεμονικόν):

> evident in this philosophical interpretation of the idea of omnipotence is the concern to display the biblical God not only as sustaining the world after the manner of Stoic thought, but also as the free Lord of the cosmos, distinguished from the world, both the sense-perceptible and the spiritual. This is deliberately opposed to all deterministic or fatalistic interpretations of the world.[402]

Thus already in Hellenistic Judaism, exposed to Greek philosophical thinking, we find another strand of thought, the second root of the doctrine of God's impotence to which I referred, alongside the analogy with the earthly ruler.

In more recent times, on the other hand, this way of thinking about God has received a yet more rigorous philosophical and speculative undergirding: God must, by definition, be like this if God is to be God. Such an attribute follows from the Godness of God. It will not do, however, simply to play off this God of reason, with whom the discussion of theodicy is concerned, against the biblical God, as Schoberth does.[403] That is possible only as long as 'theodicy' is very narrowly defined, for similar problems exercise, to varying degrees, a number of biblical authors and not just the author of Job. Nor do I find it particularly helpful to distinguish 'omnipotence' and 'almightiness', a distinction which Schoberth takes over from G. van den Brink (61); 'omnipotence' may belong more to the context of a philosophical discussion of God's nature (although the adjective *omnipotens* is often found in the Vulgate as a translation of the Hebrew divine names), 'almightiness' more to the language of the Bible and of liturgy (even though exact linguistic parallels to the idea of God as 'almighty' are harder to find in the original text of the Bible, particularly in the Old Testament, for the etymology of terms like *ṣᵉba'ot* and *šadday* is far from clear).[404] The use of the terms may belong to different contexts, but the problems must overlap if any attempt is to be made to speak rationally of the God of the biblical tradition.

Nevertheless the status of such knowledge of the Godness of God which is frequently to be found in works of Christian theology seems to me epistemologically questionable. It is questionable, not because it seeks to speak philosophically of the God of the biblical tradition, but because the philosophical basis of this speaking is itself open to question. I can only register my wonder at the ease and confidence with which many philosophers or Christian theologians seem able to argue *a priori* that God *must* be X or Y, for that belongs to the very essence of being God.[405] Rightly Carnley questions at this point Ernst Troeltsch's postulate of a universal 'religious *a priori*' and, more in the manner of Kant, argues for an interplay between experience and rational understanding or conceptualization, in order to explain the relationship between the concept of 'resurrection' and Christian experience. He sees each Christian receiving, as a given, his or her interpretative concepts, which make possible an ordering of religious experience.[406] But, as he also sees, one has to leave room for the redefinition of the concepts in the light of religious experience and that will frequently be the case with received conceptualizations. A child may, for example, learn from its parents or teachers the concept of a table, associating it perhaps with a picture in a book that shows an object with four legs and therefore assuming that having four legs is a *sine qua non* of being a table. Only later will he or she learn that objects with three or with five or more legs may also legitimately be described as 'tables'; encounters with objects and the need to 'order' them in one's understanding of the world force one into a greater flexibility in the definition and use of categories and concepts. That was also true of the concept of 'resurrection', in that what the disciples experienced after Jesus' death corresponded to none of the preconceived Jewish notions of 'resurrection', as we have seen. Similarly, however, it can be argued that the outcome of Jesus' life and activity compelled them to rethink their understanding of God and compels us too to such a rethinking that will bring our understanding of God into harmony with their experience and our own. A continuous process of redefinition is involved here, and one should not imagine that our view of God will be exempted from this.

One sees how 'omnipotence' seems to follow from the Godness of God when Keith Ward asserts that, by definition, it seems, 'God cannot be less powerful than any other being';[407] that statement, however, only holds good if being 'powerful' is something unquestionably positive, valuable and worthwhile, and precisely that traditional view seems to me to be called into question if one takes seriously the idea of a disclosure of the nature of the divine in Jesus Christ. At the very least one has to ask what one means by 'power' and 'powerful', and what constitutes them. If, for instance, one defines God as 'being-itself',[408] then what sense does it make to describe 'being-itself' as 'powerful'? Is one not inevitably guilty of a certain degree of anthropomorphism whenever one predicates such a thing of God, unless the 'power' meant is that sort of ethically indifferent power which, for instance, the forces of nature possess? Or else, on the other hand, Ward argues that since God is (by his definition, one must add) 'a reality which cannot fail to exist', God 'carries the power of existing in itself', is 'the power of being' (197); does 'power' here mean anything more than the ability to exist? But how far is this whole enterprise of discovering and defining God according to the built-in logic of the notion of God successful? At what point does it become answerable to the data of the empirical world and of that which Christians claim to be the supreme datum and divine self-disclosure, the life of Jesus of Nazareth, especially that life once it has been stripped of an incontrovertible and unmistakable, triumphant and supremely powerful 'happy end' in the resurrection of that life from the dead? For there seems to me to be something basically suspect in the notion that one can, so to speak, simply 'read off' the description of God because one knows already what is meant when one speaks of 'God'; should one not be able to check this description against something, to see whether it really matches what our senses and experience and those of our predecessors tell us? That, moreover, is a self-discipline to which most Christian theologians at least pay lip-service, regardless of how they then go about describing God.

Can one, though, allow the nature of God thus to be dictated unchallenged by the demands of logical schemes? Certainly not if one takes seriously the claim that the divine self has been revealed in Jesus, for this Jesus was hardly an all-powerful figure, but rather the reverse. Or should we reformulate this claim? The divine self has supposedly been revealed in *Christ* – but to drive a wedge between Jesus and Christ here then raises serious problems about the relationship of this Christ to Jesus, and about how one can say things about Christ which are not true also of Jesus.[409] Even if claims to know God and humanity from Jesus Christ alone have foundered, in part because information that was not gleaned from Jesus Christ alone crept in surreptitiously, in part because of the uncertainty what 'Christ' means,[410] Jesus Christ should, by definition, play a central role in shaping a *Christian* theology. On the other hand, one also comes up here against that tension between an incarnational theology and 'resurrection faith' to which Verweyen draws attention: how can one say that God has been fully revealed in the earthly life of Jesus and nevertheless see in the resurrection the decisive act of God's revelation?[411] For the incarnate Jesus seems, as we saw, to be one whose sufferings lead him to an agonized despair; it is the resurrected Christ who triumphs and prevails against all adversaries and adversity. If one distinguishes here between 'Jesus' and 'Christ', then Christian theology is indeed split in two; it has, so to speak, a 'double vision'.

(c) The creator God and human culture

Such views of the sovereign, transcendent, and all-powerful God may seem to follow naturally from the view of God as the creator who transcends the universe that has been created, but they can also seem, at first sight at least, to follow from views which see God's ways of working far more in categories of immanence. If one takes, for example, Gerd Theissen's highly innovative and suggestive, but to my knowledge surprisingly neglected, study *Biblical Faith: An Evolutionary Approach*, he sees emerging in the various scientific disciplines a single, unitary reality that underlies all the manifold phenomena of life: 'Behind everything we detect a "unitary programme" which *directs* everything.'[412] Theissen sees two forms of evolution at work in the world, 'biological' and 'cultural'. As one might expect if there is but one all-determinative reality, these are similar in certain respects: in the former, life develops through mutation and selection so that it constantly adapts anew to reality; culture too constantly develops new 'forms of adapting to the basic conditions of reality' (he lists as examples science, art and religion). It is 'only when these [forms of cultural adaptation] complement and supplement one another' that 'they do justice to the richness of reality' (8). Cultural evolution is a higher form of biological evolution,[413] but both share certain similarities: in both, variations and mutations appear; in the case of cultural developments these take traditional elements and combine them, facilitated by cultural exchange, in a new way to produce something new. At first sight cultural mutations might seem to be different in that they are intentional, in that they are deliberate answers to problems, he argues, but that would be to underestimate the element of chance, of the unforeseen, in these changes. (Where now is the 'unitary programme' that directs everything or what form does this 'direction' then take?) And whereas in the biological sphere natural 'selection' takes place, cultural evolution happens as we learn more effective patterns of behaviour. Here we might more aptly speak of 'reinforcement', either conscious or unconscious, rather

than 'selection'. Faith seeks a way of life which is compatible
with the reality which it believes underlies all, 'a central reality,
hidden from us, for which there is no better word than "God"'
(30). In other words, Theissen presupposes that cultural evolution is a reaction to a reality, an Other; it is not simply a matter
of practical utilitarianism which realizes that in the last analysis
one gets along better if one is loving and altruistic. By implication, that Other is not just the empirical world in which we live,
as it is, but something which lies behind or beneath that world.[414]

Here Theissen postulates that, were the central reality visible
to us, we would see it to be 'a reality that has an unconditional
tolerance of variations, in the face of which all human beings are
of equal value' (49).[415] It should be noted that this 'uncondition-
ally tolerant' reality would in that case be very different from any
form of rigid causality or determinism, and one's concept of God
would have to be adjusted accordingly; Theissen's talk of a 'unitary programme' which 'directs' everything needs therefore to be
set against this other view, which is anything but 'directive'. For
religion in particular is, for Theissen, 'a rebellion against the
principle of selection' (ibid.), and this is nowhere more clearly
shown than in the religion of the Christian Bible. Here there are
interesting echoes of the later writings of Charles Darwin's pupil
and follower Thomas Huxley, although Theissen makes no
mention of his work. For Huxley saw cultural progress in general
(and not just religion) as a displacement of the sovereign rule of
nature and its replacement with the rule of ethics:

> The practice of that which is ethically best . . . involves a
> course of conduct which in all respects is opposed to that
> which leads to success in the cosmic struggle for existence. In
> place of ruthless self-assertion, it demands self-restraint; in
> place of thrusting aside or treading down all competitors, it
> requires that the individual shall not merely respect, but shall
> help his fellows; its influence is directed, not so much to the
> survival of the fittest, as to the fitting of as many as possible to
> survive. It repudiates the gladiatorial theory of existence. . . .

The ethical progress of society depends not on imitating the cosmic process, still less in running away from it, but in combating it.[416]

Therefore, perhaps even more clearly than Theissen and even more so than Kaufman, as we shall see, Huxley shows how ethics demands a repudiation and reversal of the principles upon which biological selection and evolution are grounded.

If all religions are attempts 'to correspond to God' (50), then, Theissen implies, this is best done by a religion the nature of which corresponds to a God who has 'an unconditional tolerance of variation', whose face is set, so to speak, against the principle of selection.[417] But does that not then set up a tension between this and the traditional notion of a creator God who should presumably have set the rules for the process of biological evolution? Biblical monotheism asserts that the ultimately real One is on the side of those who 'would have vanished from history had the usual processes of selection prevailed' (81). If it is true that God has been finally revealed in Jesus Christ, that means that 'in the midst of history a possible "goal" of evolution is revealed: complete adaptation to the reality of God' (83).[418] So in Jesus there is revealed a love which is in solidarity with the weak (cf. Matt. 25.31–46), and which thus contradicts the processes in nature and history that are based on selection; in this love God is revealed, and if the 'central reality' that is God is shown to be love, then the pressure of selection is finally overcome. Yet the problem that arises here should not be overlooked: if one traces the processes of creation back to the creator God and the creative spirit of this God, then does this not mean that this God works creatively, directly or indirectly, through these evolutionary processes; that these processes receive, so to speak, a divine endorsement?[419] How can it then be a movement of the same spirit that resists and rejects the basic principles of the natural processes? Are we not threatened here with a dualism between the good and loving God and a lesser, possibly even evil, deity responsible for the rise of the natural world? Or can one resolve this dilemma by speaking of two levels in the cosmic order and the cosmic reality? That is a possibility to which we must return.

Theissen is, at any rate, careful to deny here a determinism that arises from the historical circumstances in which Jesus found himself. Despite the many analogies to Jesus' teaching and activity in the world of his day, what appeared in Jesus was *not* the inevitable outcome of the circumstances of his time. The situation in Palestine in the first century spawned a whole variety of different religious responses, and the movement started by Jesus also took root in quite different circumstances elsewhere in the Graeco-Roman world. After all, even in biological evolution mutations are not fully determined, and the scope for 'openness, flexibility and delight in innovation' is even greater in cultural evolution (109). Jesus, Theissen recognizes, directs a protest 'against culture, in so far as it exercises a selective pressure of adaptation' (116). In other words, cultural evolution can seemingly take different forms, and the Christian 'culture' represents a protest against the principles on which many of these forms operate.

But Jesus died, and death is, for evolution based on selection, evidence of dysfunctionality. Jesus' disciples believed that the resurrection appearances were evidence that this seeming failure was in reality victory, 'the starting point for a new development and the basis for unconditional motivation to live' (119). But perhaps Theissen here fails to do justice to the tradition that Jesus had himself in his earthly life already offered this starting-point by teaching that would-be followers must lose their lives to save them (Mark 8.35 parr., etc.). Once again, what the resurrection of Jesus seems to offer can already be found in the teaching and example of the earthly Jesus.

The themes of biological life and culture are also dealt with in another work to which I have already referred, Gordon Kaufman's *In Face of Mystery*. He also speaks of a cultural evolution, but his account places less emphasis than Theissen's on the reality to which it is a response; rather, it is a response to human beings' own awareness and conceptions. They have organized

> their lives increasingly in terms of (a) their greater awareness of their own needs, including what we might call their 'inwardly felt' needs for joy, peace, understanding, affection, and the like, and (b) their conceptions of the objects and powers in the world round about them, especially those which most directly affected them, either by significantly meeting their increasingly complex needs or by posing threats.[420]

Whereas Theissen, as we have seen, creates problems for himself in speaking too much of cultural evolution as analogous to biological evolution, despite the fact that he interprets 'religion' (all religion?), which is an important part of culture, as a 'rebellion against the principle of selection' active in biological evolution, for Kaufman, in contrast, human culture means that

> life (as a strictly biological process) has begun significantly to transcend itself: it has moved in certain crucial ways beyond blind evolutionary processes governed by natural selection, the survival of the fittest, to a process which is in certain respects self-directing, a process in which goals and objectives for life and its further evolution can be deliberately set from within (106).

In women and men have arisen 'new desires, interests, and needs which go far beyond strict biological utility, and sometimes even contradict it' (105).[421] In this ability for reflection and self-appraisal, for evaluating and setting goals, for employing language and symbolism and creating symbolic worlds, the distinctiveness of the human over against other life-forms is to be sought (107); human beings are, in his words, 'animals with "historicity"' (108), 'culture-creating beings' (110).[422]

If the problem with Theissen's account was that his insistence that cultural evolution (at least from a Christian perspective, for 'culture' is neither uniform nor develops in a single direction) involves a criticism and rejection of the principles of biological evolution conflicted with his treatment of biological and cultural evolution as analogous to one another, it is by no means clear that Kaufman has satisfactorily solved this by playing down the element of conflict between the two. Is it not arguable that the element of the analogous is to be played down, kept in bounds instead? Perhaps, however, Theissen as a Christian theologian was unwilling or unable to take that line, for the tradition of the omnipotent creator God who directs and guides the evolution of species within this world to its divinely set goal is too strongly entrenched within Christian theology. It is difficult to conceive of God working in one way at one level and then operating in a totally different way at another.

When that model of creation and evolution is called into question, as Kaufman calls it into question, would a resolution of the problem not be easier to envisage? Kaufman himself proposes two alternative models of creativity, that based on the human agent and purposive human action, which leads to the picture of God as a self-aware, all-powerful, free agent, and another one based on human history as a process of human working and purposing, workings and purposings which, like a conversation, often have unexpected, unintended consequences, a 'serendipitous' character (esp. 268–74).[423] But are these the only two models? Is no account to be taken of our experience of frustrated intentions and thwarted creativity? If the divine spirit really shares in and echoes our groans of frustration as we are confronted with the 'futility' to which creation has been subjected (Rom. 8.22, 26), is there not a place for this model of God's relation to creation, however much it may seem to conflict with the picture of a sovereign God who created the world with a word of command and saw with satisfaction that it was all good? (As long as the gap between the creation of the world and the fall of humankind was a matter of days, it was possible to argue that the 'futility' [Rom. 8.20] could be laid at the door of fallen humanity and that previously all had been in order; that has ceased to be possible with the realization just how long the universe and the world had been in existence before human beings ever had a

chance to put a spanner in the works!)[424] The paradox, the
tension is already present in Paul's claim that it is God who has
submitted the world to this 'futility' (even if he thinks of it as
solely a judgment on human sin), and yet it is God's spirit that
groans with us under that 'futility'.[425]

(d) God – personal or non-personal?

We are still left with the question of the nature of God, that
ultimate reality to which, in Theissen's eyes, the evolutionary
process, both biological and cultural, is an adjustment. This is
one aspect of his study to which Theissen does not seem to have
directed much attention. Yet the tensions in his account seem
to demand that we reckon with it. Equally, it seems to me a
problem that Kaufman has not satisfactorily resolved. Is God
responsible for the often cruel and unlovely-seeming ways of
biological selection,[426] or is God rather that impassive, inactive
reality to which nature must adjust? But if God is thought
somehow to be responsible for the forces at work in biological
selection, can the same God also be thought to lie behind the
processes at work in cultural evolution, even though these, as
Theissen has shown, often and at their best reveal the opposite of
the principles of biological evolution? And what is the role of
human decision in all this? That is the danger in the talk
of 'mutations' at this level, for the biological analogies to this
language do not involve conscious decision, while Theissen has
after all expressly declared what took place in Jesus to be a form
of protest against the pre-programming of biological selection.[427]
If that protest is a matter of free decision, then it is a human
protest against a reality that should in no way be identified with
God, or else we find ourselves left with the evil and malign
creator-god of Gnosticism.

Perhaps a more helpful starting-point here lies in what
Theissen rather misleading describes as a 'third mutation' in the
cultural evolution which he portrays, the Christian community in
the power of the Spirit.[428] For the Spirit which Theissen sees at

work in the early Christians is, like Jesus and his message, 'anti-selectionist' (131). It wars against 'works of the flesh', which are in the main biologically orientated forms of behaviour. Its 'fruits' climax in a series of 'pro-social modes of behaviour' (135). The society which this Spirit fostered was one which transcended social barriers. This Spirit is a world-transcending one, offering a new dimension to human life. Those seized by it are 'incorporated into the history of the protest against selection [which stretches] from the beginnings of Israel to Jesus of Nazareth' (140).[429] Would it not be truer to the nature of the God manifested in Jesus, as opposed to God as Jesus evidently conceived God to be, to identify that God with this Spirit that strives against, protests against the selective (and divisive) principles otherwise at work not only within biological evolution, but also within cultural evolution (or development, if one wishes to reserve 'evolution' for movements from a 'lower' form to a 'higher')?

If this God can only strive and protest against what the world is and does and against what human beings are and do, then quite manifestly this God is not omnipotent, for principles of selection continue to operate within this world. This God may appeal to us, may seek to move us and through us our world. But does not this world bear in itself some relation to the nature of this God? Is not God, then, responsible for this world? Must we cease to talk of a God who creates, and talk instead of a God who at the most recreates? But we can perhaps say more than that, even if we have ceased to regard God as omnipotent in the sense of being over and above the laws governing our world and able to change them or suspend them at will, rather than as the ultimate reason why the regularities which we observe in our world exist at all (i.e. as the ultimate answer to questions like those which the physicist Paul Davies dubs 'the Big Four': 'Why are the laws of nature what they are? Why does the universe consist of the things it does? How did those things arise? How did the universe achieve its organization?').[430] This God, who is postulated as an answer to such questions, would at any rate then be comparable

to the divine reason which the ancient Stoics believed to per-
meate the entire cosmos. It would be unthinkable for such a God
to suspend or violate the laws of creation, for would that not call
the very nature of such a God into question? Would it not mean
that God's ceasing to be that God? Or if God is 'the spiritual
reality in which the cosmos is embedded',[431] what sort of uproot-
ing of the bed of the cosmos would be involved in such irregu-
larities? (Talk of God as 'being-itself' or the 'power of being' can
perhaps be regarded as the philosopher's equivalent of this God
of the physicist.)

The case for such a concept of God, whose rationality is the
foundation of that of the universe, is to my mind a strong one, at
least when one considers the alternative or alternatives. One such
is the materialist option, 'whose unifying hypothesis' is, as Keith
Ward summarizes it, 'that all that exists consists of material
particles obeying a few ultimately simple laws, that no purpose or
moral concern or benevolent design can be observed in nature,
and that there are no acts of a supernatural being observable anywhere in nature' (110), or even that all is 'a metaphysical accident
or surd'.[432] Over against this is the mass of arguments which Paul
Davies mentions summarily in another work, *The Mind of God*,
which point to the way in which the laws of physics seem to have
been 'fine-tuned' so as to make possible the evolution of conscious life in our universe.[433] Quite apart from Ward's own
counter-argument that it 'is very counter-intuitive to suppose
that everything that exists is a material particle or complex group
of such particles', for that conflicts with the evidence of consciousness, the postulate of 'a few general laws, ultimately those
of fundamental physics' (111) seems to leave Davies' first question entirely unanswered: 'Why are the laws of nature what they
are?' Ward is also right to observe that the 'universe does seem to
be amazingly ordered, which is at least suggestive of design'
(ibid.), and to find it problematic when one arrives at such a view
of God that no interaction is possible between theological knowledge and scientific knowledge (119). For that regularity of nature
and its implicit rationality is the foundation upon which work

in the natural sciences is possible. At the same time Ward's insistence, in his discussion of Gordon Kaufman's views (123), that this God must be thought of as a personal agent, is hardly so convincing. Something that 'produces', 'draws' and 'sustains' *need* not be personal: hens produce eggs, magnets draw, and food sustains. More is needed to show that this being, this Other, can be meaningfully described as 'personal' or *must* even be thought of as such. *The case, then, for such a principle undergirding the regularities of the natural world is a strong one, but the price of this recognition threatens to be the loss of the concept of a personal God.*

Over against Kaufman himself, on the other hand, it must be said that there is the danger that his analysis of the role or function of 'God' in human thought is somewhat one-sided. It is legitimate to argue that the image or concept of 'God' 'did not serve *merely* to answer such speculative questions as 'Where did the world come from?' or 'Is there an ultimate power behind everything, and if so, what is it?'.[434] It is also legitimate to assert that 'the name "God" was believed to focus human devotion and service on that which would bring human fulfilment (salvation)' (307), as long as one does not thereby imply that this second assertion justifies us in ignoring the need to ask the 'speculative questions' as well. That would be the wrong way to approach this problem. Otherwise there is the danger that (the symbol) 'God' is reduced to a placebo: for it is precisely the role that God fulfils in answering these 'speculative questions' that is one of the main reasons for focussing our devotion and service on God. It may be that we need a 'world-picture' so as to know how to act (344–5), but we also hope that our 'world-picture' bears some relation to the world as it is, for fantasy worlds are dangerous guides to action in the real world. Without that foundation there is the danger that the devotion and service will be found to be rootless and will wither up. To start with the search for the sort of God humanity 'needs' sounds dangerously like making a God, if not in our own image, at least according to our taste. It is, in short, to be doubted whether such a utilitarian or functionalist view of 'God' is really satisfactory, despite Kaufman's efforts to resist any notions of 'God' as 'a product of self-deceit' or as 'wish-fulfilment' (e.g. 316). More than this is needed – some indication that the object of one's devotion and service corresponds to something or someone that really is and is more than just the result of wishful thinking; and Kaufman is, in the last analysis, concerned to stress that God

> is to be understood as the underlying reality (whatever it may be) – the ultimate mystery – pressing itself throughout the universe and thus also in this evolutionary-historical trajectory . . . which has produced humankind. . . . God is a reality genuinely distinct from us and all our imaginings, that which – quite apart from our own doings – has given us our being as humans and continues to nurture and sustain us, that without which we could not exist at all (317).

Once again Kaufman has seemed to side with the 'non-realists', but when it comes to the crunch there is more to his God than simply the projection of our minds.

For Kaufman, too, at first sight the case for a personal God would seem to be a strong one. For he wishes to preserve, as a feature of classical monotheism (along with God's 'absolute-ness'), God's 'humaneness' (314), the conception of God as a thoroughly moral being (315), 'God's connection with our humanness and our struggle for humaneness' (317). Yet at the same time he resists talk of God as a 'cosmic person': to speak of God the creator is rather to give expression to the conviction that some sort of intentionality or purposiveness is at work in our world (329), a way of speaking of the ordering and 'the creativity underlying and at work in all things' (330). But the notion of then living 'in rapport with the movements of life and history that provide the actual context of our human existence' becomes problematic: rapport with the movements of life, if we can rightly identify them, may square with ecological concerns, but certainly the 'movements of . . . history' are to be treated with consider-able suspicion, for some of them must surely be considered bane-ful in the extreme.[435] It has, rightly, been the task of prophetic

religion to judge between the competing currents of history and
to evaluate them.

This critical role *vis-à-vis* the movements of history is perhaps
also to be extended to apply to our stance *vis-à-vis* the movements of nature. That follows, it seems to me, if Theissen is right
to argue that the Christian cultural development involves a
protest against, and a rejection of, the principle of selection
underlying biological evolution. The inanimate creation is, moreover, not only a source of wonder, but also a source of the often
closely related emotion of terror, and it would be a piece of
one-sided romanticism to pretend that all in the natural world is
wonderful or that only humankind has spoilt this wonderful
world. Although wonder and amazement (*Staunen*) play a prominent role in Dorothee Sölle's recent account of mystical thought,
particularly in the contemplation of the world in which we live,[436]
it needs to be asked whether the groanings (*Stöhnen*) of the
distressed and afflicted should not play an equally important part.
And indeed she sees this *Staunen* resulting in either rejoicing or
tears (133): is it not in fact the case that it is the capacity of our
world to evoke wonder which makes that which is not wonderful
in it all the more distressing? If our starting-point is not heredi-
tary or original sin, as she rightly argues, it is not to be identified
with the 'original blessing' either. The insight of Gen. 3.17 is
truer to our life: it stands under a curse. And the recognition of
this reality would, it seems to me, make all the more comprehen-
sible the other strand of Sölle's book, namely the element of
resistance (*Widerstand*) in the true mystical tradition. For she
speaks of a 'hunger' which 'grows with every fresh defeat of God,
with every further destroying of the earth and its inhabitants'
(73). I suggest that these defeats are not only incurred at the hand
of human beings, but seem to be built into the very structure of
the world in which we live, if 'survival of the fittest' is the way in
which it and the life in it develop when left to themselves. So if
the prophets' objections to certain developments in history laid
claim to the guidance of God's spirit and claimed to declare
God's will on the matter, could one not also claim that God's

spirit is on our side in a critique of the way in which natural processes function and in the prophetic attempt to build social structures on very different principles from those on which the natural world has evolved? Is that not involved in the idea of the groaning of the divine spirit at the 'futility' of the world (Rom. 8.22, 26 again)? Paul Fiddes' comment is telling here. Following Moltmann, he remarks that sorrow for suffering is a form of protest against it and that therefore if we are prepared to speak of God suffering with the world, as he is, then that involves a divine protest against the suffering inherent in the natural world.[437] If the word of the prophet is a protest in God's name against the injustices of human society, then it is not so inappropriate after all to see implicit here a divine protest directed against the cruelties of the natural order, including those parts of it that lie outside the control of human beings. The mystery deepens here, however, for how can one and the same principle on the one hand undergird the regularities of the natural world and on the other protest against their workings? And, at the same time, the language of protest surely reintroduces the idea of a personal agent.

We believe, Kaufman maintains, that metaphors like 'lord' or 'creator' refer, but 'to what they refer remains in many respects mystery' (331). Correspondingly, talk of God as 'father' or 'mother' is an acknowledgment of 'the importance of these familial interpersonal relations in the creation of free selves and loving communities, and to affirm that this indispensable condition for our being fully human is itself grounded in the ultimate nature of things' (338). Personal relationship with this God is, he argues, possible and appropriate for us only in our actual interpersonal relationships with other women and men. He appeals here to I John 4.12–13, 20 and argues that:

> our personal relation with the ultimate reality with which we have to do – God – is to be found most fundamentally in and through our *interpersonal* relationships with our fellow humans.[438]

(And even if that goes further than what was actually intended by the writer of I John, I have argued that such 'going beyond' is a legitimate way of using the New Testament traditions.) These interpersonal relationships then receive, for Kaufman, a christological undergirding later in his study (chs 25–26) as he develops a 'wider Christology' that embraces not just the historical individual Jesus, but also the whole 'community of reconciliation that grew up around him and in consequence of his ministry' (401).

When all that is said, the belief and hope 'that the cosmic trajectory which has brought us into being is drawing us onward toward a humane ordering of life' (339) would seem to be a pious – and illusory – belief and hope that is contradicted by too many trajectories taking us in very different directions, if we treat this reality as present in the totality of the 'movements of life and history'. Should we not rather speak of one movement among many, which must be discerned among those many and which protests against and criticizes the others; which calls us to make hard choices and often to swim against the current? Instead, therefore, of saying that in Jesus Christ (perhaps in the 'wider' sense of that 'new interpersonal reality that came into being in connection with the man Jesus, the new spirit expressed in his action and teachings and now incarnated in the communities of his followers') 'the direction in which the human trajectory is going . . . has become visible to human eyes' (384, 388), should one not rather speak of the direction in which humanity *should* go (but may not, because it does not see it as the path which serves its selfish interests)? It may, however, be hard to see how, for instance, what underlies the principles that have led to the evolution of biological life can protest against it by setting itself against the principles that have led to the evolution of forms of biological life, but perhaps it is above all this conflict, this resistance that is rightly to be dubbed a 'mystery' – a self-criticism of the creative spirit! Here is a reality that is indeed immanent in all that is, but does not simply endorse all that is; rather, it transcends it in order to call it to be what it is not yet.

Such a God as described in the preceding account of the

creator God is still hardly a personal one in the sense affirmed by the Judaeo-Christian tradition, except perhaps in the notion of this God's protesting, but is rather an impersonal reality (Kaufman, for instance, talks as much of a 'force' or rather 'forces' or 'creativity' in the world) undergirding the rationality and orderliness of the universe in which we live. It is true that this God is not the sort of irrelevancy which Hans Weder decries in that view of God which postulates a God found at the point where our knowledge of the world has reached its highest level, a God postulated as the origin of a world-system that is otherwise self-contained and intelligible in itself. 'The idea of a something that is above all . . . does not allow us to speak intelligibly of God's incarnation.'[439] At least this God is responsible for the meaningfulness of all existence, from the greatest to the least part of it, but still this is a God who at first sight seems no more personal than a physical law or a mathematical formula or set of formulae. At the same time we need to note that, despite this, the Judaeo-Christian tradition does seem to have found room for this aspect of the existence and nature of the divine; for Jews appropriated the Stoic Logos, the divine reason, the rationality that was God, permeating the universe, and parallel to that found room too for speculation on the wisdom of God. Christian thought in turn appropriated both terms, 'Logos' and 'wisdom', and applied them to Christ. But the fact that they did this does not mean that the two notions, the impersonal and the personal, can coherently be thus put together.

Is there, however, any way in which we can hold such a view of God together with the God whom Jesus called on as 'Abba'? For although, as we have just seen, Jesus did speak of his God distributing all things regularly and indiscriminately to all, he also viewed this God as actively breaking into the world in his own ministry, to heal and to perform what were regarded as miracles, as events that were outside the normal and natural course of things. It is true that some of these healings might now be explained as 'natural', as conforming to certain laws which we have subsequently discovered; others, however, remain more intractable, like the feeding of thousands from a few loaves or the raising of the dead. And even if we dismiss these as legendary, it still remains true that Jesus expected his God to be able to intervene, and regarded this God as possessed of a moral nature and will, able to act on his behalf and on behalf of others.

Now Kaufman speaks, rather disparagingly, of theologians who in the past were 'able to persuade themselves that . . . God can quite properly be thought of both as the Unmoved Mover or Being itself (as required, supposedly, by rational philosophical reflection) and as the incarnate Son deeply involved in the vicissitudes of a very particular history – though we mere humans are unable to see how these notions can be reconciled with each other'.[440] At first sight it would seem as if Kaufman's strictures must force us to abandon the one or the other, the God to whom the orderliness of the universe points or the God to whom Jesus prayed and bore witness. Yet Kaufman himself is keen to speak of 'mystery', in the sense of a 'bafflement of mind rather than obscurity of perception' (60), in connection with talk of God, and the legitimacy of seeing an element of 'mystery' at precisely this point may be strengthened by noting *a comparable 'mystery' at the level of human existence*. It is also to be noted that Kaufman depicts the formation of religious language and symbolism as an imaginative human response to 'the great mysteries of life' (37).

At this point it may perhaps be helpful to point out a possible analogy to the 'mystery' of these two apparently incompatible views of God on the human level, namely that one of the intractable problems of philosophy is the tension between human free-will and determinism. It is true that to resort to such a human analogy might incur the charge of anthropomorphism, of making God in our own image. Yet if according to the biblical tradition human beings are made in the divine image, does that not suggest that it may be legitimate to expect there to be some analogy between human experience and the mystery of God – at least if the analogy seems to throw light on, make sense of, certain aspects of that mystery?[441] And that is, I believe, the case in this instance. It is also an analogy of which Jürgen Werbick makes a similar use: for, he argues,[442] if God is controlled by an inflexible natural order, then that is also true of human freedom; but if, on the other hand, one upholds the reality of human freedom,

> then one leaves open the possibility for people to realize their goals in the world, to make the laws of nature and the natural processes controlled by them serve their purpose, to bring their intentions to fruition in the world. Must one not also grant that God too acts as a free agent in the world and not only under the constraint of the unyielding necessity of the natural laws, and that God puts natural processes at the service of a historical plan of salvation?

Whether one is prepared to speak of God as an agent in this way or not, the analogy is there. For on the one hand we experience the ability to control our own lives to some extent. Even if external forces may control our outward lives (if we are imprisoned under the strictest of regimes, for instance, which controls every minute of our days and regulates every action which we take from brushing our teeth in the morning to putting out the light at night), we at least experience some measure of control over our inner lives, at least while we remain conscious and sane; we can decide what thoughts to think; we can even decide what words to say, as long as we are not gagged or otherwise rendered dumb.

On the other hand, our actions and our thoughts are increasingly understood as conforming to certain physical laws, as the results of certain events or changes in the chemistry and the physical make-up of our body and its central nervous system. What seems to lie within our powers to control in fact comes to be seen as more and more predictable: from the knowledge of the physical state of our bodies and particularly of our nervous systems at one point of time, coupled with a knowledge of the external stimuli or events that will impinge upon us, it seems to become increasingly possible to predict what the state of our nervous system and our resultant behaviour will be at a second, later point of time.

At the same time it must be noted that, by definition, such explanations cannot be made by those whose actions and behaviour are being thus explained. They are the sort of account that must be given by an external observer, and without the knowledge of the one being observed; otherwise the state of the central nervous system that is being observed will be altered to take account of the activity of observing itself or else in response to the awareness that it is being observed. It is true that answers have increasingly been found to the objection that such a mechanical explanation cannot account for facets of our person-hood. Comparisons are often made with artificial intelligence to show that machines could in theory replicate the functions of our minds. Relatively simple computers can, after all, be said to possess self-awareness; they can, for instance, report to us that they are not functioning properly. Yet when all that is said, I find it doubtful whether the computer will ever be made that will, unprompted, reflect on the reason for its own existence. That is to suggest that there are levels and dimensions of human existence that are hard to explain in mechanistic or deterministic terms. The most plausible response to this tension or even contradiction seems to be to regard the two accounts, the personal and the deterministic, as being on two different yet complementary levels. Paul Davies, for instance, compares the hardware and the soft-ware levels of explanation of the functioning of computers.[443] Talk of the 'mind' is a 'holistic' explanation, comparable to the software, as opposed to a reductionist account which may be likened to a description of the functioning of a computer in terms of the electronics of its hardware. There is, he thinks,

> a growing appreciation among scientists of the importance of the structural hierarchy in nature: that holistic concepts like life, organization and mind are indeed meaningful, and that they cannot be explained away as 'nothing but' atoms or quarks or unified forces or whatever (225).

What bearing has this 'structural hierarchy in nature' upon the question of the nature of God?

Applying this observation cosmically, one could argue, Davies claims, 'that there is no conflict . . . in a universe that evolves according to well-defined laws of physics but is nevertheless subject to intelligent control' (208). And if 'control' goes too far in a deterministic direction, then one can all the more easily set over against the laws of physics the 'influence' or 'appeal' of that which is intelligent, but also personal or possibly supra-personal. Such multi-level explanations are frequently necessary in the modern scientific world-view: while, on one level, particles may behave in a random and indeterminate fashion, the very existence of modern science, as well as our application of it and our every-day experience of the world, reckons with the constancy and predictability of the physical world around us. Different and seemingly self-contradictory models may be invoked to explain different facets of the phenomena around us which call for explanation. So may it not be that on one level God, the divine, the ultimate reality, 'functions' with complete regularity and con-stancy, undergirding and sustaining the universe in which we exist, but on another level 'functions' as a personal being?

Now it is true that Gordon Kaufman seeks to relate these levels by speaking of 'free action' 'emerging' (his word for it) out of 'ongoing processes of activity and striving in an organism, and ongoing sociocultural processes'.[444] Yet experientially the end-result is qualitatively different from what one would expect were the chemical and biological level the only one, and the steps by which the human being transcends, as it were, this biological and chemical level are ultimately mysterious in nature. (Though who would want to deny that sense of self-awareness that can surely be called a sort of self-transcendence? I suspect that even the most hardened materialist would find it difficult to deny the reality of this experience, for even the development of a materi-alist theory about human life presupposes precisely this sort of self-transcendence!) One can, at any rate, observe phenomena that show that these different levels are in some sort of relation to one another; one can see that if one takes tablets containing certain chemicals, one's capacity to act, to plan, to reflect upon actions and the world, to transcend the external world, may be impaired or even destroyed. But why and how these capacities are there in the first place, to be impaired or destroyed, how they ever emerged in some living beings but not in others (the majority of species), is far less clear, and we are content to live with the unsolved question of the relationship of these levels. At least we are until, as we have seen, a malfunction at one level forces us to recognize that the levels are interdependent, because the malfunctioning level brings about corresponding malfunctions in another: physical afflictions may affect our mental well-being, and mental distress is often accompanied by, or manifests itself in, physical symptoms. Until this interdependence forces itself upon our consciousness, we are usually content to let these levels of human existence continue side by side, without striving too much for a more exact definition of their precise relationship.

Would it be possible, then, to think of the existence of God as also to be understood on *two different levels*? On one level we can think of God as the one who is responsible for, who underlies the orderly functioning, of our universe; or, putting it the other way round, the orderliness of the cosmos points to such a reality of some sort. On the other can we not, must we not, also conceptualize this God as a personal being, or at least as one that is higher than, but still embracing, personality? Certainly, if the other datum in Christian theology, the life of Jesus of Nazareth, is to play a significant role in our theologizing, then this dimension seems to be present too.

It is important to note that, like the two explanations possible for the human self, these alternatives present themselves only to the *external observer*. We are not normally ourselves conscious of these two ways of describing ourselves, for by nature we think of ourselves holistically. It is 'I' that make certain decisions, think certain thoughts, do certain things, not just some part of me. However, the external observer of the human person may argue that on one level that person functions regularly and predictably according to certain physical laws, while on another that person is a free agent, making real decisions, for the external observer knows from within, as it were, what his or her own experience of being a person is, as well as observing from without the apparent phenomenon of free choice and decision being exercised by others. If what we have done breaks some law or other, then the question of our responsibility for this breach arises, and normally it will be assumed by others that, unless there are good grounds for recognizing diminished responsibility, we are indeed responsible for this action. Likewise may we not, as observers of God, · if one may thus describe theologians (!), see the divine nature, or that reality with which we are confronted, as orderly and regular on one level and at the same time free on another? On the one level God is in the regularities that make our world what it is (and make it possible to study it scientifically at all, for prediction and the experimental testing of hypotheses would be impossible in a completely random world); on another God is as free as any human person is, and we might well feel that it would be a curious God that was not indescribably more free.

We are, it is true, also often in the habit of addressing God in prayer, and it might be thought that this would become impossible were God not personal. That does not, however, necessarily follow, for we are are quite capable of speaking as if we were addressing some inanimate object or some non-person, and this need not be a sign of madness, but simply a vehicle of our communing with ourselves. Not all who seem to be talking to their pets imagine that the latter really understand what they are saying; they may rather be talking more to themselves, with the pet as a captive, non-interrupting audience, so to speak, which can be relied on not to break any confidences. Similarly, prayer might be more a matter of a 'style of thinking'[445] than an address to another person. Yet at the same time it makes a world of difference whether we think of the reality with which we are confronted as an 'it' which we can merely observe, control and dominate, or as a 'you' which stands over against us, which makes demands on us, and to which we must listen and respond. To quote Dorothee Sölle: 'nature is no "it", not just matter to be used, . . . but a living "you"'.[446]

To put it differently, we might say that the explanation of human actions calls for the holistic, higher, level, explanation if it is both to make sense and to accord with our experience. When someone declares 'I am going to do this' and then does it, does it make sense to explain this purely in terms of physical changes in his or her central nervous system? It would be like seeing a car start up and asking why it had done so; if someone then launches into an explanation of the mechanics of the engine, we might well interrupt them somewhat impatiently and say, 'Yes, that's all very well, but I didn't ask how it started, but why; I want to know who switched it on': in other words, we are asking about the personal agent responsible for this. Similarly, to ask why some-one does something that is overtly a deliberate act, e.g. when that person declares that he or she is going to do it, at some point involves mention of the decision of the individual concerned, however much one may also give an account of the factors which, consciously or unconsciously, influenced that person's decision. For if all the factors influencing a decision were unconscious, we might well question the reality of that decision as a decision; if the person was conscious of weighing up, or being influenced by, any factors, then it is hard to deny the appearance of deliberate choice.

Ultimately, too, we may well feel that to answer 'Why?' questions about our world as opposed to 'How?' ones we must speak in terms of something analogous to, even if immeasurably greater than, human decision and will. The answer to the 'Why?' questions which we ask could then be in terms of the purposes of God, purposes that are deliberate and intended: God is not simply carried along by currents of causation, as unconscious, unreflecting and powerless to alter them as a leaf carried down-stream by the course of a stream. Indeed, as we have seen, God may even be thought of as deliberately resisting those currents. Such an answer to 'Why?' questions would be a seeing of things, however faintly, however dimly, from the perspective of God, a seeing of things according to the divine spirit, according to the divine rationality of the whole, a rationality that is on a different level, qualitatively different from the rationality of the world seen as a self-sustaining, self-consistent system that is wholly explicable in terms of itself.[447] But it must be freely acknowledged that the vision and the grasp that we have of this mystery is indeed a very faint one.

(e) What sort of God?

All the same, that does not seem to justify talk of divine omnipotence. What I have said does not mean that we must endorse the omnipotent creator God of traditional Judaeo-Christian beliefs. For the analogy with human existence shows us that we are never totally free or in command of our own lives, although equally we resist the notion that our decisions and actions are wholly determined by forces outside our control. We live and decide within certain constraints, placed in a certain set of circumstances at a certain point of history. We are not free to think whatever thoughts we want either, for we have to use the conceptual apparatus that we have inherited. These may be constraints of which we are more or less conscious: we know that we live in the twentieth century and not in another; we can become aware how much our ways of thought conform to the fashions of our world and day. But the constraints placed upon us by the mechanics and the chemistry of our human nature are for the most part unnoticed; when tired or ill we may perceive the shortcomings of our equipment, but that is not the same as being aware of the regularities and the laws that govern the workings of our persons. We are not conscious of such things as the electrical impulses or the chemical changes that make up the functionings of our bodies and personalities any more than we are aware of the movement of every part of a car engine as we are driving along; that is something we are more likely to notice when something starts malfunctioning, and it is the same with our bodies and our selves. Our physical make-up and our conscious world are usually found on different levels. Similarly, the idea of God as undergirding the complex orderliness of the cosmos looks at God from one perspective, a perspective which the analogy with the experience of the human person suggests is not the level of decision-making and the exercise of power. The human person who exercises power, even if it can never be omnipotence, would not be regarded as powerful in any higher sense than a powerful motor or engine if the exercise of power were to be seen as nothing more than the ineluctable working of the chemical machine which is the human person. That person could not really be said to 'exercise' power, for such a term surely implies some conscious direction of the power, and decisions about how it is to be used and applied, and the like.

Yet it is at this level that the God who is known through Jesus, the God who seems to be reflected in the life of Jesus, seems rather to refuse to exercise power, to be prepared to suffer instead and to be thwarted. This God seems to exert influence only through a communication that can be described by the metaphor of 'speech' or 'word': the response of human beings is thus not forced upon them, but is like the voluntary answer to a word, to a communication addressed to them. It is at this point that I would put a question-mark against Cupitt's argument that a God 'out there' is a threat to human autonomy and spirituality. It is not so much the fact that God is 'out there' (although it may be questioned on other grounds whether this is an adequate or appropriate way to speak of God) that threatens autonomy and spirituality, but the nature of the God who is seen as being 'out there' and the way in which this God interacts with us and is related to us. (And could not an internalized God conceivably be just as, or at least almost as, oppressive?) So long, however, as God is regarded as appealing to us or pleading with us, rather than coercing us or browbeating us, then full scope is left for the development of human spirituality, although it can still be asked whether this is in the last analysis a purely human venture, as Cupitt seems to suppose, or whether it is rather the human response to a (or the) divine spirit moving amongst us.

If one could similarly describe God's relation to other elements of the cosmos, animate and inanimate, in a way which was not in terms of the operation of the all-powerful upon the powerless, then it might be far easier to reconcile the idea of God with the suffering in this world. Could one not then speak, not of a God who imposes this orderliness on the world, an order which entails suffering, but of a God whose orderliness *and suffering* is reflected in the world? And not just in the suffering of human beings, we may add, but in the whole travail of creation, from first to last. That qualification is necessary in that it is not clear how much is meant, for instance, when Moltmann speaks of 'human history' being 'taken up into this "history of God"' in Jesus' death on the cross and then continues: 'There is no suffering which in this history of God is not God's suffering.'[448] And it would be strange if Christ's death could be described as the 'beginning' of God's suffering, for Christ's death was by no means the 'beginning' of human suffering, let alone of the suffering on other creatures,[449] or if God were spoken of as so 'constituting himself' then.[450] Moltmann himself sees the story of God's suffering stretching back into the sufferings of Israel, perhaps even back to the act of creation itself – at least if God's self-humiliation, self-restriction there is to be seen as part of God's suffering.[451] Fiddes detects here a corresponding shift in Moltmann's thought in later works.[452] Again the human analogy may be of some help: an individual within a group may inflict suffering on the other members of the group by maltreating them, but a close-knit group will also suffer if one member suffers, and the distress may even be communicated to the non-human, e.g. to pets or domestic animals. Is such a model so unthinkable for understanding the relationship between God and the cosmos? For a theodicy that confines itself to the malaise in the world that can be attributed to the actions of human beings is simply incomplete, and takes no account of the suffering and pain of the world for which humans cannot be blamed.

That is also true of a theodicy which takes account of the suffering of human beings which human beings have not caused, but not of sufferings which the natural order also inflicts upon higher forms of animal life besides the human. Even in so carefully argued a work as Paul Fiddes' *The Creative Suffering of God*, there is a tendency in discussing natural evil to treat the problem from a human perspective alone:[453] 'natural evil' refers to evil in the natural world that impinges upon humanity and causes humanity (and God, he argues) to suffer. Also problematic is the suffering involved for those other life-forms which are capable of experiencing physical and mental pain like fear and terror. These latter in turn may be, but need not be, occasioned by other creatures; they may also be inflicted by non-animate phenomena like a forest fire. At any rate, it is important to note the concessions in relation to divine omnipotence and sovereignty which are forced upon theologians when they attempt to do justice to the phenomenon of natural evil: one must speak, Fiddes concedes, 'of the fall of nature, like that of man, as being a strange factor to God', and so 'the whole of creation and not just mankind is envisaged as having some kind of free response to its creator' (225). He refers to various attempts to come to terms with this: Arthur Peacocke's appeal to an element of 'randomness',[454] or process theologians' view 'that all actual entities are self-creative and therefore free', 'that all levels of actuality can enjoy some experience of feeling and some freedom' (227). Whatever one thinks of these (and I must confess that I find them stretching my credulity overmuch),[455] Fiddes' own 'open-ended' conclusion is noteworthy:

> Some overall vision of the 'responsiveness' and 'resistance' of creation to the Spirit of God is needed for a doctrine of creative evolution, for a proper theodicy, and certainly for the claim with which we have been most concerned – that God suffers conflict with a non-being which is alien to him.

'Somehow,' he concludes, 'we must think of nature as generating something strange to God if we are to say that he suffers within it' (228–9).

In the case of the orderliness of the cosmos, however, one

should not think of this as the result of rules imposed by God upon the creation so much as a reflection of an orderliness, a rationality and consistency in that reality which we call God, a reality which also bears in itself the reality of suffering; a reality which, though transcending personality, nonetheless reflects the human experience of personality as both orderly and ordered on the one hand, through its very physical constitution, and as purposive, volitional and emotional on the other. Seen from the one perspective this reality is impersonal and ineluctable; seen from the other it strives towards a goal and suffers on account of all that thwarts that goal.[456] Perhaps in that very tension, that bipolarity, it becomes most appropriate to ascribe personality to God or at least to compare God with persons: a creature wholly under the control of rules, programmed, is no person but a robot; experience seems to tell us that it is as we are able to make and choose our own programme that we are most fully and properly persons, or at least it is in our awareness of a choice of pro-grammes and our ability to evaluate them, regardless of whether they are practical possibilities for us or not. Personhood, as we experience it, is found, at any rate in part, in the ability to view various choices and courses from outside as it were, so that if one is compelled to follow a certain course, one at least knows whether one follows it willingly or unwillingly and can evaluate it. One might appropriately describe this as a capability of self-transcendence. (However, it must be noted that this capacity of self-transcendence is a strictly limited one: people's physical natures, for instance, place certain constraints upon them, in that they must die; and the choice of actions that one can conceptu-alize, let alone perform, is not an infinite one either. Self-transcendence on the human level, in other words, in no way implies omnipotence or an infinite capacity.) If it is legitimate to think of God in terms of human personality at all,[457] then this line of argument suggests that what may seem to us to be two alter-native ways of viewing God, the impersonal and the personal, may not be alternatives at all, but complementary aspects. These are, at any rate, it must be stressed, ways of *our* viewing God, our experiencing God, our encounter with the ultimate reality of life; whether our perception of God's nature corresponds to that nature in fact is a further, perhaps ultimately unanswerable, question.

At any rate I find myself in this world confronted by a reality which awakes awe mingled at times with terror, even if I personally have hitherto been spared the experience of the world at its most terrible. It is a world of complex and yet seemingly ordered wonder, and yet it is also a world in which human beings have arisen, who, although themselves very much part of its natural order, betray a capacity to transcend this order, while at the same time utilizing its orderliness, transcending it either by producing yet greater and more complex order or by plunging it into chaos and destruction. I find it hard, on the one hand, to treat this experience of order as simply a construct of human minds, however much it may tax to the full the capacities of that mind to discover the principles governing its orderliness. I find it equally hard, on the other, to view the reality of self-transcendence found in human beings as somehow simply the result of the ongoing, ultimately random and fortuitous workings of a system of things which just happens to be there and to be just like this.[458] If what has emerged is indeed 'higher' than the raw stuff of inanimate matter from which it emerged and human life is the 'highest' form that has yet emerged on this earth, then I want and need to ask whether this 'highest' form does not in some fashion and degree correspond to some dimension of the world, the reality in which we find ourselves; some such conviction came to expression in the Old Testament in the talk of humanity as being made in God's image. Reality as I experience it has, in other words, a sort of recognizable 'shape' which is as it were the framework within which I must try to understand it, but a 'shape' that nonetheless somehow seems to involve a two-faced reality, two apparently irreconcilable aspects, that of the impersonal and inflexible order and that of the existence of creative, self-transcending persons. Nevertheless, I am at the same time aware that, as in a microcosm, these two aspects are part of my own constitution and existence, which, despite all the tensions that arise between 'flesh' and 'spirit', I experience as a unity. I am not, however, simply projecting my own nature into a macrocosmic setting, for I find it undeniable that that is how the larger world, the greater reality actually is, and therefore my attempts to find meaning, to invoke the word 'God' to explain this world, are attempts to come to terms with a reality independent of myself which seems to combine these two at first sight irreconcilable elements; I would not readily grant that either of them is illusory, either in myself or in the macrocosm.

Don Cupitt clearly recognizes these two seemingly irreconcilable dimensions in a brief passage in his *Taking Leave of God* (105–7). There is what he calls 'the little interventionist God' whose roots lie in the 'small tribal deity', and there is 'the lawlike cosmic God'. The former is needed to give the latter personal qualities 'and to stop him from fading into emptiness and vacuity'. The latter, however, is also 'needed to give breadth and universality to the little interventionist God and stop *him* declining into a fantasy guardian-spirit'. Both 'need each other – and yet they do not go well together'. Cupitt's own solution is to say that 'God's lawlike aspect is a principle, the religious requirement, and God's personal aspect is a mythical representation . . . of the requirement's effect and impact upon us'; they represent respectively 'the demand and the promise of the spiritual life'. But is that enough? What 'religious requirement', for instance, does the lawlike cosmic God entail except perhaps wonder (and, again, sometimes horror and terror) at the orderliness of nature? Our response, mixed as it may be, is directed at the nature that surrounds us, but how far is that of the slightest ethical relevance? Does it not teach us to be as cruel and self-assertive as nature teaches us to be, if we wish to succeed, to rise as high as we can? What sort of 'spirituality' is that? On this basis can it be more than the demand of the most radical of the ancient Cynics that one should live according to nature (as opposed to the more metaphysically conceived life according to nature of the Stoics)? Treating 'God' as simply a symbol 'of what it is that the believer finds himself up against in the religious life' (99) does not, for me, explain the elements of protest and critique (even of forms of religious life) that I believe to be necessary, necessary also for the existence of those spiritual values whose worth Cupitt himself recognizes (e.g. 82).

It may be helpful to note at this stage two further examples of such a dichotomy, such a bipolarity, such a paradoxicality. A glance at the literature on that elusive and variegated topic, mysticism, will show that mysticism or the mystical search for God may be portrayed either as a journey out of oneself, as ecstasy, or as a journey into the depths within oneself. The former is perhaps more typical of older forms of mysticism, the latter of newer (although it has older, oriental precedents). But it is at first sight surprising that these two options should exist. The fact that they do can be regarded as a witness to the human sense that these two mysteries, of the cosmos and of the human person, are analogous, not alternatives but complementary, and that the one offers clues to the other. (It may be granted that the clues to the cosmic are more often found in the personal rather than *vice versa*; that is hardly surprising, for the human person lies nearer to hand, is more familiar.) And the validity of the appeal to the approaches of mysticism lies in the recognition that in talking of God we are confronted with mystery, and that the divine is not to be analysed and dissected as upon some philosophical marble slab; it cannot be so treated and remain the divine.

Equally, it is the experience both of mystics and indeed of religion as a world-wide phenomenon that it embraces both the highly personal approach to God and approaches which view the ultimate reality in non-personal ways. 'God', the divine, the real, reality, seems to combine these two aspects or dimensions. To quote John Hick:

One whose spiritual life is formed by Christian prayer and sacrament is led to experience the Real as the divine Thou, whereas one who practises advaitic yoga, or Buddhist zazen, is thereby brought to experience the Real as the infinite being-consciousness-bliss of Brahman, or as the limitless emptiness of *sunyata*, which is at the same time the fullness of immediate reality as 'wondrous being'.[459]

It is Hick's argument that these approaches are complementary, are both valid. But that only holds good when both in fact correspond to something in the nature of what he terms 'the Real', when somehow this ultimate reality is indeed like this, embraces these two aspects in itself, however paradoxical that may seem to our analytical eyes.

When I look at myself, these two contrasting elements, of ordered matter and self-transcending reflection and self-awareness, stand in uneasy tension, so that I find it easier to suppose that this aspect, too, corresponds to something on the macrocosmic level, that the 'groaning' of the divine spirit with our spirits to which Paul refers, as we have seen, expresses an appropriate relationship between these two dimensions of reality, whatever philosophical difficulties or bafflement this suggestion may occasion. Just as I, for instance, 'groan' at signs of aging which are difficult to transcend, so too it makes sense to think of the divine spirit being more than a little disgruntled at the workings of the natural order and in no way regarding it as the best of all possible worlds. In other words, the relation between these two dimensions is not necessarily one of complacent acceptance and endorsement of the one by the other. Rather, they can and should be seen as standing in tension with one another. The transcendence or self-transcendence of the one entails a critique and judgment of the other.

'God' may indeed remain very mysterious in all this, but I would want to argue that this is both healthy and inevitable. I must indeed confess to a deep-seated unease at the way in which so many theologians can embark upon the most complex of language-games on the basis either of the philosophical notion of 'God' as the highest being or on that of the accumulated wisdom of Christian tradition. Is it not the case that an account which speaks with too great a confidence and with too great a precision and abundance of detail about the nature of God is *ipso facto* suspect? Should not common sense and a sense of proportion tell us that such declarations are inappropriate and display a hybris that ill befits the theologian, most of all the Christian theologian? For too often these language-games that are still played today awake in me the feeling that this is a fantasy, a make-believe, for we do not really know so much about God and should not pretend that we do. That follows if God, if reality, really is as mysterious as at least some theologians acknowledge it to be, and I can only bear witness that, if my wrestlings with faith and understanding are anything to go by, both God and reality are indeed most mysterious. To play such games may be in order if it increases our understanding of reality as it is, but this criterion entails that we must come down to earth again, as it were, and ask anew what we really know and how this all measures up to reality.

Taking Jesus of Nazareth as a starting-point for reflection about God also justifies speaking of God as 'suffering', as I have argued above. How is one then to reconcile 'suffering' with 'omnipotent' as usually understood? (Or with talk of God as 'supremely happy', for that matter?)[460] It may be going too far to speak of God as actually 'crucified', as Moltmann does, following Luther,[461] but surely not when one speaks of God as suffering with Jesus, and suffering, too, with the rest of creation? What is difficult here is to hold together the notion of a suffering God with talk of God's omnipotence or even of God's power, except in the sense of the moral power exercised by suffering righteousness and love. For omnipotence should mean that God could have created such a world that neither God's creatures nor their creator need suffer, a world like that which is promised as the next world in the apocalyptic hope, and the message of the resurrected Jesus seems to be that God has indeed the power to rescue humanity from suffering. That inevitably raises the question why God has not done so instead of simply suffering with them.

Now the omnipotent God seems to be the God that conforms to philosophers' notions of what God should be like in order to be God. This God fits their schemes and their definitions. The view that I have been advocating here as an alternative is not simply the God of biblical tradition, for the simple reason that the biblical tradition points in more than one direction here, and what I am proposing here is clearly at variance with a major part of this tradition. A suffering God who is not omnipotent, who must suffer with creation because no easy answer, no quick solution to its woes lies to hand, seems at first sight to be a nonsense to the philosophers and a betrayal of the traditional God to the devotees of the Bible. One is reminded of the way in which the message of the crucified Christ is folly to the Greeks and a stumbling-block to the Jews (I Cor. 1.22–23). But such a view of God takes very seriously certain central thrusts of the biblical message, and at the same time avoids many of the pitfalls that beset other philosophical attempts to define the relation of God to a world which is not all that we would wish it to be, not all that we think it should be if a loving and at the same time all-powerful God were indeed responsible for it.

A critic might well retort that all this talk of tensions, of paradox, of mystery, is just a tacit admission that all talk of 'God' is simply, in the last analysis, incoherent nonsense. And it is scarcely a stringent argument that I have advanced or can advance; more a matter of a groping after understanding. Moreover, John Hick, in his reply to an atheistic treatment of the question of life after death, grants that 'the universe is religiously ambiguous in the sense that it is capable of being thought and experienced in both religious and naturalistic ways'.[462] Yet he does not say that it is *equally* capable of being thought and experienced in both these ways, and that is perhaps significant: both ways may be a matter of faith, but in differing degrees and ways. For I return, on the one hand, to my unease, even incredulity, at the idea that the universe just happens to be the way it is, happens to have developed as it is, with the forms of life that it contains. We find ourselves, in short, in a cosmos which seems to manifest purpose and design, even if it does not move to any goal by the shortest and most effective route. What

Kaufman calls 'serendipitous' seems better accounted for by postulating an organizing principle which is not omnipotent, but which must struggle to achieve its goals despite the resistance of the workings of nature. Whether one ascribes this purposiveness to 'God' depends more than anything else upon our definition of 'God'. I return also, on the other hand, to the observation of how many of these of these seemingly incoherent paradoxes and elements of mystery are reproduced, microcosmically, in human nature and in our experience of being human. Despite that, how many of us can help proceeding as if we and other human beings were free responsible agents, at least within a limited sphere which, it may be granted, is more limited for some than for others?[463] Hick's insistence that the religious interpretation is 'entirely reasonable and rational' is therefore defensible as long as the word 'rational' is not taken to imply that one can fully explain or grasp the nature of the religious reality any more than one's own nature or that of the reality of the world within which we live.

Once we recognize the uncertainty that surrounds the resurrection of Jesus and thus our own future, the way in which one thinks of God is, depending on one's viewpoint, robbed of the security of a certain framework of thought or else freed from the encumbrance of a world-view and of a view of God's relation to that world which to my mind has become increasingly difficult to sustain as our understanding of our world has grown and expanded. One pays for that freedom, of course, with a certain rootlessness, a wonder and at the same time bewilderment at the mind-blowing and elusive nature of the idea of God, a struggling with the sheer difficulties of conceptualization. The cosy familiarity of the omnipotent God, who has at least once revealed that omnipotence unmistakably, in the raising of Jesus from the dead, has gone, as has the easy anthropomorphism of the acting and intervening God. One now has to struggle with the conflict, the seeming inconsistency between a God big enough to be related and relevant to an immense cosmos, and a God who is yet near enough and intimate enough to suffer with us and share our ultimate helplessness: a God, that is, who is fullness itself and yet is empty, source of all and at the same time at the mercy of all. If the paradoxical is one of the hallmarks of mystical language,[464] then this way of viewing and speaking of God richly deserves the epithet 'mystical'. That which confronts us in our world and, I have argued, in our very selves, is a thoroughly paradoxical mystery. And yet that mysterious God draws nearer to us as a suffering God than when regarded as the sovereign and almighty 'Mr Fix-it' who has demonstrated his irresistible power once and for all by raising Jesus. Moreover, the reality of that suffering is not to be undermined by the thought that it is not really necessary, that God could have dispensed with all that agony and humiliation.

10

A Vulnerable Faith

I spoke earlier of vulnerability, the vulnerability of God and the vulnerability of a faith that does not find the protection of firm proofs of its validity in the resurrection stories, and I argued that such a form of faith was appropriate if God was like that. But it could be suggested that, by pleading agnosticism about what what happened on Easter Day and by seeking to detach the validity of Christ's call to follow him from any decisions about what did or did not happen on that day, I have in fact made the Christian faith invulnerable, in the sense of being incapable of falsification or refutation. For an insubstantial spectre cannot be wounded if it has nothing to it that can be wounded. Similarly a faith without substance or content, as some would regard the form and the shape of Christian faith that I am proposing, has nothing about it or in it to be refuted. Yet it is hardly appropriate to describe the sort of Christian faith that I have sketched out as invulnerable. On the contrary, it is all too vulnerable, for it is deprived of all those props and undergirdings that are so frequently given to Christian faith by affirming the resurrection of Jesus as an objective historical event. It is, and remains, faith in the God of Jesus, that God whom Jesus served even to the point of an agonizing and humiliating death. However, as Hoffmann reminds us,[465] neither with the earthly nor the risen Jesus can we ever prove historically that 'God was with him'. The Jesus whose wonders and healing could even be reinterpreted by his critics as the product of collusion with Beelzebul (Mark 3.22 parr.) was not one who placed himself above and beyond the uncertainties of human faith and human ability to perceive or not to perceive. It is such 'confirmation' of the truth of the Christian faith, on the other hand, which can all too easily lead to a triumphalist 'theology of glory' against which the charge of 'invulnerability' can be rather more easily be made to stick; to see that, one only has to look at some of the more triumphant hymns which Christians sing, particularly at Easter-time. How often are the theologies enshrined in such hymns really open to the possibility of being fatally wounded by falsification or refutation? For, if the event of the resurrection is placed beyond historical questioning by being classified as not 'historical', or if the case is tacitly considered to remain proven until something turns up that would count as falsification (discovering in Palestine a skeleton conveniently labelled 'Jesus of Nazareth, king of the Jews'?), then this cannot really be considered anything but the most hypothetical vulnerability.

By contrast, the version of Christian faith that I have described is vulnerable at all points, for all that it can appeal to is the intrinsic worth of the life Jesus lived and the message that he delivered, and the inherent value of the quality of the life which is lived in this world by the community which follows him. That appeal or warrant is very vulnerable indeed, particularly since its very challenge of self-denying love for God and for one's fellows gives its hearers a vested interest in a self-justifying and self-protecting repudiation of its claims.

Yet I can see no other way for Christians to go once they see how mysteriously inscrutable this founding event of the Christian church really was, once they see that intellectually a form of agnosticism, of suspension of judgment, is the only adequate response to the nature of the evidence. And those of Jesus' followers, I suspect, whose lives most closely mirror the way of life of Christ would be least affected by this shift in perspective, for they have found the meaning and the worth of their living in a costly service of God and of others here in this suffering world, and do not look for triumphalist manifestations of divine power either in this world or in another.[466]

The real difficulty that I can see in this position is rather a pastoral one: how are Christians of this persuasion to hold out comfort and help and hope to those who do not share their views, either because they hold more traditional religious views or because they have no faith or hope at all? What are we to say to those who are caught in abject misery or pain, and cannot find the comfort of Christ in the midst of their suffering? Or to those overwhelmed by a bereavement? If they look to the Christian faith expecting it to offer them at least the comfort of another life in another world where God 'will wipe away every tear from their eyes, and death shall be no more, neither shall there be mourning nor crying nor pain any more, for the former things have passed away' (Rev. 21.4, RSV), what will this form of faith have to say to them? 'Discover Christ in the midst of your sufferings and fears and find your comfort and your joy there'? That may very well not be what people in such a position either want to or are ready to hear.

It is, however, important to identify here precisely where this pastoral problem arises and what its nature is. For, put more concretely, this is a pastoral problem that arises in two contexts, which in this respect differ significantly and should not be confused with one another: on the one hand it is a problem in speaking to those who themselves face death, and on the other it is a problem in supporting those bereaved. With those facing death one must ask what it is that troubles them, and one could name at least three possible scenarios: if it is their present pain or distress, then often death will be regarded as a welcome release from that;[467] if it is a feeling of guilt and regret for a (at least supposedly) misspent life, then what would the certainty of an after-life do to help in that situation? Might it not even exacerbate the situation, particularly if the person believed in eternal torment and were unable to accept forgiveness? For what such a person needs to hear is God's word of forgiveness and reconciliation *now*. Or is it, thirdly, the fear of the unknown that terrifies that person? Now undoubtedly it might then help that person to be able to say that one knows what awaits us beyond the grave, but that is precisely what the evidence of the New Testament, rightly and critically read, does not provide; as we saw, it differs from other literature of the time in refraining from giving it. At this point, Leslie Houlden notes,[468] Jesus' resurrection is being used for a purpose very different from 'the concerns of the original proclamation of the resurrection'. What the Gospels do offer is the example of Jesus himself, going with all his doubts and uncertainties into the teeth of a terrible death, ready to trust God to that point where trust seems to have broken down in a cry of dereliction which is nevertheless directed, however accusingly, to his God (Mark 15.34 par.). Can we too face death with the confidence that God is there, even to be reproached?

The needs of the bereaved are rather different: they have lost someone and feel that loss; perhaps also feel regret and guilt as they look back at their relations with, and treatment of, the one who is now dead. One might be tempted here to offer them the prospect of a reunion with the departed one, even the chance to make amends for what was not right in their life, in an after-life. One might offer them that, but with a good conscience? For we have seen how even in the theology of a Barth the notion of personal, individual survival after death becomes problematic. Indeed D. Z. Phillips refers to Mark 12.25 parr., 'For when they rise from the dead they neither marry nor are given in marriage, but are as the angels in heaven', and continues:

> Now tied up with marital relationships is a complex of other relationships: child–parent relationships, relationships between brothers and sisters, relationships between lovers, and so on. . . . how can one speak of taking up and continuing these relationships after death? What is to be made of the hope of meeting fathers, mothers, brothers, sisters, friends, lovers, after death?[469]

To come to terms with this personal loss is one thing, and grateful remembering of what that departed person meant in his or her life can offer a healing reappraisal and reorientation. If that memory is clouded with guilt or regret or shame, then the pastoral problem is acuter. However, even if it were possible to point to an after-life as a panacea, I doubt whether that would be appropriate or healthy. The question is rather how that guilt- or shame-ridden bereaved person is going to live now, in this world, together with those who also live on in this world.

On the other hand – and that is the gain in this way of looking at things and above all of looking at God – one no longer needs to explain to the suffering how God could have let it happen like that, when it was fully within God's power to order it otherwise. This God does not deserve to be cursed, is not to be resented or blasphemed as heartless, if even the one who was as near to him as an only son to his father had to be allowed to suffer an agonizing and unjust death. Or one can identify oneself all too well with the heartrending doubts of that faithful, but suffering righteous one who demanded to know whether his God had after all forsaken him.

Anyway, can or should one trim the truth as one perceives it to meet 'consumer demand' (or one's own personal emotional needs)? That is a constant temptation for Christian theologians, particularly if their livelihood depends on satisfied customers. One of the saddest, and most frustrating, experiences that I have had as a theological teacher is of an immensely gifted and intelligent student who saw very clearly the challenges presented by biblical criticism; yet he also saw the effect which sharing the insights of biblical criticism would be likely to have upon the faith of his future parishioners, and he chose to set his face against those insights and the use of them, and instead to use the Bible as his congregation were accustomed to use it and expected him to use it. In this I am reminded of the scene in Brecht's *The Life of Galileo* in which a little monk who has studied mathematics, physics and astronomy confesses to Galileo that he wishes to turn his back on the insights of these sciences because he realizes how they will subvert the faith of the simple peasants of the Campagna amongst whom he grew up:

I see their eyes grow frightened! I see them dropping their spoons on the hearth-stone, I see how they feel cheated and betrayed. So there is no eye resting upon us, they say. We must look after ourselves, untaught, old and worn out as we are?

The little monk then praises as compassionate the decree of the Holy Congregation banning the teachings of Copernicus; he himself will keep silent for the sake of 'the peace of mind of our unfortunate people'.[470] So to ignore the insights that I believe scientific study has brought us is something that I could not bring myself to do, for I would feel that such a course would not only destroy my integrity but, perhaps more importantly, would fail to treat my fellow human beings with the respect that they deserve. For I would in effect be saying: 'I have wrestled with these insights and have come to terms with them and can live with them and their consequences, but you are not ready for, or capable of, doing that, now or at any time in the future.' So too with the matter of Jesus' resurrection and life after death: if an agnostic 'Not proven' is the most that we can say about either of these, then I think it better to acknowledge that clearly and unambiguously, and then to work out one's Christian theology and practice accordingly.

That is going to be most problematic at the pastoral level, since by the nature of things one may find oneself touching on these matters with people who are at a desperately low ebb and at their most vulnerable; then, of all times, is not the moment to start engaging them in a restructuring of the Christian faith. In honesty, at moments like these I myself can do little more – but also no less – than to throw myself, here and now, upon the love and mercy of a God who, if we can learn anything about the divine nature from the fate of Jesus, above all suffers with us, and whose love and mercy is all the more credible precisely because that God suffers with us, and is not one who sits back and watches us suffer, when it would be fully in the power of the divine to intervene. I can, therefore, only encourage those who suffer to do likewise. Whatever God can or will do, we believe that it will be in love, for the life and death of Jesus shows us no other God. Such a trust in another, however, is always extremely vulnerable on the human level.

Yet vulnerability is, I believe, no counter-argument, above all for a theology that is Christian and indeed takes as its starting-point the suffering Christ and finds there the clue to the nature of God. There we find a vulnerability that is actually wounded, even to the point of death; there we find perplexity to the point of despair and unbelief and a cry of desolation. Would it not be presumptuous to expect or wish a revelation of God with cast-iron guarantees and the possibility of a correspondingly unshakeable faith?

Bibliography of Works Cited

(Abbreviated titles, where used, are shown in square brackets. Otherwise I have tried to follow the conventions for abbreviations of the Society of Biblical Literature as published in its *Handbook* and in *Journal of Biblical Literature* 117, 1998, 555–79.)

1. Sources

K. Berger and C. Colpe (eds), *Religionsgeschichtliches Textbuch zum Neuen Testament*, NTD Textreihe 1, Göttingen: Vandenhoeck & Ruprecht 1987 [*Textbuch*]

J. H. Charlesworth (ed.), *The Old Testament Pseudepigrapha* (2 vols), London: Darton, Longman and Todd 1983, 1985 [*OTP*]

Septuaginta, ed. A. Rahlfs, Stuttgart: Württembergische Bibelanstalt, ⁷1962

H. F. D. Sparks (ed.), *The Apocryphal Old Testament*, Oxford: Clarendon Press 1984 [*Apoc. OT*]

(a) Christian authors

The Apostolic Fathers, ed. K. Lake, LCL, London: Heinemann and New York: Macmillan 1912–13

Augustine, *De civitate Dei*, CSEL 40, Prague and Vienna: Tempsky and Leipzig: Freytag 1898–1900

—, *Das Enchiridion ad Laurentium sive de fide, spe et caritate*, PL 40, Paris: Migne 1865

Die Bekenntnisschriften der evangelisch-lutherischen Kirche, Göttingen: Vandenhoeck & Ruprecht ⁶1967 [*Bekenntnisschriften*]

Didascalia et Constitutiones Apostolorum, ed. F. X. Funk (2 vols), Paderborn: Schoeningh 1905

Epiphanius, *Panarion*, ed. K. Holl, GCS 25, 31, 37, Leipzig: Hinrichs 1915–33; Vol. 37, ed. J. Dummer, Berlin: Akademie Verlag ²1980

Eusebius, *Historia ecclesiastica*, ed. J. E. L. Oulton and H. J. Lawlor, LCL, London: Heinemann and New York: Macmillan 1927–8

W. Foerster and R. McL. Wilson (eds), *Gnosis: A Selection of Gnostic Texts* 1: *Patristic Evidence*, Oxford: Clarendon Press 1972

Irenæus, *Adversus Hæreses*, ed. W. W. Harvey, Cambridge: Cambridge University Press 1857

Jerome, *Epistulæ*, ed. I. Hilberg, CSEL 54–6, Vienna: Tempsky and Leipzig: Freytag 1910–96

—, *Lettres*, ed. J. Labourt (8 vols), Paris: Belles Lettres 1949–63

E. J. Goodspeed, *Die ältesten Apologeten*, Göttingen: Vandenhoeck & Ruprecht 1914

Origen, *Contra Celsum*, ed. P. Koetschau, GCS 2–3, Leipzig: Hinrichs 1899

J. M. Robinson (ed.), *The Nag Hammadi Library*, Leiden: Brill 1977, ³1988

A. de Santos, *Los evangelios apocrifos*, Biblioteca de autores Christianos 148, Madrid: La Editorial Catolica ²1963

W. Schneemelcher and R. McL. Wilson (eds), *New Testament Apocrypha* (2 vols), Cambridge: James Clarke and Louisville: Westminster John Knox Press 1991, 1992, ET of W. Scheemelcher, *Neutestament-liche Apokryphen in deutscher Übersetzung* (2 vols), Tübingen: Mohr-Siebeck ⁶1989, ⁵1990 [Schneemelcher]

Tertullian, *Opera*, CChr Ser. lat., Turnhout: Brepols 1954

(b) Graeco-Roman authors

A. J. Malherbe, *The Cynic Epistles*, SBLSBS 12, Missoula: Scholars Press 1977

Chariton, *Callirhoe*, ed. G. P. Goold, LCL, Cambridge, MA and London: Harvard University Press 1995

Demetrius, *On Style*, ed. D. C. Innes and W. R. Roberts, LCL, Cambridge, MA and London: Harvard University Press 1995

Diodorus Siculus, *Bibliotheca*, ed. C. H. Oldfather *et al.*, LCL, London: Heinemann and New York/Cambridge MA: Harvard University Press 1933–67

Josephus, *Opera*, ed. H. St. J. Thackeray, R. Marcus *et al.*, LCL, London: Heinemann and New York/Cambridge MA: Harvard University Press 1926–65

Papyri Græcæ magicæ, ed. K. Preisendanz (2 vols), Leipzig 1928–31, Stuttgart: Teubner ²1974 [*PGM*]

Philo Alexandrinus, *Opera*, ed. F. H. Colson, G. H. Whitaker and R. Marcus, LCL, London: Heinemann and New York/Cambridge MA: Harvard University Press 1929–62

Pliny, *Epistulæ*, ed. R. A. B. Mynors, Scriptorum classicorum bibliotheca Oxoniensis, Oxford: Clarendon Press 1963

Plutarch, *Vitæ parallelæ*, ed. B. Perrin, LCL, London: Heinemann and New York/Cambridge MA: Harvard University Press 1914–26

Sources for the Study of Greek Religion, ed. D. G. Rice and J. E. Stambaugh, SBLSBS 14, Scholars Press 1979 [*Sources*]

Suetonius, *De vita Cæsarum*, ed. J. C. Rolfe, LCL, London: Heinemann and Cambridge, MA: Harvard University Press ²1951

2. Secondary literature (excluding most dictionary articles):

K. Aland, 'Bemerkungen zum Schluss des Markusevangeliums', in E. E. Ellis and M. Wilcox (eds), *Neotestamentica et Semitica: Studies in Honour of Matthew Black*, Edinburgh: T. & T. Clark 1969, 157–80 ['Bemerkungen']

—, 'Der Schluss des Markusevangeliums', in M. Sabbe (ed.), *L'Évangile selon Marc: Tradition et rédaction*, BETL 34, Gembloux: Duculot and Leuven: Leuven University Press 1971, 435–70 ['Schluss']

M. Albertz, 'Zur Formengeschichte der Auferstehungsberichte', *ZNW* 21, 1922, 259–69 = Hoffmann, *Überlieferung*, 259–70 ['Formengeschichte']

G. Altner, 'Schöpfung als Prozess – Gott im Geschehen der Welt', in W. H. Ritter *et al.*, *Der Allmächtige: Annäherung an ein umstrittenes Gottesprädikat*, Göttingen: Vandenhoeck & Ruprecht 1997, 68–96 ['Schöpfung']

P. Avis, 'The Resurrection of Jesus: Asking the Right Questions', in id. (ed.), *The Resurrection of Jesus Christ*, London: Darton, Longman and Todd 1993, 1–22 ['Resurrection']

A. J. Ayer, *The Concept of a Person and Other Essays*, London: Macmillan 1963 [*Concept*]

—, *Language, Truth and Logic*, London: Gollancz ²1946 [*Language*]

P. Badham, 'God, the Soul and the Future Life', in Davis, *Death*, 36–52 ['God']

—, 'The Meaning of the Resurrection of Jesus', in Avis, *Resurrection*, 23–38 ['Meaning']

I. G. Barbour, *Issues in Science and Religion*, London: SCM Press 1966 [*Issues*]

—, *Religion in an Age of Science*, London: SCM Press 1990 [*Religion*]

M. Barker, *The Risen Lord: The Jesus of History as the Christ of Faith*, SJT Current Issues in Theology, Edinburgh: T. & T. Clark 1996

K. Barth, *Church Dogmatics* (13 vols, Edinburgh T. & T. Clark 1936–69), ET of *Die kirchliche Dogmatik* (13 vols, Zürich: TVZ 1932–65) [*CD*]

—, *Dogmatics in Outline*, London: SCM Press 1949, ET of *Dogmatik im Grundriss*, Zürich: EVZ 1947 [*Dogmatics*]

—, *The Faith of the Church: A Commentary on the Apostles' Creed*, London: Collins 1960; ET of *La Confession de Foi de l'Église* [*Faith*]

—, *The Epistle to the Romans*, London: Oxford University Press 1933, ET of *Der Römerbrief*, Zürich: Evangelischer Verlag 1919, [15]1989; ET is of the sixth edition

C. K. Barrett, *Jesus and the Gospel Tradition*, London: SPCK 1967 [*Jesus*]

S. Barton and G. N. Stanton (eds), *Resurrection: Essays in Honour of Leslie Houlden*, London: SPCK 1994

H. W. Bartsch, 'Inhalt und Funktion des urchristlichen Osterglaubens', *ANRW* II 25,1, 1982, 794–843 ['Inhalt']

F. C. Baur, *Christenthum und die christliche Kirche der drei ersten Jahrhunderte*, Tübingen: Fues 1860, reprinted Stuttgart and Bad Cannstatt: Frommann 1966 [*Christenthum*]

J. Becker, *Auferstehung der Toten im Urchristentum*, SBS 82, Stuttgart: Katholisches Bibelwerk 1976 [*Auferstehung*]

—, 'Das Gottesbild Jesu und die älteste Auslegung von Ostern', in G. Strecker (ed.), *Jesus Christus in Historie und Theologie: Neutestamentliche Festschrift für Hans Conzelmann zum 60. Geburtstag*, Tübingen: Mohr-Siebeck 1975, 105–26 = Hoffmann, *Überlieferung*, 203–27 ['Gottesbild']

—, *Jesus von Nazaret*, Berlin and New York: de Gruyter 1996 [*Jesus*]

—, *Das Evangelium nach Johannes*, ÖTK 4/1–2, Gütersloh: Gerd Mohn and Würzburg: Echter Verlag 1979, [3]1991 [*JohEv*]

P. Benoit, 'Marie-Madeleine et les disciples au tombeau selon Jean 20[1–18]', in: W. Eltester (ed.), *Judentum, Urchristentum, Kirche. FS J. Jeremias*, BZNW 26, Berlin: Töpelmann 1964, 141–52 ['Marie-Madeleine']

K. Berger, *Die Auferstehung des Propheten und die Erhöhung des Menschensohnes: Traditionsgeschichtliche Untersuchungen zur Deutung des Geschickes Jesu in frühchristlichen Texten*, SUNT 13, Göttingen: Vandenhoeck & Ruprecht 1976 [*Auferstehung*]

H. D. Betz, 'Zum Problem der Auferstehung Jesu im Lichte der griechischen magischen Papyri', in id., *Hellenismus und Urchristentum: Gesammelte Aufsätze* 1, Tübingen: Mohr-Siebeck 1990, 230–61 ['Problem']

E. Bickermann, 'Das leere Grab', *ZNW* 23, 1924, 281–92 = Hoffmann, *Überlieferung*, 271–84 ['Grab']

J. Blinzler, 'Die Grablegung Jesu in historischer Sicht', in Dhanis, *Resurrexit*, 56–107 ['Grablegung']

E. L. Bode, *The First Easter Morning: The Gospel Accounts of the Women's Visit to the Tomb of Jesus*, AnBib 45, Rome: Biblical Institute 1970 [*Morning*]

D. Bonhoeffer, *Letters and Papers from Prison*, London: SCM Press ²1971, ET of *Widerstand und Ergebung – Briefe und Aufzeichnungen aus der Haft*, Munich: Christian Kaiser Verlag 1959 [*LPP*]

M. J. Borg, *Jesus: A New Vision: Spirit, Culture, and the Life of Discipleship*, San Francisco: Harper 1987 [*Jesus* 1987]

—, *Jesus in Contemporary Scholarship*, Valley Forge: TPI 1994 [*Jesus* 1994]

G. Bornkamm, *Jesus of Nazareth*, London: Hodder & Stoughton 1960, ET of *Jesus von Nazareth*, UB 19, Stuttgart: Kohlhammer 1956, ¹⁵1995 [*Jesus*]

W. Bousset, *Kyrios Christos: Geschichte des Christusglaubens von den Anfängen des Christentums bis Irenaeus*, Göttingen: Vandenhoeck & Ruprecht ⁵1965

H. Braun, 'Das "Stirb und werde" in der Antike und im Neuen Testament', in id. *Gesammelte Studien zum Neuen Testament und seine Umwelt*, Tübingen: Mohr-Siebeck ²1967, 136–58 = E. Wolff and W. Matthias (eds), *Libertas Christiana. FS Delekat*, BEvT 26, Munich: Christian Kaiser Verlag 1957, 9–29 ['"Stirb"']

B. Brecht, *The Life of Galileo*, London: Methuen 1960, ET of *Leben des Galilei*, Berlin: Suhrkamp 1955

I. Broer, 'Der Glaube an die Auferstehung Jesu und das geschichtliche Verständnis des Glaubens in der Neuzeit', in Verweyen, *Osterglaube*, 47–64 ['Glaube']

—, '"Seid stets bereit, jedem Rede und Antwort zu stehen, der nach der Hoffnung fragt, die euch erfüllt" (1 Petr 3,15): Das leere Grab und die Erscheinungen Jesu im Lichte der historischen Kritik', in id. and Werbick, *'Herr'*, 29–62 ['"Seid stets bereit"']

I. Broer, *Die Urgemeinde und das Grab Jesu: Eine Analyse der Grablegungsgeschichte im Neuen Testament*, SANT 31, Munich: Kösel Verlag 1972 [*Urgemeinde*]

I. Broer, and J. Werbick (eds), *'Der Herr ist wahrhaft auferstanden' (Lk 24,34): Biblische und systematische Beiträge zur Entstehung des Osterglaubens*, SBS 134, Stuttgart: Katholisches Bibelwerk 1988 [*'Herr'*]

R. E. Brown, *The Death of the Messiah* (2 vols), New York and London: Doubleday 1994 [*Death*]

S. Brown, 'Reader Response: Demythologizing the Text', *NTS* 34, 1988, 232–7

F. F. Bruce, 'The Epistles of Paul', in H. H. Rowley and M. Black (eds), *Peake's Commentary on the Bible*, London: Nelson 1962, 927–39 ['Epistles']

R. Bultmann, 'Karl Barth, 'The Eschatology of the Gospel of John' , in id., *Faith and Understanding*, 165–83, ET of 'Die Eschatologie des Johannes-Evangeliums', *Zwischen den Zeiten* 6, 1928, 4–22 = id., *Glauben und Verstehen* 1, Tübingen: Mohr-Siebeck ⁴1961, 134–52 ['Eschatology']

—, *The History of the Synoptic Tradition*, Oxford: Blackwell ²1968, ET of *Die Geschichte der synoptischen Tradition*, FRLANT NF 29, Göttingen: Vandenhoeck & Ruprecht 1921, ¹⁰1995 [*History*]

—, *The Gospel of John*, Oxford: Blackwell and Philadelphia: Westminster Press 1971, ET of *Das Evangelium des Johannes*, MeyerK 2, Göttingen: Vandenhoeck & Ruprecht ¹⁰1941, ²¹1986 [John]

—, 'New Testament and Mythology: The Problem of Demythologizing the New Testament Proclamation', in *New Testament and Mythology and Other Basic Writings*, Philadelphia: Fortress Press and London: SCM Press 1985, 1–43, ET of 'Neues Testament und Mythologie: Das Problem der Entmythologisierung der neutestamentlichen Verkündigung', in H. W. Bartsch (ed.), *Kerygma und Mythos* 1, Hamburg: Herbert Reich-Evangelischer Verlag, ²1951, 15–48 ['NT and Mythology']

—, 'The Primitive Christian Kerygma and the Historical Jesus', in C. E. Braaten and R. A. Harrisville (eds), *The Historical Jesus and the Kerygmatic Christ*, New York and Nashville: Abingdon Press 1964, 15–42, ET of *Das Verhältnis der urchristlichen Christusbotschaft zum historischen Jesus*, Sitzungsberichte der Heidelberger Akademie der Wissenschaften, phil.-hist. Klasse, 3. Abh., Heidelberg: Winter 1960 = id., *Exegetica: Aufsätze zur Erforschung des Neuen Testaments*, ed.

E. Dinkler, Tübingen: Mohr-Siebeck 1967, 445–69 ['Primitive Christian Keryma']

—, 'The Problem of Hermeneutics', in *New Testament and Mythology and Other Basic Writings*, 69–93, ET of 'Das Problem der Hermeneutik', *ZTK* 47, 1950, 47–69 = *Glauben und Verstehen* 2, Tübingen: Mohr-Siebeck 1952, ⁴1965, 211–35 ['Problem']

—, 'Karl Barth, *The Resurrection of the Dead*', in id., *Faith and Understanding*, London: SCM Press 1969, 66–94, ET of 'Karl Barth, "Die Auferstehung der Toten"', *Theologische Blätter* 5, 1926, 1–14 = id.,*Glauben und Verstehen* 1, Tübingen: Mohr-Siebeck ⁶1966, 38–64 ['Resurrection']

—, *Theology of the New Testament* (2 vols), London: SCM Press 1952, 1955, ET of *Theologie des Neuen Testaments*, ed. O. Merk, UTB 630, Tübingen: Mohr-Siebeck ⁹1984 [*Theology*]

H. von Campenhausen, 'The Events of Easter and the Empty Tomb', in id., *Tradition and Life in the Church: Essays and Lectures in Church History*, London: Collins 1968, 42–89, ET of *Der Ablauf der Osterereignisse und das leere Grab*, Sitzungsberichte der Heidelberger Akademie der Wissenschaften, phil.-hist. Kl., 1952, ⁴1977 = id., *Tradition und Leben: Kräfte der Kirchengeschichte*, 1960, 48–113 ['Events of Easter']

P. Carnley, *The Structure of Resurrection Belief*, Oxford: Clarendon Press 1987 [*Structure*]

S. Coakley, 'Is the Resurrection a "Historical" Event? Some Muddles and Mysteries', in Avis, *Resurrection*, 85–115 ['Resurrection']

H. Conzelmann, 'Jesus von Nazareth und der Glaube an den Auferstandenen', in H. Ristow and K. Matthiae (eds), *Der historische Jesus und der kerygmatische Christus: Beiträge zum Christusverständnis in Forschung und Verkündigung*, Berlin: Evangelische Verlagsanstalt 1960, 188–99 ['Jesus']

—, *An Outline of the Theology of the New Testament*, London: SCM Press 1968, ET of *Grundriss der Theologie des Neuen Testaments*, UTB 1446, Tübingen: Mohr-Siebeck 1967; ⁴1987, ed. A. Lindemann

F. H. Cook, '*Memento mori*: The Buddhist Thinks about Death', in Davis, *Death*, 154–71 ['*Memento*']

W. L. Craig, 'Pannenbergs Beweis für die Auferstehung Jesu', *KuD* 34, 1988, 78–104 ['Beweis']

—, 'The Historicity of the Empty Tomb of Jesus', *NTS* 31, 1985, 39–67 ['Historicity']

J. M. Creed, 'The Conclusion of the Gospel according to Saint Mark', *JTS* 31, 1929–30, 175–80 ['Conclusion']

J. D. Crossan, *The Cross That Spoke: The Origins of the Passion Narrative*, San Francisco: Harper & Row 1988 [*Cross*]

—, *Who Killed Jesus? Exposing the Roots of Anti-Semitism in the Gospel Story of the Death of Jesus*, San Francisco: Harper 1995

'Empty Tomb and Absent Lord (Mark 16:1–8)', in W. H. Kelber (ed.), *The Passion in Mark: Studies on Mark 14–16*, Philadelphia: Fortress Press 1976, 135–52 ['Tomb']

D. Cupitt, *Christ and the Hiddenness of God*, London: Lutterworth Press 1971; London: SCM Press ²1985) [*Christ*]

—, 'The Resurrection: A Disagreement (A Correspondence with C. F. D. Moule, 1971)', in: Don Cupitt, *Explorations in Theology* 6, London: SCM Press 1979, 27–41

—, *The Sea of Faith*, London: BBC Publications 1984; London: SCM Press ²1994 [*Sea*]

—, *Taking Leave of God*, London: SCM Press and New York: Crossroad Publishing Company 1980

M. E. Dahl, *The Resurrection of the Body: A Study of I Corinthians 15*, SBT 36, London: SCM Press 1962

D. J. Davies, 'Rebounding Vitality: Resurrection and Spirit in Luke-Acts', in M. D. Carroll *et al.* (eds), *The Bible in Human Society: Essays in Honour of John Rogerson*, JSOTSup 200, Sheffield: Sheffield Academic Press 1995, 205–24 ['Vitality']

P. Davies, *God and the New Physics*, London: Dent 1983, Harmondsworth: Penguin Books 1984 [*God*]

—, *The Mind of God*, New York: Simon & Schuster 1992

S. T. Davis, '"Seeing" the Risen Jesus', in Davis *et al.*, *The Resurrection*, 126–47 ['"Seeing"']

– (ed.), *Death and Afterlife*, New York: St Martin's Press 1989 [*Death*]

—, D. Kendall and O'Collins (eds), *The Resurrection: An Interdisciplinary Symposium on the Resurrection of Jesus*, Oxford: Oxford University Press 1997

H. Dawes, *Freeing the Faith: A Credible Christianity for Today*, London: SPCK 1992

É. Dhanis (ed.), *Resurrexit: Actes du symposium international sur la résurrection de Jésus (Rom 1970)*, Vatican: Editrice Vaticana 1974

M. Dibelius, *Jesus*, London: SCM Press 1963, ET of *Jesus*, SG 1130, Berlin: de Gruyter 1939, ⁴1966

C. Dietzfelbinger, 'Paraklet und Anspruch im Johannesevangelium', *ZTK* 82, 1985, 389–408 ['Paraklet']

C. H. Dodd, 'The Appearances of the Risen Christ: An Essay in Form-Criticism of the Gospels', in D. E. Nineham (ed.), *Studies in the Gospels: Essays in Memory of R. H. Lightfoot*, Oxford: Blackwell 1967, 9–35 ['Appearances']

D. J. Doughty, 'Citizens of Heaven: Philippians 3.2–21', *NTS* 41, 1995, 102–122 ['Citizens']

E. Drewermann, *Das Markusevangelium* (2 vols), Olten and Freiburg im Breisgau: Walter 1987, 1988

D. C. Duling, 'The Promises to David and Their Entry into Christianity – Nailing Down a Likely Hypothesis', *NTS* 20, 1973/74, 55–77 ['Promises']

J. D. G. Dunn, *The Evidence for Jesus: The Impact of Scholarship on Our Understanding of How Christianity Began*, London: SCM Press 1985 [*Evidence*]

—, *Jesus and the Spirit: A Study of the Religious and Charismatic Experience of Jesus and the First Christians as Reflected in the New Testament*, London: SCM Press 1975 [*Jesus*]

—, *The Partings of the Ways between Christianity and Judaism and Their Significance for the Character of Christianity*, London: SCM Press and Philadelphia: TPI 1991 [*Partings*]

R. Feldmeier, 'Nicht Übermacht noch Impotenz: Zum biblischen Ursprung des Allmachtsbekenntnisses', in W. H. Ritter *et al.*, *Der Allmächtige: Annäherung an ein umstrittenes Gottesprädikat*, Göttingen: Vandenhoeck & Ruprecht 1997, 13–42 ['Nicht Übermacht']

J. Fenton, 'The Ending of Mark's Gospel', in Barton and Stanton (eds), *Resurrection*, 1–7 ['Ending']

P. S. Fiddes, *The Creative Suffering of God*, Oxford: Clarendon Press 1988, [*Suffering*]

P. Fiedler, 'Vorösterliche Vorgaben für den Osterglauben', in Broer and Werbick (eds), *'Herr'*, 9–28 ['Vorgaben']

K. M. Fischer, *Das Ostergeschehen*, Göttingen: Vandenhoeck & Ruprecht [2]1980

J. A. Fitzmyer, *The Gospel according to Luke X–XXIV*, AB 28A, New York and London: Doubleday 1985 [*Luke*]

A. G. N. Flew, *The Logic of Immortality*, Oxford: Blackwell 1987 [*Logic*]

J. Frey, *Eugen Drewermann und die biblische Exegese*, WUNT 2/71, Tübingen: Mohr-Siebeck 1995 [*Drewermann*]

J. Frey, *Die johanneische Eschatologie* 1. *Ihre Probleme im Spiegel der Forschung seit Reimarus*, WUNT 96, Tübingen: Mohr-Siebeck 1997; 2. *Zeitverständnis und Eschatologie in den johanneischen Texten*, Habilitationsschrift, Evangelischer-Theologischer Fakultät, Tübingen 1997 [*Eschatologie*]

G. Friedrich, 'Die Auferweckung Jesu, eine Tat Gottes oder ein Interpretament der Jünger?', *KuD* 17, 1971, 153–87 = id., *Auf das Wort kommt es an: Gesammelte Aufsätze*, Göttingen: Vandenhoeck & Ruprecht 1978, 319–53 ['Auferweckung']

—, 'Lk 9,51 und die Entrückungschristologie bei Lukas', in P. Hoffmann *et al.* (eds), *Orientierung an Jesus: Zur Theologie der Synoptiker, FS J. Schmid*; Freiburg, etc.: Herder 1973, 48–77 = id., *Auf das Wort kommt es an*, 26–55 ['Lk 9,51']

P. Geach, 'Immortality', in id., *God and the Soul*, London: Routledge & Kegan Paul 1969, 17–29

S. M. Gilmour, 'The Christophany to More than Five Hundred Brethren', *JBL* 80, 1961, 248–52 ['Christophany']

J. Gnilka, *Das Evangelium nach Markus* (2 vols), EKK 2, Zürich etc.: Benziger and Neukirchen-Vluyn: Neukirchener Verlag, [4]1994 [*MkEv*]

C. Gore, *Dissertations on Subjects Connected with the Incarnation*, London: John Murray [2]1896 [*Dissertations*]

M. Goulder, 'Did Jesus of Nazareth Rise from the Dead?', in Barton and Stanton (eds), *Resurrection*, 58–68 ['Jesus of Nazareth']

H. Grass, *Ostergeschehen und Osterberichte*, Göttingen: Vandenhoeck & Ruprecht 1956, [4]1970 [*Ostergeschehen*]

D. R. Griffin, 'Life after Death, Parapsychology, and Post-Modern Animism', in Davis, *Death*, 88–107 ['Life']

K. Grobel, 'Revelation and Resurrection', in J. M. Robinson and J. B. Cobb (eds), *New Frontiers in Theology* 3: *Theology as History*, New York: Harper & Row 1967, 155–75 ['Revelation']

G. R. Habermas and A. G. N. Flew, *Did Jesus Rise from the Dead? The Resurrection Debate*, San Francisco: Harper & Row 1987 [*Did Jesus Rise?*]

F. Hahn, *The Titles of Jesus in Christology: Their History in Early Christianity*, London: Lutterworth Press 1969, ET of *Christologische Hoheitstitel: Ihre Geschichte im Urchristentum*, UTB 1873, Göttingen: Vandenhoeck & Ruprecht 1963, [5]1995 [*Titles*]

N. Q. Hamilton, 'Resurrection Tradition and the Composition of

Mark', *JBL* 84, 1965, 415–21 ['Resurrection Tradition']

A. E. Harvey, '"They Discussed among Themselves What This 'Rising from the Dead' Could Mean" (Mark 9.10)', in Barton and Stanton (eds), *Resurrection*, 69–78 ['Mark 9.10']

V. A. Harvey, *The Historian and the Believer: The Morality of Historical Knowledge and Christian Belief*, New York: Macmillan and London: SCM Press 1966 [*Historian*]

D. M. Hay, 'Pauline Theology after Paul', in E. E. Johnson and D. M. Hay (eds), *Pauline Theology* 4: *Looking Back, Pressing On*, SBL Symposium Series, Atlanta: Scholars Press 1997, 181–95 ['Pauline Theology']

M. Hengel, *The Charismatic Leader and His Followers*, Studies of the NT and Its World, Edinburgh: T. & T. Clark 1981, ET of *Nachfolge und Charisma: Eine exegetisch-religionsgeschichtliche Studie zu Mt 8,21f und Jesu Ruf in die Nachfolge*, BZNW 34, Berlin: de Gruyter 1968 [*Charismatic Leader*]

—, 'Maria Magdalena und die Frauen als Zeugen', in O. Betz *et al.*, *Abraham unser Vater: Juden und Christen im Gespräch über die Bibel. FS O. Michel*, Leiden: Brill 1963, 243–56 ['Maria']

J. Hick, *Death and Eternal Life*, London: Collins 1976 [*Death*]

—, *Evil and the God of Love*, London: Macmillan 1966 [*Evil*]

—, 'Present and Future Life', *HTR* 71, 1978, 1–15 ['Life']

—, *The Metaphor of God Incarnate: Christology in a Pluralistic Age*, London: SCM Press and Louisville: Westminster/John Knox Press 1993 [*Metaphor*]

E. Hirsch, *Osterglaube: Die Auferstehungsgeschichten und der christliche Glaube*, Tübingen: Katzmann 1988

P. Hoffmann, 'Auferstehung Jesu Christi II/1: Neues Testament', *TRE* 4, 1979, 478–513 ['Auferstehung']

– (ed.), *Zur neutestamentlichen Überlieferung von der Auferstehung Jesu*, Wege der Forschung 522, Darmstadt: Wissenschaftliche Buchgesellschaft 1988 [*Überlieferung*]

O. Hofius, 'Das Evangelium und Israel: Erwägungen zu Römer 9–11', *ZTK* 83, 1986, 297–324 = id., *Paulusstudien*, WUNT 51, Tübingen: Mohr-Siebeck 1989, 175–202 ['Evangelium']

M. D. Hooker, *The Gospel according to St Mark*, BNTC, London: A. & C. Black 1991 [*Mark*]

J. L. Houlden, *Backward into Light: The Passion and Resurrection of Jesus according to Matthew and Mark*, London: SCM Press 1987 [*Backward*]

J. L. Houlden, *Connections: The Integration of Theology and Faith*, London: SCM Press 1986

—, 'The Resurrection and Christianity', *Theology* 99, 1996, 198–205 ['Resurrection']

T. H. Huxley, *Evolution and Ethics*, London: Macmillan 1894, reprinted ed. J. Paradis and G. C. Williams, Princeton: Princeton University Press 1989

J. Jeremias, *Heiligengräber in Jesu Umwelt (Mt. 23,29; Lk. 11,47): Eine Untersuchung zur Volksreligion der Zeit Jesu*, Göttingen: Vandenhoeck & Ruprecht 1958 [*Heiligengräber*]

—, *Jerusalem in the Time of Jesus: An Investigation into Economic and Social Conditions during the New Testament Period*, London: SCM Press 1969, ET of *Jerusalem zur Zeit Jesu: Eine kulturgeschichtliche Untersuchung zur neutestamentlichen Zeitgeschichte*, Göttingen: Vandenhoeck & Ruprecht ³1962 [*Jerusalem*]

—, *New Testament Theology* 1: *The Proclamation of Jesus*, London: SCM Press 1971, ET of *Neutestamentliche Theologie* 1: *Die Verkündigung Jesu*, Gütersloh: Gütersloher Verlagshaus Gerd Mohn 1971, ⁴1988 [*Theology*]

G. Josipovici, *The Book of God: A Response to the Bible*, New Haven and London: Yale University Press 1988

E. Käsemann, 'Blind Alleys in the "Jesus of History" Controversy', in id., *New Testament Questions of Today*, London: SCM Press and Philadelphia: Fortress Press 1969, 23–65, ET of 'Sackgassen im Streit um den historischen Jesus', in id. *Exegetische Versuche und Besinnungen* 2, Göttingen: Vandenhoeck & Ruprecht 1964, ²1965, 31–68 ['Blind Alleys']

—, *The Testament of Jesus: A Study of the Gospel of John in the Light of Chapter 17*, London: SCM Press and Philadelphia: Fortress Press 1968, ET of *Jesu letzter Wille nach Johannes 17*, Tübingen: Mohr-Siebeck 1966, ⁴1980 [*Testament*]

G. D. Kaufman, *In Face of Mystery: A Constructive Theology*, Cambridge, MA and London: Harvard University Press 1993 [*Mystery*]

—, *Theology for a Nuclear Age*, Manchester: Manchester University Press and Philadelphia: Westminster Press 1985 [*Theology*]

A. Kee, *From Bad Faith to Good News: Reflections on Good Friday and Easter*, London: SCM Press and Philadelphia: TPI 1991 [*Bad Faith*]

U. Kellermann, *Auferstanden in den Himmel: 2 Makkabäer 7 und die Auferstehung der Märtyrer*, SBS 95, Stuttgart: Katholisches Bibelwerk 1979 [*Auferstanden*]

J. N. D. Kelly, *Early Christian Creeds*, London: Longmans ²1960 [*Creeds*]

H.-J. Klauck, *Die religiöse Umwelt des Urchristentums* (2 vols), Stuttgart etc.: Kohlhammer, 1995, 1996 [*Umwelt*]

J. S. Kloppenborg, '"Easter Faith" and the Sayings Gospel Q', in R. Cameron (ed.), *The Apocryphal Jesus and Christian Origins*, Semeia 49, SBL 1990, 71–99 ['"Easter Faith"']

D.-A. Koch, *Die Bedeutung der Wundererzählungen für die Christologie des Markusevangeliums*, BZNW 42, Berlin and New York: de Gruyter 1975 [*Bedeutung*]

T. Koch, '"Auferstehung der Toten": Überlegungen zur Gewissheit des Glaubens angesichts des Todes', *ZTK* 89, 1992, 462–83 ['"Auferstehung"']

W. Kramer, *Christ, Lord, Son of God*, SBT 50, London: SCM Press 1966, ET of *Christos Kyrios Gottessohn: Untersuchungen zu Gebrauch und Bedeutung der christologischen Bezeichnungen bei Paulus und den vorpaulinischen Gemeinden*, ATANT 44, Zürich and Stuttgart: Zwingli Verlag 1963 [*Christ*]

H. Küng, *On Being a Christian*, New York: Doubleday and London: Collins 1978, ET of *Christ sein*, Munich: Piper Verlag 1974 [*Christian*]

—, *Credo. The Apostles' Creed Explained for Today*, London: SCM Press 1993, ET of *Credo: Das Apostolische Glaubensbekenntnis – Zeitgenossen erklärt*, Munich: Piper Verlag 1992 [*Credo*]

P. Lapide, *The Resurrection of Jesus: A Jewish Perspective*, Minneapolis: Augsburg Publishing House 1983, ET of *Auferstehung: Ein jüdisches Glaubenserlebnis*, Stuttgart: Calwer Verlag 1977, ⁶1986

K. Lehmann, *Auferweckt am dritten Tag nach der Schrift: Früheste Christologie, Bekenntnisbildung und Schriftauslegung im Lichte von 1 Kor 15,3–5*, QD 38, Freiburg: Herder 1968) [*Auferweckt*]

—, 'Zur Frage nach dem "Wesen" der Erscheinungen des Herrn: Thesen zur hermeneutischen Struktur der Ostererzählungen', in Dhanis, *Resurrexit*, 297–315 ['Frage']

C. S. Lewis, *Miracles: A Preliminary Study*, London: Bles 1947

J. Lieu, 'The Women's Resurrection Testimony', in Barton and Stanton (eds), *Resurrection*, 34–44 ['Testimony']

A. T. Lincoln, 'The Promise and the Failure – Mark 16:7, 8', *JBL* 108, 1989, 283–300 ['Promise']

B. Lindars, *New Testament Apologetic: The Doctrinal Significance of the Old Testament Quotations*, London: SCM Press 1961 [*Apologetic*]

—, 'The Resurrection and the Empty Tomb', in Avis, *Resurrection*, 116–35 ['Resurrection']

J. Lindblom, *Gesichte und Offenbarungen: Vorstellungen von göttlichen Weisungen und übernatürlichen Erscheinungen im ältesten Christentum*, Acta reg. Soc. humaniorum litterarum Lundensis 65, Lund: Gleerup 1968 [*Gesichte*]

A. Lindemann, Review of Lüdemann, *Auferstehung*, in *Wege zum Menschen* 46, 1994, 503–13

—, 'Die Osterbotschaft des Markus', *NTS* 26, 1979/80, 298–317 ['Osterbotschaft']

E. Linnemann, 'Der (wiedergefundene) Markusschluss', *ZTK* 66, 1969, 255–87 ['Markusschluss']

G. Lohfink, 'Der Ablauf der Osterereignisse und die Anfänge der Urgemeinde', *TQ* 160, 1980, 162–76

T. Lorenzen, *Resurrection and Discipleship: Interpretive Models, Biblical Reflections, Theological Consequences*, Maryknoll: Orbis Books 1995 [*Resurrection*]

G. Lüdemann, 'Zwischen Karfreitag und Ostern', in Verweyen, *Osterglaube*, 13–46 ['Karfreitag']

—, *The Resurrection of Jesus*, London: SCM Press 1995, ET of *Die Auferstehung: Historie, Erfahrung, Theologie*, Göttingen: Vandenhoeck & Ruprecht ¹1994 and Stuttgart: Radius ²1994 [*Resurrection*]

U. Luz, 'Aufregung um die Auferstehung Jesu: Zum Auferstehungsbuch von G. Lüdemann', *EvT* 54, 1994, 476–82 ['Aufregung']

H. K. McArthur, '"On the Third Day" (1 Cor xv.4b and Rabbinic Interpretation of Hosea vi.2)', *NTS* 18, 1971/2, 81–6 ['"Third Day"']

J. I. H. McDonald, *The Resurrection: Narrative and Belief*, London: SPCK 1989 [*Resurrection*]

R. MacMullen, *Paganism in the Roman Empire*, New Haven and London: Yale University Press 1981 [*Paganism*]

J. L. Magness, *Sense and Absence: Structure and Suspension in the Ending of Mark's Gospel*, Semeia Studies, Atlanta: Scholars Press 1986 [*Sense*]

W. Marxsen, *Mark the Evangelist*, Nashville: Abingdon Press 1969, ET of *Der Evangelist Markus: Studien zur Redaktionsgeschichte des Evangeliums*, FRLANT 67, Göttingen: Vandenhoeck & Ruprecht 1956, ²1959

—, *The Resurrection of Jesus of Nazareth*, London: SCM Press 1970, ET of *Die Auferstehung Jesu von Nazareth*, Gütersloh: Gütersloher Verlagshaus Gerd Mohn 1968 [*Resurrection*]

—, 'The Significance of the Message of the Resurrection for Faith in Jesus Christ', in Moule (ed.), *Significance*, 15–50, ET of *Die Auferstehung Jesu als historisches und als theologisches Problem*, Gütersloh: Gütersloher Verlagshaus Gerd Mohn 1964 ['Significance']

H. Merklein, *Auferstehung und leeres Grab (Mk 16,1–8)*, Stuttgart: Katholisches Bibelwerk 1994 [*Auferstehung*]

—, 'Mk 16,1–8 als Epilog des Markusevangeliums', in C. Focant (ed.), *The Synoptic Gospels: Source Criticism and the New Literary Criticism*, BETL 110, Leuven: Leuven University Press 1993, 209–38 ['Mk 16,1–8']

B. M. Metzger, 'A Suggestion Concerning the Meaning of I Cor xv.4b', *JTS* 8, 1957, 118–23 ['Suggestion']

P. W. Meyer, 'Pauline Theology', in E. E. Johnson and D. M. Hay (eds), *Pauline Theology 4: Looking Back, Pressing On*, SBL Symposium Series, Atlanta: Scholars Press 1997, 140–60

J. Moltmann, *The Crucified God: The Cross of Christ as the Foundation and Criticism of Christian Theology*, London: SCM Press 1974, ET of *Der gekreuzigte Gott: Das Kreuz Christi als Grund und Kritik christlicher Theologie*, Munich: Christian Kaiser Verlag ⁶1993 [*God*]

—, *Theology of Hope: On the Ground and the Implications of a Christian Eschatology*, London: SCM Press 1967; ET of *Theologie der Hoffnung: Untersuchungen zur Begründung und zu den Konsequenzen einer christlichen Eschatologie*, BEvT 38, München: Christian Kaiser Verlag ⁸1969 [*Theology*]

—, *The Trinity and the Kingdom of God: The Doctrine of God*, London: SCM Press 1981, ET of *Trinität und Reich Gottes; Zur Gotteslehre*, Munich: Christian Kaiser Verlag 1980 [*Trinity*]

R. Morgan, 'Flesh Is Precious: The Significance of Luke 24.36–43', in Barton and Stanton (eds), *Resurrection*, 8–20 ['Flesh']

R. Morgan and J. Barton, *Biblical Interpretation*, Oxford: Oxford University Press 1988

F. Morison, *Who Moved the Stone?*, London: Faber & Faber 1930

C. F. D. Moule (ed.), *The Significance of the Message of the Resurrection for Faith in Jesus Christ*, SBT 2/8, London: SCM Press 1968 [*Significance*]

J. Muddiman, '"I Believe in the Resurrection of the Body"', in Barton and Stanton (eds), *Resurrection*, 128–38

U. B. Müller, *Die Entstehung des Glaubens an die Auferstehung Jesu: Historische Aspekte und Bedingungen*, SBS 172, Stuttgart: Katholisches Bibelwerk 1998 [*Entstehung*]

—, 'Die Parakletenvorstellung im Johannesevangelium', *ZTK* 71, 1974, 31–77 ['Parakletenvorstellung']

W. Nauck, 'Die Bedeutung des leeren Grabes für den Glauben an den Auferstandenen', *ZNW* 47, 1956, 243–67 ['Bedeutung']

K. Nielsen, 'The Faces of Immortality', in Davis (ed.), *Death*, 1–30 ['Faces']

D. E. Nineham, *Saint Mark*, Pelican NT Commentaries, Harmondsworth: Penguin Books 1963 [*Mark*]

—, 'Some Reflections on the Present Position with Regard to the Jesus of History', *Historicity and Chronology in the New Testament*, Theological Collections 6, London: SPCK 1965, 1–18 ['Reflections']

J. M. Nützel, 'Zum Schicksal der eschatologischen Propheten', *BZ* 20, 1976, 59–94 ['Schicksal']

K.-H. Ohlig, 'Thesen zum Verständnis und zur theologischen Funktion der Auferstehungsbotschaft', in Verweyen (ed.), *Osterglaube*, 80–104 ['Thesen']

B. C. Ollenburger, 'If Mortals Die, Will They Live Again? The Old Testament and Resurrection', *Ex auditu* 9, 1993, 29–44 ['Mortals']

A. G. Padgett, 'Advice for Religious Historians: On the Myth of a Purely Historical Jesus', in: Davis *et al.*, *The Resurrection*, 287–307 ['Advice']

W. Pannenberg, *Jesus – God and Man*, Philadelphia: Westminster Press and London: SCM Press 1968, ET of *Grundzüge der Christologie*, Gütersloh: Gütersloher Verlagshaus Gerd Mohn 1964, [7]1990 [*Jesus*]

—, 'Response to the Discussion', in J. M. Robinson and J. B. Cobb (eds.), *New Frontiers in Theology* 3: *Theology as History*, New York, etc.: Harper & Row 1967, 221–76 ['Response']

—, 'The Revelation of God in Jesus of Nazareth', in Robinson and Cobb (eds), *New Frontiers* 3, 101–33 ['Revelation']

—, *Systematische Theologie* (3 vols), Göttingen: Vandenhoeck &

Ruprecht, 1988–93 [*SystTheol*]

H. Paulsen, 'Mk XVI 1–8', *NT* 22, 1980, 138–75 = (shortened) Hoffmann, *Überlieferung*, 377–415

A. R. Peacocke, *Creation and the World of Science*, Oxford: Clarendon Press 1979

—, *God and the New Biology*, London: Dent 1986

T. Penelhum, 'Christianity', in H. Coward (ed.), *Life after Death in World Religions*, Maryknoll: Orbis Books 1997, 31–47

P. Perkins, *Resurrection: New Testament Witness and Contemporary Reflection*, London: Geoffrey Chapman 1984

—, 'The Resurrection of Jesus of Nazareth', in B. Chilton and C. A. Evans (eds), *Studying the Historical Jesus: Evaluations of the State of Current Research*, NTTS 19, Leiden: Brill 1994, 423–42 ['Resurrection']

N. Perrin, *The Resurrection Narratives: A New Approach*, London: SCM Press 1977

M. C. Perry, *The Easter Enigma: An Essay on the Resurrection with Special Reference to the Data of Psychical Research*, London: Faber & Faber 1959 [*Enigma*]

R. Pesch, 'Zur Entstehung des Glaubens an die Auferstehung Jesu: Ein Vorschlag zur Diskussion', *TQ* 153, 1973, 201–28 (cf. 270–83) ['Entstehung' 1973]

—, 'Zur Entstehung des Glaubens an die Auferstehung Jesu: Ein neuer Versuch', *Freiburger Zeitschrift für Philosophie und Theologie* 30, 1983, 73–98 = Hoffmann, *Überlieferung*, 228–55 ['Entstehung' 1983]

—, *Das Markusevangelium* (2 vols), HTKNT 2, Freiburg, etc.: Herder 1976/77, Vol. 1, [5]1989; Vol. 2, [4]1991 [*MkEv*]

D. Z. Phillips, *Death and Immortality*, London: Macmillan 1970 [*Death*]

P. Pokorný, *The Genesis of Christology: Foundations for a Theology of the New Testament*, Edinburgh: T. & T. Clark 1987, ET of *Die Entstehung der Christologie*, Berlin: Evangelische Verlagsanstalt 1984 and Stuttgart: Calwer Verlag, 1985 [*Genesis*]

H. S. Reimarus, *Fragments* (ed. C. H. Talbert), Philadelphia: Fortress Press 1970 and London: SCM Press 1971

J. M. Robinson, 'Jesus: From Easter to Valentinus (or to the Apostles' Creed)', *JBL* 101, 1982, 5–37 ['Jesus']

—, 'Revelation as Word and as History', in J. M. Robinson and J. B. Cobb (eds), *New Frontiers in Theology* 3: *Theology as History*, New York: Harper & Row 1967, 1–100 ['Revelation']

J. M. Robinson and H. Koester, *Trajectories through Early Christianity*, Philadelphia: Fortress Press 1971 [*Trajectories*]

W. Rordorf, *Sunday: The History of the Day of Rest and Worship in the Earliest Centuries of the Christian Church*, London: SCM Press 1968

C. Rowland, 'Interpreting the Resurrection', in Avis (ed.), *Resurrection*, 68–84

G. Ryle, *The Concept of Mind*, London: Hutchinson 1949

E. P. Sanders, *Judaism: Practice and Belief 63 BCE–66 CE*, London: SCM Press and Philadelphia: TPI 1992 [*Judaism*]

L. Schenke, *Auferstehungsverkündigung und leeres Grab: Eine traditionsgeschichtliche Untersuchung von Mk 16,1–8*, SBS 33, Stuttgart: Katholisches Bibelwerk 1968 [*Auferstehungsverkündigung*]

E. Schillebeeckx, *Jesus: An Experiment in Christology*, London: Collins 1979, ET of *Jezus, het verhaal van een levende*, Bloemendaal: Nelissen 1974 [*Jesus*]

R. Schnackenburg, *The Gospel according to St John*, New York: Crossroad Publishing Company 1990, ET of *Das Johannesevangelium*, HTKNT 4, Freiburg, etc.: Herder Verlag 1965–75 [*John*]

W. Schoberth, 'Gottes Allmacht und das Leiden', in W. H. Ritter *et al.*, *Der Allmächtige: Annäherung an ein umstrittenes Gottesprädikat*, Göttingen: Vandenhoeck & Ruprecht 1997, 43–67 ['Allmacht']

L. Schottroff, 'Heil als innerweltliche Entwicklung: Der gnostische Hintergrund der johanneischen Vorstellung vom Zeitpunkt der Erlösung', *NovT* 11, 1969, 294–317 ['Heil']

W. Schrage, 'Theologie und Christologie bei Paulus und Jesus auf dem Hintergrund der modernen Gottesfrage', *EvT* 36, 1976, 121–54 ['Theologie']

F. Schüssler Fiorenza, 'The Resurrection of Jesus and Roman Catholic Fundamental Theology', in Davis *et al.*, 213–48 ['Resurrection']

A. Schweitzer, *The Quest of the Historical Jesus*, London: A. & C. Black [3]1954, ET of *Von Reimarus zu Wrede: Eine Geschichte der Leben-Jesu-Forschung*, UTB 1302, Tübingen: Mohr-Siebeck [9]1984 [*Quest*]

E. Schweizer, 'Auferstehung – Wirklichkeit oder Illusion?', *EvT* 41, 1981, 2–19 ['Auferstehung']

—, 'Der Menschensohn (Zur eschatologischen Erwartung Jesu)', *ZNW* 50, 1959, 185–209 = id., *Neotestamentica: German and English Essays 1951–1963*, Zürich and Stuttgart: Zwingli Verlag 1963, 56–84 ['Menschensohn']

A. F. Segal, 'Life after Death: The Social Sources', in Davis *et al.*, *The*

Resurrection, 90–125 ['Life']

—, 'Paul's Thinking about Resurrection in Its Jewish Context', *NTS* 44, 1998, 400–19 ['Paul's Thinking']

E. Segal, 'Judaism', in H. Coward (ed.), *Life after Death in World Religions*, Maryknoll: Orbis Books 1997, 11–30

P. Selby, *Look for the Living: The Corporate Nature of Resurrection Faith*, London: SCM Press 1976 [*Look*]

D. Sölle, *Mystik und Widerstand: 'Du stilles Geschrei'*, Hamburg: Hoffmann & Campe 1997 [*Mystik*]

D. F. Strauss, *The Life of Jesus Critically Examined*, translated by George Eliot, reissued Philadelphia: Fortress Press 1972 and London: SCM Press 1973, ET of *Das Leben Jesu, kritisch bearbeitet* (2 vols), Tübingen: Osiander 1835/6 [*Life*]

P. Stuhlmacher, 'The Resurrection of Jesus and the Resurrection of the Dead', *Ex auditu* 9, 1993, 45–56 ['Resurrection']

R. Swinburne, 'Evidence for the Resurrection', in Davis *et al.*, 191–212 ['Evidence']

J. E. Taylor, *Christians and the Holy Places: The Myth of Jewish-Christian Origins*, Oxford: Clarendon Press 1993 [*Christians*]

—, 'Golgotha: A Reconsideration of the Evidence for the Sites of Jesus' Crucifixion and Burial', *NTS* 44, 1998, 180–203 ['Golgotha']

V. Taylor, *The Historical Evidence for the Virgin Birth*, Oxford: Clarendon Press 1920 [*Evidence*]

G. Theissen, *Biblical Faith: An Evolutionary Approach*, London: SCM Press 1984, ET of *Biblischer Glaube in evolutionärer Sicht*, Munich: Christian Kaiser Verlag 1984 [*Faith*]

—, and A. Merz, *The Historical Jesus*, London: SCM Press and Minneapolis: Fortress Press 1998, ET of *Der historische Jesus: Ein Lehrbuch*, Göttingen: Vandenhoeck & Ruprecht 1996 [*Jesus*]

P. Tillich, *Systematic Theology* (3 vols), Chicago: Chicago University Press 1951–63 and London: Nisbet 1953–64, reissued London: SCM Press 1978 [*SystTheol*]

E. Troeltsch, 'Über historische und dogmatische Methode in der Theologie', in id., *Gesammelte Schriften* 2: *Zur religiösen Lage, Religionsphilosophie und Ethik* (1922), reprinted Aalen: Scientia 1962, 729–53 ['Methode']

G. Vermes, *Jesus and the World of Judaism*, London: SCM Press 1983 [*Jesus*]

H. Verweyen , '"Auferstehung": Ein Wort verstellt die Sache', in id., *Osterglaube*, 105–44 ['"Auferstehung"']

—, *Osterglaube ohne Auferstehung? Diskussion mit Gerd Lüdemann*, QD 155, Freiburg, etc.: Herder Verlag 1995 [*Osterglaube*]

—, 'Die Sache mit den Ostererscheinungen', in Broer and Werbick (eds), *'Herr'*, 63– 80 ['Sache']

A. Vögtle, 'Wie kam es zur Artikulierung des Osterglaubens?', *BibLeb* 14, 1973, 231–44; 15, 1974, 16–32, 102–20, 174–93 ['Artikulierung'] – and R. Pesch, *Wie kam es zum Osterglauben?*, Düsseldorf: Patmos Verlag 1975 [*Osterglauben*]

S. Vollenweider, 'Grosser Tod und grosses Leben: Ein Beitrag zum buddhistisch-christlichen Gespräch im Blick auf die Mystik des Paulus', *EvT* 51, 1991, 365–82 ['Grosser Tod']

'Ostern – der denkwürdige Ausgang einer Krisenerfahrung', *TZ* 49, 1993, 34–53 ['Ostern']

N. Walter, 'Eine vormatthäische Schilderung der Auferstehung Jesu', *NTS* 19, 1972–3, 415–29 ['Schilderung']

K. Ward, *Religion and Creation*, Oxford: Clarendon Press 1996 [*Religion*]

F. Watson, '"He Is Not Here": Towards a Theology of the Empty Tomb', in Barton and Stanton (eds), *Resurrection*, 95–107 ['"He Is Not Here"']

A. J. M. Wedderburn, *Baptism and Resurrection: Studies in Pauline Theology against Its Graeco-Roman Background*, WUNT 44, Tübingen: Mohr-Siebeck 1987 [*Baptism*]

—, 'The Body of Christ and Related Concepts in 1 Corinthians', *SJT* 24, 1971, 74–96 ['Body']

—, 'Some Recent Pauline Chronologies', in *ExpTim* 92, 1981,103–8 ['Chronologies']

—, 'The Theology of Colossians', in A. T. Lincoln and A. J. M. Wedderburn, *The Later Paulines*, New Testament Theology, Cambridge: Cambridge University Press 1993, 3–71, 167–9, 173–8 ['Colossians']

—,'Paul and the Story of Jesus', in id. (ed.), *Paul and Jesus: Collected Essays*, JSNTSup 37, Sheffield: Sheffield Academic Press 1989, 161–89

—, 'Paul and "Biblical Theology"', in S. Pederson (ed.), *New Directions in Biblical Theology: Papers of the Aarhus Conference, 16–19 September 1992*, NovTSup 76, Leiden, etc.: Brill 1994, 24–46 ['Paul']

—, 'The Problem of the Denial of the Resurrection in I Corinthians XV', *NovT* 23, 1981, 229–41 ['Problem']

—, 'Traditions and Redaction in Acts 2.1–13', *JSNT* 55, 1994, 27–54 ['Traditions']

H. Weder, *Neutestamentliche Hermeneutik*, Zürcher Grundrisse zur Bibel, Zürich: Theologischer Verlag 1986 [*Hermeneutik*]

C. H. Weisse, *Die evangelische Geschichte kritisch und philosophisch bearbeitet*, Leipzig: Breitkopf & Härtel 1838 [*Geschichte*]

K. Wengst, *Christologische Formeln und Lieder des Urchristentums*, SNT 7, Gütersloh: Gütersloher Verlagshaus Gerd Mohn 1972 [*Formeln*]

—, 'Glaubensbekenntnisse IV: Neues Testament', *TRE* 13, 1984, 392–9

—, *Ostern – ein wirkliches Gleichnis, eine wahre Geschichte: Zum neutestamentlichen Zeugnis von der Auferweckung Jesu*, Munich: Christian Kaiser Verlag 1991 [*Ostern*]

J. Werbick, 'Die Auferweckung Jesu – Gottes "eschatologische Tat"? Die theologische Rede vom Handeln Gottes und die historische Kritik', in Broer and Werbick (eds), *'Herr'*, 81–132 ['Auferweckung']

U. Wilckens, *Resurrection: Biblical Testimony to the Resurrection: An Historical Examination and Explanation*, Atlanta: John Knox Press 1978, ET of *Auferstehung: Das biblische Auferstehungszeugnis historisch untersucht und erklärt*, Gütersloh: Gütersloher Verlagshaus Gerd Mohn ⁵1992

—, 'Die Auferstehung Jesu: Historisches Zeugnis – Theologie – Glaubenserfahrung: Eine Auseinandersetzung mit Gerd Lüdemann', *Pastoraltheologie* 85, 1996, 102–20 = id., *Hoffnung gegen den Tod: Die Wirklichkeit der Auferstehung Jesu*, Neuhausen-Stuttgart: Hänssler 1996, 28–62 ['Auferstehung Jesu']

—, 'Der Ursprung der Überlieferung der Erscheinungen des Auferstandenen: Zur traditionsgeschichtlichen Analyse von 1. Kor 15,1–11', in W. Joest and W. Pannenberg (eds), *Dogma und Denkstrukturen*, FS E. Schlink, Göttingen: Vandenhoeck & Ruprecht 1963, 56–95 = Hoffmann, *Überlieferung*, 139–93 ['Ursprung']

M. F. Wiles, 'A Naked Pillar of Rock', in Barton and Stanton (eds), *Resurrection*, 116–27 ['Pillar']

F. Young, 'The Mark of the Nails', in Barton and Stanton (eds), *Resurrection*, 139–53 ['Mark']

W. Zager, 'Jesu Auferstehung – Heilstat Gottes oder Vision? Das Ostergeschehen in historisch-kritischer und psychologischer Perspektive', *Deutsches Pfarrerblatt* 96, 1996, 120–3 ['Auferstehung']

Notes

1. Lüdemann, 'Karfreitag', 17, quotes a letter from Theodosius Harnack to his son Adolf in 1886, in which the fact of the resurrection is described as a *'bombenfest'* foundation, not just for Christianity, but even for the Trinity.

2. Moltmann, *Theology*, 165–6. Over against this J. L. Houlden comments in an unpublished paper entitled 'Is the historical reliability of the resurrection necessary to Christianity?', a copy of which he very kindly sent me, that when a meeting of British New Testament scholars debated the evidence for and against the resurrection of Jesus in autumn 1991 (his own paper was delivered at the corresponding meeting in the following year), the dispassionate and restrained character of the discussion and the cheerfulness in the bar afterwards suggested, rather, 'that both unbelief and Christianity can (or at any rate *will*) manage very well *whatever* the historical reliability of the resurrection. Whatever makes Christianity stand or fall, it is not the resurrection.' Some of the same ground is covered in his 'Resurrection', but this blunt assertion is muted there (though doubtless implicit). (And Hansjürgen Verweyen refers to the disinterest that teachers of religion encounter when the word 'resurrection' is mentioned, *Osterglaube*, 7.) Paul Avis represents a mediating position ('Resurrection', 19): a Christian faith without belief in the resurrection is indeed Christian faith, but 'a sombre, indeed a tragic, faith'.

3. Pokorný, *Genesis*, 61.

4. Very puzzling here is Lorenzen's assertion (*Resurrection*, 2) that he is not asking whether the resurrection is true or false because 'the answer to that question is not at our our disposal as Christian theologians who accept the authority of the biblical message'; I could understand this acceptance as meaning that one should not pose the question at all, but to say that it can be posed but not answered is surprising. And

this assertion begs the question of the nature of the 'authority' of this message and what follows from it.

5. Jeremias, *Theology*, 305. This verdict by Jeremias is problematic: if such behaviour by the Roman governor were unusual, then this is surely more reason for the historian to doubt the account of the governor's actions than for the mysterious 'fanatics' to remedy the governor's aberration by putting Jesus' body where it properly belonged. Or does Jeremias mean by the 'fanatics' the Jewish authorities, who might understandably have been much put out by the unusual favour ostensibly wrung from the governor by one from amongst their own ranks, Joseph of Arimathea, and by his subsequent burial of Jesus, if one accepts the Gospels' account of this?

6. Reimarus, *Fragments*, 161.

7. Taylor, *Evidence*, 127–8.

8. Gore, *Dissertations*, 64.

9. Despite all the critical acumen of Grass's work, this is ultimately his justification for speaking of 'objective visions', i.e. visions that are not self-induced but come from God (*Ostergeschehen*, 248): 'faith and the church would have no more right to exist were there no living, exalted Lord'.

10. It *may* be that there are circumstances which would amount to a complete falsification of a historical claim. If bones which could be shown to be definitely those of Jesus – a condition that is rather unlikely to be met – were discovered in a Palestinian grave, then this might amount to a falsification of the claim that Jesus is risen, or at least of one understanding of what is meant by saying that Jesus is risen. If 'Jesus is risen' means that the physical body of the earthly Jesus left his grave then that discovery would falsify that claim. But unlikely hypothetical situations are hardly helpful to our enquiry here.

11. Van Harvey, *Historian*, 107–9, criticizing H. Zahrnt, *The Historical Jesus*, London: Collins and New York: Harper & Row 1963.

12. Nineham, 'Reflections', 16; cf. Fischer, *Ostergeschehen*, 12.

13. Much of this handling of what is 'historical' is reminiscent of the more general claims about the meaningfulness of statements in logical positivism; cf. e.g. Ayer, *Language*, 9: 'a statement is held to be literally meaningful if and only if it is either analytic or empirically verifiable.'

14. In this respect Carnley's appeal to events like the First World War to show that there *are* indeed historical judgments the falsification of which may be considered impossible (*Structure*, 134) is really beside the point when one comes to an event of the first century, and

particularly an event of the kind that the resurrection of Jesus seems to have been.

15. So, rightly, Marxsen, 'Significance', 14.

16. Probably to be dated to the second century (C. Maurer and W. Schneemelcher in Schneemelcher, 1, 221). The resurrection event is described in 9.35–42. However, there are those who claim that the traditions in this Gospel are often older than our canonical Gospels: e.g. Nikolaus Walter, who thinks that a similar account to that of this Gospel lies behind our Gospel of Matthew ('Schilderung'; cf. Grass, *Ostergeschehen*, 26), and above all in the English-speaking world J. D. Crossan (*Cross*). It is, however, unlikely that Matthew knew a more pronouncedly miraculous version of the story and toned it down, for this evangelist does not seem to be one to shun the miraculous.

17. Grobel, 'Revelation', 171–2.

18. Baur, *Christenthum*, 39–40.

19. Hoffmann, *Überlieferung*, 2; cf. Fischer, *Ostergeschehen*, 31.

20. Cf., e.g., Suetonius, *Nero* 57.

21. Cf. Küng, *Christian*, 349: if the raising of Jesus was an act of God, 'it can *not* be a *historical* event in the strict sense . . . an event which can be verified by historical science with the aid of historical methods'; cf. also his *Credo*, 150: whereas the disciples' faith is a historical event that can be investigated by historical means, the resurrection itself is not historical, but a 'real event in the sphere of God'. Also Meyer, 'Pauline Theology', 158.

22. Padgett, 'Advice', 302–3.

23. Grass, *Ostergeschehen*, 12–13.

24. Becker, 'Gottesbild', 205.

25. Quite why it should be *so* contentious, at least in the German-speaking world, I find a little puzzling, since so much that Lüdemann says and has said subsequently has been said before, and much of it would be taken for granted in critical academic circles. Ulrich Luz goes somewhat further: Lüdemann's book contains *nothing* that New Testament scholars would not regard as self-evident or at least as long-recognized possible hypotheses ('Aufregung', 477). True, Lüdemann has perhaps said it more bluntly and provocatively than most, helped (or hindered, depending on how one views the controversy) by the media.

26. Barth, *CD* III.2, 471f.: the resurrection story is one of those which contain very little 'Historie', and he describes it as having a narrow '"historical" fringe'. Earlier, in his Romans commentary (195,

203) he had described it as 'non-historical'. For a fuller account of the discussion between Barth and Bultmann here see Carnley, *Structure*, esp. 108–43. With Barth's stance may be compared that of Stuhlmacher, 'Resurrection', 50, who denies that 'the Easter events are "objective facts"' and prefers to speak of 'events in space and time which are not objectifiable'. But the crucified body of Jesus *was* an object like any other corpse.

27. Bultmann, 'Problem', 89; it should be noted that 'occur' and 'history' (or in Ogden's translation 'story') represent two words whose relationship to one another is more immediately perceptible in German, '*geschehen*' and '*Geschichte*'. Cf. also the question posed by Marxsen, *Resurrection*, 120–1 (his italics): 'How can an event be called *historical* if it cannot be established by historical methods? . . . how can it be maintained that an event has happened if historical research cannot do so? . . . If one is dealing with an event, one is dealing with something which is within the competence of the historian. . . . historical judgments are in principle open to examination, although whether this examination will produce results is another matter.' See also Van Harvey, *Historian*, 157–8: 'Barth, in effect, claims all the advantages of history but will assume none of its risks.'

28. Bultmann, 'Problem', 90.

29. Lüdemann, *Resurrection*, 4. Just as impregnable as Barth's position is that which William Craig adopts in response to Pannenberg's arguments ('Beweis', 87–95, esp. 94): by virtue of the Spirit's witness we know that the content of faith is true and therefore that historical proof will ultimately confirm this, even if that does not seem to be the case at a particular point of time. Such absolutist claims for the Spirit seem to me to be dangerous in the extreme. How can one be so sure that it is the Spirit that convinces one of this truth (rather than, say, one's own preferences or wishful thinking)?

30. Pannenberg, *Jesus*, 99.

31. Lüdemann, *Resurrection*, 2; cf. the short discussion and bibliography on Pannenberg's position in Lorenzen, *Resurrection*, 17–25.

32. Pannenberg, *SystTheol* 2, 404 and n. 115.

33. Cited in Robinson, 'Revelation', 33 (his italics); cf. Craig, 'Beweis', 80: are these alternative falsifications or must all of them first be fulfilled in order to falsify the traditions of Jesus' resurrection? (Robinson's evaluation of where the burden of proof is made to lie suggests the latter.)

34. Pannenberg, 'Response', 274.

35. Moltmann, *Theology*, 174–5, 177, 180. Similarly, Pannenberg wishes to distance the historicity of the resurrection of Jesus from the application of the principle of analogy as customarily used in historical questioning, although he speaks rather of '*Gleichartigkeit*' (*Syst Theol 2*, 403). See, however, the critique of Pannenberg's arguments here in Coakley, 'Resurrection', esp. 88–94.

36. Cf. Zager, 'Auferstehung', 123, as well as the more modern evidence cited by Lüdemann, *Resurrection*, 126–8. Further in Ch. 4 below.

37. Bultmann, 'NT and Mythology', 36; cf. Conzelmann, 'Jesus', 191.

38. Bultmann, 'NT and Mythology', 39–40; with the last sentence cf. Marxsen, *Resurrection*, 141: 'in our historical enquiry into the background of our texts, we do not come upon the fact of Jesus' resurrection; we come upon the faith of the primitive church after Jesus' death'.

39. Bultmann, *Theology* I, 45.

40. Bultmann, 'Primitive Christian Kerygma', 42.

41. Marxsen, 'Significance', 40; *Resurrection*, 77, 126. For Marxsen, however, the 'cause', the '*Sache*', of the pre-Easter Jesus was already an eschatological proclamation.

42. That the proclamation of the first Christians was an unquestionable datum is an assumption which Bultmann's pupil Ernst Käsemann challenged when he sought to justify the theological relevance of the question of the historical Jesus. That is particularly clear in his 'Blind Alleys' article, e.g. 50: 'the real problem . . . is how to use the critical method to separate the true message from falsifications of it, and to do this we need the help of the very One who was at that very time the historical Jesus'. So too Hoffmann asks (*Überlieferung*, 10) whether the 'that' of Jesus which is for Bultmann God's final revelation does not function as an alibi for a free kerygma that becomes ever further removed from history as the place of revelation and for quite arbitrary theological speculations.

43. E.g. Marxsen, *Resurrection*, 89–96.

44. For Pesch too ('Entstehung' 1983, 233), Bultmann's interpretation of the resurrection means that it is the '*Entscheidungstat*' of the disciples alone which is significant.

45. Bornkamm, *Jesus*, 9, 15; cf. Bultmann, *Theology* 1, 26: 'faith, being personal decision, cannot be dependent upon a historian's labour'; Carnley, *Structure*, 132–3.

46. Drewermann, *Das Markusevangelium* 2, 699.

47. A statement about the past like 'Pigs have always had four legs' (and 'God has raised Jesus from the dead' is also *prima facie* such a statement) cannot in practice be verified because we no longer have access to the remains of all deceased pigs, but the statement could in theory be falsified by finding the skeleton of a three- or five-legged pig.

48. A quick glance e.g. at Reimarus (pp. 161–94 of Talbert's ed.) will show how the following list of discrepancies could be added to, for instance with the question when the spices for anointing Jesus were actually bought.

49. It may well be that, as R. E. Brown, *Death*, 1019, 1195, 1276, argues, there was a tradition that three women had observed Jesus' death, but that this trio was variously identified (see his table on p. 1016, which also records the women present at the burial and at the tomb on Easter morning); in the accounts of Easter morning the presence of Mary of Magdala is the one common element. To be noted is also the first person *plural* of John 20.2, even if its significance has been widely dismissed (e.g. Grass, *Ostergeschehen*, 54).

50. That despite the fact that anointing was apparently no longer necessary after Joseph of Arimathea's ministrations (cf., e.g., Grass, *Ostergeschehen*, 20).

51. As Reimarus noted, the question of Mark 16.3 (and indeed the whole venture to anoint the body) is hardly compatible with Matthew's story of the guards at the tomb. Reimarus saw this as a decisive reason to reject Matthew's story (ed. Talbert, 162, 168).

52. Grass, *Ostergeschehen*, 32: the two figures are a common motif of the narrative technique of folk-tales.

53. But the disciples on the way to Emmaus seem to exclude that by implication: Luke 24.22–23.

54. Strauss, *Life*, 727.

55. For further examples, and appropriate comments, cf. Carnley, *Structure*, 18–19 n. 20.

56. Morison is also unlikely to endear himself to modern tastes when he writes of Pilate's wife: 'Now does anyone with personal knowledge of the immemorial characteristics of women suppose for a moment that an incident like this [Caiaphas' supposed nocturnal visit to Pilate to arrange for Jesus' arrest and trial] would pass without Claudia wanting to know something about it?' (49–50)! Cf. 73: 'women are specially prone to unforeseen delays when engaged in joint expeditions'.

57. See Ch. 7 (c) below.

58. Cf. Grass, *Ostergeschehen*, 35–40. Even the scene with Mary in

John 20 is problematic, and Wengst, *Ostern*, 76, mentions that mediae-val Easter plays found it difficult to decide whether Jesus should appear as a gardener or a royal figure.

59. Grass, *Ostergeschehen*, 14.

60. Mark 16.12, REB (italics added).

61. At this point this ending of Mark differs from Luke, for there the two disciples find, when they rejoin the others, that these have been prepared for their news by the appearance to Peter and are already convinced of the resurrection (24.34). This and features like the specific powers promised to the disciples in Mark 16.17–18 suggest that the author of this ending to Mark was not solely dependent on our canoni-cal Gospels for the contents of his summary account, but drew on other traditions as well.

62. Cf. Grass, *Ostergeschehen*, 49.

63. Not so wide of the mark is Cupitt's comparison of what he calls 'psi-theories' or 'vision theories' of the resurrection with pheno-mena like the sighting of UFOs (or the Loch Ness monster): *Christ*, 144–50.

64. Küng, *Christian*, 350 (his italics).

65. McDonald, *Resurrection*, esp. 105–9 on the Emmaus story and its sequel.

66. Cf. ibid., 141: 'The corporeal aspect of the risen Jesus finds expression in the concept of "the body of Christ" in which believers participate, rather than in the notion of a reanimated corpse', and stories of the empty tomb point to the fact that Jesus' 'life belongs to the future, to lived experience and the shaping of history'. This sounds impressive, but on sober reflection one is left with the suspicion that the author's rhetoric has taken flight away from the text and has left the evangelist himself far behind.

67. Cf. now Frey, *Eschatologie*.

68. So the definition of Bultmann, 'NT and Mythology', 10 and 42 n. 5.

69. Cf. Schweizer, 'Auferstehung', 10.

70. This could, however, be simply a literary and apologetic device, heightening and underlining the sense of the miraculous.

71. Cf. Perkins, *Resurrection*, 181.

72. So Berger, *Auferstehung*, esp. 146; Pesch, 'Entstehung' 1973, esp. 222–5; Vögtle, 'Artikulierung', 20; this view also exerted considerable influence on Eduard Schillebeeckx, *Jesus*, e.g. 458, 507.

73. For a short account in English of this interpretation of the rise of

the belief in the resurrection see F. Schüssler Fiorenza, 'Resurrection', 219–23. See also the critical article of Nützel, 'Schicksal'.

74. According to the numbering of *OTP* 1,748.

75. Nützel, 'Schicksal', 60–7, 87.

76. Wintermute edited this work for *OTP* 1, 721–53, Kuhn for Sparks, *Apoc. OT*, 753–73. Schneemelcher's verdict, appealing to W. Schrage, is that the Jewish original goes back no earlier than the second half of the third century CE and that this was edited by Christians at the start of the fourth: 2, 626.

77. *OTP* 2, 379–99. Rightly Nützel, 'Schicksal', 82–4, argues that the additions in the version of the Lives which Isidore of Seville records come from a later Christian hand.

78. Müller, *Entstehung*, 51, traces the failure of these earlier accounts back to this attempt to find parallels specifically for the tradition of the martyrdom of eschatological prophetic figures.

79. Müller, *Entstehung*, 53, argues that it is in fact Mark 6.14b that reflects earlier, non-Christian tradition, for it is John who is there the object of veneration and it is on his account that these powers are at work in Jesus.

80. See also the critique in Vögtle-Pesch, *Osterglauben*, 74–85.

81. Müller, *Entstehung*, 31–5.

82. Kellermann, *Auferstanden*, esp. 81; cf. 137, where the relation of this belief to the traditions of Jesus' resurrection is mentioned. Whether Daniel's resurrection is in fact meant to be earthly or would be so understood seems to me a moot point.

83. Cf. Fiedler, 'Vorgaben', 25–6.

84. Lapide, *Resurrection*, 88–9. Lapide's rather remarkable argument is dismissed by Drewermann as a form of 'late-Jewish fundamentalism' which distorts the symbol of the resurrection into a historical fact (*Das Markusevangelium* 2, 670 n.).

85. Thus Pesch, even in his 1983 article, where he distances himself from the views of Berger, seems to take an unwarranted short-cut when he speaks of the resurrection appearances as visions in which Jesus appeared as the son of man and in which the disciples saw the fulfilment of the promise of his resurrection given in his 'son of man' sayings ('Entstehung' 1983, 243). That seems to presuppose, for a start, that the passion and resurrection predictions of the Gospels are more historically reliable than many would like to grant.

86. Schweizer, 'Menschensohn', 68; and yet he grants that it could just be an abbreviation of Mark 9.31, to avoid repetition. However, the

third passion prediction (10.32–33) is not so brief and is remarkable, rather, for its deletion of any Jewish role in Jesus' passion.

87. Becker, *Auferstehung*, 12–13; cf. Rowland, 'Interpreting the Resurrection', 71.

88. Perkins, *Resurrection*, 75.

89. And if *they* did not expect the resurrection, then, asks Reimarus, *a fortiori* how could one expect the chief priests to expect or fear such an event and consequently have a guard placed at the tomb (ed. Talbert, 165)? Cf. also Grass, *Ostergeschehen*, 24.

90. Perkins, 'Resurrection', 432–3, seems to wish to strip this line of reasoning of its force; her first argument, however, from the social sciences, namely that Jesus and his disciples lacked clout with the Jerusalem authorities, seems irrelevant to this issue. This may explain why Jesus was summarily condemned and why none of his other followers could petition for his body, but that is not the same as explaining their unpreparedness for his death and resurrection. The second line of argument, from the relations between charismatic leaders and their followers, may show that things could fall apart when the strong authority of of the charismatic leadership was suddenly removed. But Perkins then seems to argue that the removal of the leader meant a removal of divine grace and power, so that a renewed sense of that grace and power would imply that the leader was once more present with them. Too many different arguments and sorts and levels of argument are mingled together here to carry conviction.

91. Kee, *Bad Faith*, 59; with this contrast H. Verweyen's report of a confirmation candidate's answer to the question, 'What were Jesus' last words on the cross?': 'I don't care. I'll be resurrected in three days anyway' ('"Auferstehung"', 105)! (Symptomatic of the creeping docetism of much popular Christian piety?)

92. Cf. Barrett, *Jesus*, 78. Even that, however, is questioned by Perkins, who holds it 'difficult to argue that Jesus clearly taught that he personally would be vindicated or exalted like the *maskilim* of Dan 12' (*Resurrection*, 80).

93. Lohfink, 'Ablauf', 169, argues, however, that nothing in Jewish eschatological expectations made it necessary that all the events of the end would unfold on a single day; he argues, therefore, for an incredibly heightened eschatological expectation of the proximity of the end, yet concedes that it has left little trace in the traditions except, perhaps, for Matt. 27.51–53.

94. So Wengst, *Ostern*, 37: the assertion that Jesus had been raised,

never to die again, and had already been so raised, was astonishing; cf. Pannenberg, 'Revelation', 114–15.

95. Cf. e.g. Dunn, *Evidence*, 60.

96. Küng, *Christian*, 345 (his italics).

97. Cf. Dibelius, *Jesus*, 131.

98. So, rightly, Broer, *Urgemeinde*, 282.

99. *Didascalia* 2, 59, 2 (ed. Funk).

100. Tertullian, *De oratione* 23.2 (1, 271)

101. Cf. Conzelmann, *Outline*, 66; Fischer, *Ostergeschehen*, 71.

102. 15.9; it seems to be implied that the ascension took place on a Sunday, perhaps even on Easter Day itself, as suggested by Luke 24.51, according to the text offered by Nestle-Aland[26] and *UBSGNT*.

103. Justin, *Apol.* 1.67.7 (ed. Goodspeed, p. 76).

104. As it still is in a number of languages: e.g. Spanish, *domingo*; Italian, *domenico*; French, *dimanche*, etc.

105. Rordorf, *Sunday*, 233; cf. also 219: 'The selection of Sunday as the day for worship must in some way be connected with the resurrection of Jesus, which according to the evidence in the Gospels took place on a Sunday.' See also Swinburne, 'Evidence', 207–12. Bode's scepticism at this point (*Morning*, 132–45) is in fact not too damaging to Rordorf's general case, for if indeed it was rather the visit to Jesus' tomb which was remembered in the special status of the first day of the week, it remains true that the visit remained the *terminus ante quem* for the resurrection to which the empty tomb in turn was thought to witness.

106. E.g. Pliny, *Ep.* 10.96.7.

107. Cf. Matt. 16.21; 17.23; 20.19; Luke 9.22; 18.33; 24.7, 46; Acts 10.40. On the tradition contained in I Cor. 15.3ff, cf. Ch. 7 below.

108. LXX: 'on the third day we shall rise (ἀναστησόμεθα) and we shall live in his presence.'

109. Cf. Conzelmann, *Outline*, 66; McArthur, '"Third Day"', 85; Metzger, 'Suggestion', 119–20. It may have been interpreted in later rabbinic exegesis as referring to the general resurrection, but this could as easily be an argument for the rabbis' ignorance of any use of this passage by Christians (but cf. Grass, *Ostergeschehen*, 137: the suppression of the time-references in the Targum is a polemical response to Christian use of the text; cf. also Fischer, *Ostergeschehen*, 73). Also to be noted is Craig's argument ('Historicity', 47) that the absence of any linking of the resurrection with the third day in earlier Jewish literature is significant; indeed it is 'after seven days' that is found if any timing is mentioned (IV Ezra 7.31).

110. McArthur, "'Third Day'", 85.

111. Ibid., 83.

112. Cf. Conzelmann, *Outline*, 66.

113. All that Lindars, *Apologetic*, 62, can point to is the quotation of Hos. 6.6 in Matt. 9.13 and 12.7 and a possible allusion to 6.9 in Luke 10.30, very different uses of the text from the one that concerns us here.

114. Cf. von Campenhausen, 'Events of Easter', 45–7.

115. Lehmann, *Auferweckt*, 263–72; Bode, *Morning*, 119–26; it is to be noted that their starting-point is the relatively late Genesis Rabbah. Fischer's use of rabbinic sources also betrays a similar lack of caution when he seems to suggest that the Pirke R. Eliezer (51) is earlier than the New Testament or is evidence for the eschatological interpretation of Hos. 6.2 in 'contemporary Judaism' (*Ostergeschehen*, 72, 83).

116. Rom. 8.32 is probably an allusion to Abraham's readiness to offer his son, Heb. 6.13–14, the only express citation, to the oath which God subsequently swore to Abraham.

117. At least in Philo, *Vit. Mos.* 1.163, but Josephus, *Ant.* 2.315 has τριταῖοι.

118. E.g. above all Ps. 16.10 (Acts 2.27, 31; 13.35) and, if one couples Jesus' exaltation with his resurrection, Ps. 110.1 (Mark 12.36 parr.; 14.62 parr.; Acts 2.34–35; I Cor. 15.25; Heb.1.13); cf. Lindars, *Apologetic*, ch. 2. Similarly A. F. Segal's suggestion that it is above all Dan.12.2 that is meant ('Paul's Thinking', 416) would entail that the 'third day' is not part of the fulfilment.

Would one not expect early Christians also to be tempted to see a promise of Jesus' resurrection in references to God's raising up (usually forms of ἀνίστημι, the cognate verb to ἀνάστασις, resurrection, although for the verb 'raise' in connection with Jesus' resurrection the verb ἐγείρω is preferred in the New Testament; cf., however, Eph. 5.14; I Thess. 4.14, where ἀνίστημι is used intransitively: 'arise', a prophet like Moses (Deut. 18.15; cf. Acts 3.22; 7.37) or a successor to David (e.g. Isa. 11.10 in Rom. 15.12; cf. II Sam. 7.12; Jer. 23.5 LXX; 30.9 = LXX 37.9) or other messianic figures (e.g. Num. 24.17; cf. TestJud 24.1)? Cf. also Duling, 'Promises'. But there is surprisingly little evidence of such texts playing a role in early Christian apologetics specifically in connection with the resurrection of Jesus.

119. Cf. Metzger, 'Suggestion', 121. Hahn, *Titles*, 180, also avoids tying 'according to the scriptures' too tightly to 'on the third day'.

120. E.g. Mark 8.31 parr. and the other passion predictions; cf. also Luke 24.26; Acts 17.3.

121. Cf. Lüdemann, *Resurrection*, 47.

122. Cf. Craig, 'Historicity', 45, 49; also Hahn, *Titles*, 180–1.

123. Lindars, 'Resurrection', 126; the phrase here is, anyway, διὰ τριῶν ἡμερῶν (John 2.19 ἐν τρισὶν ἡμεραῖς, as in Mark 15.29 par.).

124. It is striking and perplexing that this charge of the temple saying is never linked to Jesus' action in the temple (Mark 11.15–17 parr.). Or was it in fact originally so linked in the actions and charges of the Jewish authorities against Jesus, but the connection was suppressed by the early Christians as too damaging to their reputation and Jesus'?

125. Apart, that is, from the reading of D W it. It may also be doubted whether the distinction 'made with hands' – 'not made with hands' in Mark's version of the charge can plausibly be traced back to Jesus. The prediction of the rebuilding of the temple or a better temple is not, however, inconceivable (cf. I Enoch 90.28–29).

126. Von Campenhausen, 'Easter Events', 47.

127. Sanders, *Judaism*, 130.

128. So, rightly, Lüdemann, *Resurrection*, 32.

129. However, von Campenhausen, 'Easter Events', 84, argues that Jerusalem, the city of Jesus' enemies, was no place in which to expect his reappearance, so that the disciples would have awaited him in his home and theirs, Galilee. Yet Jesus had evidently regarded Jerusalem as so important that he went there despite the obvious risks; did that no longer count for anything with his disciples? Or did they hold that Jerusalem had now had its chance and had rejected it? But if that were so, what persuaded them to return there, as eventually they (or at least their leaders) most certainly did?

130. The suggestion of Lapide (*Resurrection*, 66) that the whole tradition of Galilean appearances arose from a mistranslation of *galîla'*, district, is unconvincing.

131. Cf. e.g. Paulsen, 'Mk XVI 1–8', 168 (409). See further in Ch. 7 (c).

132. Cf. Grass, *Ostergeschehen*, 76; with some justification he sees Luke 5.1–11 as a variant form of this tradition, which Luke could not use as an Easter story because it belonged to a Galilean setting; accordingly he projected it back into the ministry of Jesus, even though Peter's confession in v. 8 would be more appropriate after his denial of Jesus. Does the explanation for the smaller number lie at least partly in the fact that not all of the twelve had been fishermen before?

133. Gospel of Peter 14.58–60 (evidently the tax-collector Levi was prepared to learn a new trade!).

134. Cf. Lüdemann, *Resurrection*, 145–6; Pokorný, *Genesis*, 111; even the manuscript tradition seems to be in some uncertainty how far the place was from Jerusalem (see J. F. Strange, in *Anchor Bible Dictionary* 2,497–8: certainty only reigned from the fourth century on, when it was decided that the location was the city that was given the name of Nicopolis).

135. E.g. Fitzmyer, *Luke*, 1563: he baldly states that Cleopas is a shortened form of Kleopatros, while Clopas is a Graecized form of a Semitic name, either *qlwp'* or *qlwpw*. That does not take sufficient account of a natural tendency for Semitic names to be assimilated to already existing Graeco-Roman names if they were near enough in form.

136. Lüdemann, *Resurrection*, 145.

137. One needs to recall here the oft-cited summary of Moses' legislation given by the first-century Jewish historian, Josephus, in *Ant.* 4.219: 'From women let no evidence be accepted, because of the levity and temerity of their sex' (translation LCL; an elaboration on Deut. 17.6; 19.15 that is paralleled in later rabbinic texts: cf. Jeremias, *Jerusalem*, 374); cf. also von Campenhausen, 'Easter Events', 73; Hengel, 'Maria', 246.

138. Lieu, 'Testimony', 42.

139. See further Ch. 6 (a).

140. Strauss, *Life*, 715. Jeremias, *Theology*, 304–5, follows the suggestion of Benoit, 'Marie-Madeleine', that John 20 preserves a version of the discovery of the empty tomb earlier than that found in Mark 16.1–8, a version in which Mary Magdalene alone discovers the empty tomb; this would be more convincing were it not for the 'we' of 20.2, which may suggest a deletion of other witnesses (for dramatic effect?) rather than a harmonization with the Synoptic accounts, for in the latter case why should the other women not also have been mentioned in v. 1? Mary only needs to be there alone for the encounter with Jesus in v. 14.

141. Cf. Grass, *Ostergeschehen*, 55, on the tensions between vv. 2 and 11.

142. Cf. Hengel, 'Maria', 251.

143. Lüdemann, *Resurrection*, 118.

144. Cf. von Campenhausen, 'Easter Events', 77–87, but contrast Grass, *Ostergeschehen*, 116.

145. Lüdemann, *Resurrection*, 32; cf. Broer, *Urgemeinde*, 291; contrast, e.g., Fischer, *Ostergeschehen*, 50.

146. Fischer, *Ostergeschehen*, 27.

147. Matthew and Mark, however, only mention the presence of women (Matt. 27.55–56; Mark 15.40–41). Pheme Perkins notes the parallel of Mark 6.29: despite similar perils involved in being associated with an executed leader, John the Baptist's disciples retrieved his body for burial ('Resurrection', 431–2).

148. And Marxsen is prepared to dismiss the entire tradition of a flight to Galilee (*Mark the Evangelist*, 81–2 n. 101).

149. Lohfink, 'Ablauf, 163.

150. Cf. Theissen and Merz, *Jesus*, 498–9; Merklein, *Auferstehung*, 18. On the other hand Vollenweider, 'Ostern', 36–7, lists the following factors which might have contributed to the subsequent evolving of such a tradition: 1. the traditional role of women in burial rites (although Jesus had apparently already been buried, by a man or men, at least after a fashion); 2. the role of socially inferior persons in receiving revelations is a regular *topos* of biblical, Jewish and Christian literature; 3. the same argument about 'poor witnesses' could apply in many other miracle stories of the ancient world.

151. Cf. Blinzler, 'Grablegung', 93–6; R. E. Brown, *Death*, 1207–11.

152. E.g. Crossan, 'Tomb', 152 (however, for him it is the Roman soldiers who buried Jesus, though this is historically less likely than the Jewish authorities, who might well be concerned about matters of defilement). But cf. Broer, *Urgemeinde*, 205–29. He then argues (250–63) that Acts 13.29b is to be attributed to Luke's redaction and not to any independent tradition.

153. That would only really make sense according to John's chronology of the Passion, according to which Jesus dies on the eve of Passover, rather than holding his last meal on that evening as in the Synoptic accounts. It would at any rate be serious enough to defile the land on the eve of Passover.

There is a noticeable tendency in the Gospel accounts to claim Joseph as a follower of Jesus: for Mark he is merely one who was awaiting God's kingdom (15.43; cf. Luke 23.52), but for Matthew and John he is a disciple (Matt. 27.57; John 19.38: a secret one) and for the Gospel of Peter a friend of Jesus (2.3 – he was also a friend of Pilate! Cf. 6.23). Brown, *Death*, 1223, speculates that he may have become a follower of Jesus after the resurrection, but that remains nothing more than speculation.

154. Cf. Grass, *Ostergeschehen*, 181.
155. Brown, *Death*, 1210.
156. *Pace*, e.g., Nauck, 'Bedeutung', 261–2.
157. In Eusebius., *Hist. eccl.* 2.23.18.
158. Jeremias, *Heiligengräber*, 145.
159. Taylor, 'Golgotha', esp. 196–7, revising her earlier *Christians*. She notes that *Ep. Apost.* 9 places the burial of Jesus at the 'place of a skull'; she also appeals to the details of the finding of the tomb in Gospel of Peter 13.55–56, but the verb παρακύπτειν, 'stoop', to which she appeals as evidence for the value of this Gospel's traditions, is also found in Luke 24.12 and John 20.5, 11. She also surmises that this larger area known as Golgotha, in which the crucifixion also occurred, may have included a common burial pit (188).
160. Betz, 'Problem', 246.
161. Dunn, *Evidence*, 68; cf. *Jesus*, 120.
162. Justin, *Dial.* 78.5.
163. Origen, *Contra Celsum* 1.51.
164. Jerome, *Ep.* 46.11.1; 58.3.5; 108.10.2; 147.5.
165. Cf. Brown, *Death*, 1251: Mark is only interested in their observing and makes no mention, for instance, of their lamenting, as one might expect.
166. Carnley, *Structure*, 58.
167. The persistent tradition that something happened 'on the third day' is hard to reconcile with Margaret Barker's thesis that Jesus' 'resurrection' in fact took place in the visionary experience at his baptism (*The Risen Lord*). Even if 'resurrection' could mean that (would Paul describe himself as 'risen' because of the experience referred to in II Cor 12?), it is asking rather much to claim that Jesus from then on knew himself to be 'the Lord', when this insight has left so little trace in the Gospel accounts. (Or is one to treat the Fourth Gospel as 'historical' in this sense? But then why are the Synoptics so reticent?)
168. Dunn, *Evidence*, 74. He refers particularly to Luke 24.39 and I Cor. 15.50 respectively. See also Grass, *Ostergeschehen*, 40; Lorenzen, *Resurrection*, 80; A. F. Segal, 'Paul's Thinking', 419 (who even entertains the notion that the Gospel accounts were written as polemic against Paul's notion). In this, at least, Dunn and J. L. Houlden are at one, for the latter also asserts, in the unpublished paper referred to at the beginning of this book (n. 2), that 'it is not possible to say, with anything approaching precision, exactly what this resurrection is

supposed to have been . . . the claims [of the New Testament writers] do not tally'.

169. Strauss, *Life*, 735.

170. Cf. Gal 1.14; Phil 3.6.

171. At least Jesus' family are not mentioned among his followers and supporters during his ministry, and if the NEB is correct in its translation of Mark 3.21, οἱ παρ᾽ αὐτοῦ (contrast RSV), then their view of him and his activities was an unfavourable one: 'when his family heard of this, they set out to take charge of him; for people were saying that he was out of his mind', or perhaps even 'set out to seize him; for they [i.e. his family] were saying that he was out of his mind'. The apocryphal Gospel of the Hebrews (Schneemelcher, §7) is the first extant record of an appearance of the risen Jesus to James, but also seems to assume that he was present at the Last Supper.

172. Dunn, *Evidence*, 74; cf. Marxsen, 'Significance', e.g. 28–9.

173. Lohfink, 'Ablauf', 168–9.

174. Pannenberg, *Jesus*, 77, rightly distinguishes 'the resurrection of the dead in the Christian hope for the future from those resuscitations of corpses which are otherwise reported occasionally in ancient literature as especially marvellous miracles' – and Jesus' resurrection was seen as part of that final resurrection (cf. id., *Syst Theol* 2, 404).

175. Friedrich, 'Auferweckung', 335; cf. Vögtle and Pesch, *Osterglauben*, 111–12.

176. Müller, *Entstehung*, 55–60, has most recently shown how far from dominant this expectation was in the Judaism of that time (contrast Lindars, 'Resurrection', 121).

177. So Perry, *Enigma*, esp. 237–8, argues that there was a decisive shift after a period of forty days from a 'physical body' type of appearance to one of a 'heavenly glory'. In other words, the nature of the resurrection appearances did indeed vary and varied drastically. What Luke describes as the ascension marks the transition from the one type to the other. In a somewhat similar fashion Lindblom, *Gesichte*, 104–13, distinguishes the earthly 'Christ-epiphanies' that occurred before Pentecost from the heavenly 'Christophanies' that occurred afterwards (amongst which he numbers the appearances to the more than five hundred, James, the apostles and Paul) – yet what reliable evidence is there in the sources for any such distinction and any such change at that point of time? There is the ascension, but even if one does not question that as a peculiarly Lukan theologoumenon, what grounds has one for assigning all these 'Christ-epiphanies' to the post-ascension phase?

178. The same applies at the beginning of the Gospels of Matthew and Luke: before the point at which Mark takes up his story (the baptism of John) the other two diverge sharply; thereafter they have far more in common.

179. Cf. further in Ch. 7 (c) below.

180. Cf. Strauss, *Life*, 740: 'when Paul . . . places the Christophany which occurred to himself in the same series with the appearances of Jesus in the days after his resurrection: this authorizes us, so far as nothing else stands in the way of such an inference, to conclude that, for aught the apostle knew, those earlier appearances were of the same nature with the one experienced by himself' (similarly Lüdemann, *Resurrection*, 30). But Ohlig, 'Thesen', 87–8, questions whether that was in fact the case (however Paul understood it).

181. Cf. Carnley, *Structure*, 237.

182. Cf. Carnley, *Structure*, 207–9, 219; also W. Michaelis, 'ὁράω', *TDNT* 5, 1967, 315–67, here 358; but cf. also Vögtle, 'Artikulierung', 30–1.

183. Cf. also Gal 1.16: God decided ἀποκαλύψαι τὸν υἱὸν αὐτοῦ ἐν ἐμοί.

184. Lüdemann, *Resurrection*, e.g. 54, 69; cf. Fischer, *Ostergeschehen*, 78.

185. This distinction is above all associated with the name of Hans Grass, who insisted that the visions in question were 'objective', induced by God, not by the psyche of the disciples and Paul (see especially *Ostergeschehen*, 247–9). It is a distinction also adopted by S. T. Davis, '"Seeing"', who distinguishes here between 'seeing' and 'visualizing', and interestingly links the necessity of 'visualizing' as opposed to normal 'seeing' to the nature of the object thus 'visualized'. This is 'not the sort of object that human eyes, working normally and unaided by God, can see' (128; and yet Davis himself opts for 'seeing' as more appropriate in the case of the resurrection appearances). Is something similar also implied by Cupitt and Moule's talk of 'veridical religious experiences' (Cupitt, 'The Resurrection', 38)? Finally G. Lohfink should be mentioned, with his insistence that a 'genuine vision' consists both of a human act and a divine ('Ablauf', 167).

Pannenberg, *Jesus*, 95, is correct to point out that the word 'vision' may tell us something about 'the subjective mode of experience, not something about the reality of an event experienced in this form'. Coakley, however, is also right to draw attention to problems in Pannenberg's following comments, in which he argues that the 'psychiatric concept of vision' is 'primarily derived from the investigation of mentally ill persons' and 'cannot be applied without further ado to phenomena in the history of religions', particularly, in the case of the resurrection appearances, if a 'psychological event . . . without a corresponding extrasubjective reality' is meant. For Pannenberg would not wish to deny that Paul had visions, as he says he had (II Cor. 12.1), and Coakley questions whether Pannenberg would regard the apostle as mentally ill ('Resurrection', 97). But some psychiatrists might well, like the Roman governor Festus according to Acts 26.24, consider Paul mentally unstable, so that Coakley's argument here is more an *ad hominem* one, the *homo* being in this case Pannenberg.

186. Marxsen, 'Significance', 29. Carnley too (e.g. *Structure*, 71, 83) voices his puzzlement with the application of this distinction.

187. Küng, *Credo*, 108; cf. Hoffmann, 'Auferstehung', 494.

188. Bartsch's observation is also to be noted here, namely that the formula with ὤφθη was never used of prophetic visions, but of God's saving presence in the time of the patriarchs, of the wilderness wanderings and of the kings David and Solomon ('Inhalt', 835), and, with a corresponding change of tense, of the eschatological time of salvation. It is, however, otherwise with the form ἑόρακα or ἑώρακα: 'Inhalt', 829–30.

189. Ohlig, 'Thesen', 86.

190. Similarly Cupitt, *Christ*, 165–6, argues that their recognition of Jesus was of the same order as the assertion of the identity of Edward Heath and the Prime Minister; it was a case of seeing that the Jesus whom they had known was the Lord.

191. And when they talk of their 'dreams' (as Martin Luther King did), then one is not necessarily to think of insights that came to them in their sleep.

192. E.g. Philo, *Deus imm.* 144: τὸ ὁρατικὸν γένος.

193. Cf. Wedderburn, *Baptism*, 254–66.

194. Acts 26.13–14 is not explicit, but presumably implies that Paul's companions also saw the light if they too fell to the ground.

195. So, e.g., Hick, *Metaphor*, 25. For this reason it seems to me questionable whether Dunn's more complex account of the conceptualization of the resurrection of Jesus in which he detects three stages (a physical raising of Jesus' body to heaven, a move away from the idea of the restoration of the flesh in Paul's account, and then a swing back to a physical view) is nearly so likely (*Jesus*, 120–1).

196. For a similar emphasis that the risen Christ was no ghost cf. *Epistula apostolorum* §11 (Schneemelcher, 1, 211). Contrast Paul's readi-

ness to call the risen Christ a 'spirit' in I Cor. 15.45. Betz shows how the (often potentially dangerous) presence of the spirits, πνεύματα, of the dead near graves was a standard feature of folk religion in those days, and sees in Luke's account a deliberate rejection of this misunderstanding of the resurrection ('Problem', 247–50).

197. A tradition going back at least to Trito-Isaiah (cf 65.17); contrast the discussion in Philo's *On the Eternity of the World*.

198. It is also an attractive suggestion that Paul's ultimate hope for Israel in Rom. 11.25–32 is likewise coloured by Paul's own experience of how God had brought one wayward Jew to faith in Christ: cf. Hofius, 'Evangelium', 320/198.

199. Pokorný, *Genesis*, 124–5. How far his own phrase and category 'eschatological visions' (127) is any improvement is questionable; to my mind it tells us nothing about the nature of the experiences involved, but only classifies their content and interprets it within a certain theological framework.

200. So Vollenweider, 'Ostern', 39, describes the category of visions as '*schwankender Boden*', shaky ground.

201. Lüdemann, in contrast to others (he cites as an example Eugen Drewermann; on Drewermann's attitude to historical criticism see Frey, *Drewermann*, 172–84), clearly sees his use of psychology as complementary to historical criticism, and not as an alternative (*Resurrection*, 7). Müller, too, thinks it impossible to disregard psychological factors if one wishes to throw any light on these events (and adds that it is implied in the attitude of some that these events should remain in darkness: *Entstehung*, 77). And that is in principle correct: the historian can and should seek the aid of any means available that may help to explain why the human actors in history have behaved as they have done. Thus to Lindemann's question in his review of Lüdemann (p. 505) whether it is legitimate to want to know more about Paul's religious life than his writings themselves tell us I would want to reply: 'In principle, yes, if we can or could.' F. C. Baur, on the other hand, roundly declared that 'no psychological analysis can penetrate into the inner, mental process through which the disciples' unbelief . . . was turned into belief in [Jesus'] resurrection' (*Christenthum*, 40). My criticisms here focus rather on evidence which seems to point in a very different direction, namely Paul's own utterances. In that respect the 'conflict' which D. F. Strauss saw earlier in Paul's situation, and which Zager, 'Auferstehung', perhaps rather misleadingly compares with Lüdemann's accounts without fully noting the differences, may be truer

to the texts, the conflict namely between Paul's loyalty to Jewish traditions which he saw being undermined by the Christian movement, and
that which he nevertheless found appealing in their lives (cf. *Life*, 741).
K.-H. Ohlig's criticism is rather different: psychogenic visions such as
Lüdemann postulates are generally characterized by non-traditional or
highly personal elements. What the witnesses to Jesus' resurrection
'saw' stemmed, however, from the symbols and theology of the apocalyptic tradition ('Thesen', 88).

202. It is also the line taken about the same time by Michael Goulder
('Jesus of Nazareth'), with often very similar arguments and analogies.

203. Lüdemann, *Resurrection*, 83.

204. But cf. Doughty, 'Citizens'. I am not, however, fully persuaded
by Doughty's arguments for the inauthenticity of this section of the
letter or by the rationale offered for the composition of this supposedly
pseudonymous piece. Nor am I persuaded, on the other hand, that Rom
7.7–25 is simply a retrospective analysis of Paul's own past experience
of the Jewish law, as Lüdemann argues (more fully in his 'Karfreitag',
33–40); the account is rather to be seen as a composite picture of
the human self, unaided by the Spirit of God, as it is confronted by
the command of God. This picture contains elements drawn from
scriptural exegesis (the Adam story) and from Paul's view of the history
of Israel, as in 1.18–32. Rom. 7.7–25 describes the experience of
humanity in general, however much it may draw, *inter alia*, upon Paul's
own experience, his own past seen in the light of his later experience as
a Christian. If a psychological explanation is to be sought to account for
the conversion of this particular individual, Paul, then it is surely more
convincing to look to experiences which are more peculiarly and
specifically his, like his leading role in persecuting the early Christians,
as the trigger for this change. In that respect Strauss's account
mentioned above, which is at the same time a second strand in
Lüdemann's explanation, seems better suited to account for the crisis in
this one individual and very specific life, for Lüdemann not only
appeals to Rom. 7 as evidence of Paul's unconscious difficulties with the
law, but also reckons with Paul's 'unconscious Christianity' which
caused him to be drawn to Jesus and the early Christian movement and
yet at the same time to recoil with ferocious violence from this object of
his unconscious longings. But Phil.3 must remain the Achilles' heel of
Lüdemann's account, and Lindemann's question in his review (508) is
a legitimate one, namely how one can justify the difference in the treatment of this passage compared to that of the rest of Paul's writings.

205. Lüdemann's psychological explanation of Peter's experience is rather different: it arose out of an experience of grieving, and a grieving exacerbated by guilt-feelings due to his denial of Jesus; Lüdemann here compares studies of instances of grieving which have resulted in the grieving person seeming to see the dead person once more (*Resurrection,* 97–100; cf. the similar suggestion in Müller, *Entstehung,* 68; Vollenweider, 'Ostern', 41; also *CIL* VI, 3.21521 = Berger and Colpe, *Textbuch,* §134); where Lüdemann cites the findings of a Harvard study, Goulder mentions the similar findings of a Welsh doctor ('Jesus of Nazareth', 60; see also Cupitt, *Christ,* 144, on the study of Gorer; for an altogether more sympathetic and constructive evaluation of such phenomena cf. Griffin, 'Life', 104; yet if one believes that such visions of a dead person occur more generally, then the vision of Jesus ceases to have any unique significance). That the guilt-feelings in the case of Peter and the disciples stemmed ultimately from deep-seated tensions in the circle of the disciples which are reflected in the 'Satanswort' of Mark 8.33 (124) is an unnecessary further step in Lüdemann's argument; the disciples' failures during Jesus' last days would have been sufficient. With Lüdemann's attempt at a psychological explanation one may contrast Marxsen's attitude (*Resurrection,* 127): 'The way in which Peter's faith was sparked off after Good Friday is unimportant.' What will not do is to compare 'near-death' experiences, as Hick does (*Metaphor,* 24), in which people near death but subsequently resuscitated have reported an experience of seeing something like a bright light or brightly shining figure (which Christians may often identify with Christ); for there is no suggestion that those early Christians like Peter and Paul were themselves near death.

206. NHC III 91, 10, 13, tr. D. M. Parrott in Robinson, *Library,* 222.

207. Gilmour, 'Christophany', traces this suggestion back to Weisse, *Geschichte,* 2, 417; cf. also, more recently, Jeremias, *Theology,* 308; Lüdemann, *Resurrection,* 100–8 (who classifies it as an example of 'mass-ecstasy'); Wedderburn, 'Traditions', 52.

208. Cf. also II Cor. 3.17.

209. Grass, *Ostergeschehen,* 226–32.

210. Ibid., 198–207.

211. Barker, *The Risen Lord,* 5, does, however, reckon it amongst them; cf. also Lindars, 'Resurrection', 127.

212. Cf. Hoffmann, 'Auferstehung', 492.

213. Grass, *Ostergeschehen,* 241.

214. Dunn, *Jesus,* 103.

215. Similarly Robinson, 'Jesus', 10, draws attention to the way in which what he terms 'luminous appearances' continued and became subject to an 'increasingly dubious interpretation' ('dubious' at least in the eyes of the orthodox). Lohfink, on the hand, thinks that no distinction is to be drawn between these earlier visionary experiences and later ecstatic and visionary experiences in the early church: 'Ablauf', 165.

216. Robinson, 'Jesus', 24.

217. Davies, 'Vitality', 212–13; the talk of 'rebounding violence or conquest' here does not seem to me a particularly well-chosen formulation.

218. Carnley, *Structure*, 249 n. 31, his italics.

219. Particularly puzzling is the reference to the 'experience of the Spirit as a post-mortem event' (*Structure*, 260), unless by that is meant '*post mortem Christi*'!

220. Pannenberg, 'Revelation', 128.

221. Carnley, *Structure*, 262.

222. Schweitzer, *Quest*, 397: 'Jesus means something to our world because a mighty spiritual force streams forth from Him and flows through our time also'; cf. 399–400.

223. Tillich, *Systematic Theology* 2,156–7.

224. Verweyen, '"Auferstehung"', 115.

225. Cf. Wedderburn, 'Problem', esp. 240–1.

226. E.g. Craig, 'Historicity', 40–1; Nauck, 'Bedeutung', 247–8 (he also claims that Paul's whole argument presupposes this).

227. Merklein, *Auferstehung*, 5.

228. Lüdemann, *Resurrection*, 46; cf. also Grobel, 'Revelation', 174–5.

229. Cf. Wedderburn, *Baptism*, 368–9.

230. Selby, *Look*, 124, his italics; cf. also 85, 153, 164.

231. Ibid., 45–6; he rightly says that if this shift in meaning is being used, the shift should be clearly stated; are we to assume that since he does not plainly say that this is what he is doing, he does not intend to make this move?

232. Moltmann, *Theology*, 164.

233. Marxsen, *Resurrection*, 126. Compare with this John Kloppenborg's conclusion that for the Sayings Gospel (i.e. Q) 'Jesus arose in his words' ('"Easter Faith"', 92).

234. Lindemann observes (in his review of Lüdemann, 511) that the Easter message of the first Christians did not suggest that forgiveness could be experienced through the resurrection, but the message of

the risen Jesus to Peter comes near to that (Mark 16.7; cf. John 21.15–17).

235. Lüdemann, *Resurrection*, 90–1 and 177 (he refers here, as often, to the work of Emanuel Hirsch, *Osterglaube*, 74–80, 206–22).

236. Similar dangers perhaps attend the German '*Osterglaube*'.

237. If it is merely a faith that something will happen in the future, then the situation is somewhat different: one has to ask what are the warrants for supposing that. If the warrant is in fact that something of the sort has already happened, as in this case, then the criteria are in part the same as those for determining whether something is already the case. The difference is that one must in addition show that what is already the case, particularly if it is something exceptional, warrants the expectation of something similar in the future.

238. Wiles, 'Pillar', 124–5.

239. Coakley, 'Resurrection', 88.

240. I therefore have difficulty in seeing why Alan Padgett can so curtly dismiss Lüdemann's account as 'patently absurd' ('Advice', 304).

241. Müller, *Entstehung*, 61.

242. Broer, '"Seid stets bereit"', 56.

243. Wilckens, 'Auferstehung Jesu', 117.

244. Troeltsch, 'Methode', esp. 731–4.

245. Habermas and Flew, *Did Jesus Rise?*, 33, cf. 61; Cupitt, 'The Resurrection', 35.

246. Luz, 'Aufregung', 479.

247. Lüdemann, 'Karfreitag', 27; Luz had in fact argued that Lüdemann's certainty that Jesus' corpse had simply decomposed stemmed from the application of the principle of analogy: it is our experience that corpses decompose (which is not quite universally true – there is the practice of mummification or embalming; but then Jesus was no Pharaoh or hero of a victorious revolution, but a condemned criminal).

248. Swinburne, 'Evidence', 200 (his italics).

249. Morgan, 'Flesh', 9 – the 'reverence' here would, at any rate, be on my part a reluctance to force the data to say more than they in fact can.

250. Cf. Broer, '"Seid stets bereit"', 48: for many the resurrection has to fulfil the role which in the past was filled by the Gospels as a whole, but in particular by the miracles, resurrection and virgin birth together.

251. Kaufman, *Mystery*, 19–20.

252. Particularly through the work of Robinson and Koester, *Trajectories*.

253. Another popular technical term today is *Wirkungsgeschichte*, sometimes translated 'history of influence' (as, for instance, in English translations of the Evangelisch-Katholische Kommentare, which regularly contain sections on the '*Wirkungsgeschichte*' of particular passages), in which an account is given of the way in which a text, large or small, has been understood, applied and appropriated by its readers down the centuries.

254. Cf. Koester and Robinson, *Trajectories*, 14: 'To be sure, the term *trajectory* may suggest too much determinative control at the point of departure, the angle at which the movement was launched, the torque of the initial thrust. . . . [Whereas the] future is open . . . we move among a plurality of spinning worlds, with conflicting gravitational fields pulling upon us. In this sense one is free to redefine one's trajectory . . . one's freedom [consists] in knowing the direction of the trajectory along which one is being borne, assessing alternate movements, and then taking relevant steps to redirect one's course towards a better outcome.'

255. Thus there is a good deal to be said for the translation of 'trajectory' by '*Entwicklungslinien*', 'lines of development', in the German edition of Robinson and Koester's book. This was the preference expressed by a former colleague of mine with much experience of the trajectories of little white balls on their way to and/or past small holes in the ground, and I can certainly see the benefit in this instance: 'lines of development' are far less predictable and, more important still, can fork out in different directions. Cf. the recent example of D. M. Hay's conclusion, that the members of the 'Pauline school' 'did not feel constrained to move in a single direction in extending the apostle's legacy' ('Pauline Theology', 189–90).

256. One only needs to look at the varying interpretations of the phrase 'the kingdom of God', so often used by Jesus, along with the very different uses made of his teaching about it, or at the history of interpretation of a text like the Sermon on the Mount, to see this point.

257. That, too, has its analogies in Paul's handling of the Old Testament; see Wedderburn, 'Paul'.

258. It may be correct to see here a different perception of the role of the Paraclete over against 14.26, where the Paraclete reminds the disciples of all that Jesus has already told them (cf., e.g., Becker, *JohEv*, 595; Müller, 'Parakletenvorstellung', 74).

259. Cf. e.g. Dietzfelbinger, 'Paraklet', 404–5: 'The evangelist wants his word *about* Jesus to be seen as the *word of Jesus* which is to be spoken today. . . The Gospel of John sees itself as the word of the Paraclete' (his italics; this formulation is to be preferred to Bultmann's identification of the Paraclete and the word of the community: 'Eschatology', 177); on the attendant risks of this procedure cf. 406–8.

260. This is probably reflected in Irenaeus, *Haer.* 3.11.9 (ed. Harvey 3.11.12: Harvey sees the Montanists as rejecting the Fourth Gospel because it promised the Paraclete to the apostles whereas Montanus claimed it for himself); Schnackenburg, *JohEv* 1, 200, notes that, along with the Book of Revelation, the Fourth Gospel 'also suffered from [the Montanists'] misguided appeal to the Johannine doctrine of the Spirit' and interprets Irenaeus' reference as being rather to opponents of Montanism who went too far in their opposition!

261. Kaufman, *Mystery*, 62.

262. This is a theme that I have also explored briefly in 'Colossians', 64–71.

263. Cf., e.g. S. Brown, 'Reader Response', esp. 232: 'If meaning is actually generated by the experience of reading, rather than residing "in" the text, then we must accept a Copernican revolution in interpretive theory. For the reading experience is guided not by the "intention of the author", to which appeal is so often made, but by the interest of the reader.' That is all very well as long as (a) it is recognized that a given text can have several meanings and that one of those will usually be at least one meaning intended by the original author (it is an irritating feature of Morgan and Barton, *Biblical Criticism*, esp. 258, that this work continues to talk of 'the meaning' of a text, a phrase which seems to stem from an outdated hermeneutic, and to apply it to a literary criticism which should surely recognize a plurality of meanings – as the quotation of Via's reference to 'a multiplicity of possible meanings' on this same page shows); (b) for many who read the biblical text their 'interest' is going to be in hearing what that original author was saying; (c) the meaning for readers in different contexts, situations and centuries will of course differ; and (d) it is to be asked of what significance the 'context' of a text is here, and whether that 'context' is purely literary and textual or also includes the historical setting of the text (as well as of its readers then and down the centuries).

264. Cf. Rom. 4.24; 8.11; 10.9; I Cor. 6.14; 15.12, 15, 20; II Cor. 4.14; Gal. 1.1; I Thess. 1.10; 4.14. Apart from the variation in the designation of the one raised (Jesus, Christ, the Lord, etc.), it is to be

noticed that this statement can take an active or a passive form ('God raised'; 'Christ was raised', the latter in I Cor. 15 alone, presumably under the influence of the credal formulation of v. 4; but cf. v. 15) or an intransitive one ('Jesus was raised', only in the double formulation 'died and rose' in I Thess 4.14, which is also unusual in that the verb ἀνίστημι is used, not ἐγείρω). It is widely supposed that the double statement of I Cor. 15.3–4, involving both the death and resurrection of Jesus, is a later development, and that credal statements about Jesus' resurrection originally circulated independently, perhaps in the form 'God raised Jesus (from the dead)' (it is also to be noted that 'from the dead' is omitted in I Cor 15.4). Cf., e.g., Kramer, *Christ*, 28–33; Wengst, *Formeln*, 27–33 (also in *TRE* 13, 392).

265. Pauline chronology (and indeed that of the death of Jesus) presents many problems, but too late a date for Paul's conversion creates difficulties with Gal. 1.18; 2.1; cf. Wedderburn, 'Chronologies'. Lüdemann's acceptance of a date between 30 and 33 for the rise of the traditions contained here (*Resurrection*, 38) is thus by no means implausible. And yet, early and highly valuable as this tradition may be, one needs to treat with caution statements like von Campenhausen's: this tradition 'meets all the demands of historical reliability that could possibly be made of such a text as things stand' ('Easter Events', 44).

Although the formula here may be early, the evidence for an Aramaic original is hardly overwhelming. It may, therefore, be likelier that this tradition arose in a Greek-speaking milieu, though in one strongly influenced by the Greek of the LXX. But see the survey of the pros and cons here in Lehmann, *Auferweckt*, 97–115. If Jerusalem is a likely place of origin, as many suppose, then that would point to the circle of the Hellenists there as a likely candidate for the authors of this tradition.

266. The form ὤφθη may be used absolutely in Rev. 1.1.19; 12.1, 3 (a usage which Bartsch explains as due to the fact that the seer is here describing, not a vision given to himself alone, but a revelation granted to all, so that it is superfluous to name the recipients: 'Inhalt', 811), but usually it is followed by a dative in the LXX, e.g. in the theophanies in Genesis (cf., however, Gen. 17.7: καὶ ὤφθη ἡ δόξα κυρίου; cf. Bartsch, 'Inhalt', 820–7; Hahn, *Titles*, 175.

267. Cf. Bartsch, 'Inhalt', 804–5; Hahn, *Titles*, 179; Hoffmann, 'Auferstehung', 493; Lüdemann, *Resurrection*, 35; Müller, *Entstehung*, 16–17.

268. *Pace* Wilckens, 'Ursprung', 163; cf. Lüdemann, 'Karfreitag', 22.

269. It may be asked whether this list is in chronological order (so von Campenhausen, 'Easter Events', 44) or rather whether Paul thought it was. The use of ἔπειτα and εἶτα and ἔσχατον in vv. 23, 24, 26 suggests that he understood it so (so also Grass, *Ostergeschehen*, 96–8; Lehmann, *Auferweckt*, 31), but, particularly if here he has gathered together disparate traditions, that is no guarantee that the appearances were in fact in this sequence. Paul may have been none too clear about the order, except that he was the last, and this was perhaps held against him by his opponents and critics. At any rate Strauss already saw that any attempt to coordinate this listing with the accounts of appearances in the Gospels led to results which he described as 'ridiculous' (*Life*, 723, 726).

270. Dodd, 'Appearances', 28; Hahn, *Titles*, 175.

271. So, e.g., von Campenhausen, 'Easter Events', 44; Hahn, *Titles*, 175.

272. *Pace* Wilckens, 'Ursprung', 152.

273. That it was *Christ* who was also raised may be due to the combination of a statement about the resurrection with one about Christ's death. We saw that earlier statements about the resurrection probably referred to God's raising *Jesus*.

274. Albertz, 'Formengeschichte', 265.

275. This oblique reference is in itself puzzling: did not Luke know of a story of Peter's experience of which he could tell? The disputed text of 24.12 (a 'Western non-interpolation'), which is so strongly reminiscent of John 20.6, is no help, since it mentions only a seeing of the grave-clothes (ὀθόνια, as in John 20.6) and no appearance of Jesus himself. Peter's response is not faith, but wonder (contrast the beloved disciple in John 20.8). Has Luke suppressed details of this appearance as too unavoidably bound up with a Galilean setting to fit his Jerusalem-centred account (so von Campenhausen, 'Easter Events', 49f.; Lohfink, 'Ablauf', 164)? What is also surprising is that the two disciples on the way to Emmaus tell of 'certain' (plural) of their number who had gone to the tomb and had verified the women's account (v. 24) – and that despite the rather dismissive (but nevertheless quite probably ironic) v. 11! And even Ignatius, *Smyrn.* 3.2, which Lüdemann mentions in this connection (*Resurrection*, 85), mentions only an appearance to those with Peter, not just Peter alone (similarly John 21.1–14). Moreover, accounts which appear in a pre-Easter setting but which in the eyes of some are post-Easter stories that have been projected back in to the life of Jesus (e.g. Mark 9.2–8 parr.; Luke

5.1–11; Matt. 16.17–19) cannot count as appearances to Peter *alone*, for in these scenes he is always in the company of other disciples, even when in some cases he is the main *dramatis persona*. It seems to me to go well beyond the evidence to suppose that Mark has added Peter's two companions to the story of the transfiguration (*pace* Robinson, 'Jesus', 9); such trios – and Jesus also appears with two others here – are a regular feature of such stories (cf. Gen. 18.2). The appearance to Peter *alone*, which plays such an important role in many reconstructions of the rise of belief in Jesus' resurrection (e.g., as already mentioned, for Marxsen, *Resurrection*, 95–6; contrast Müller, *Entstehung*, 20–1), proves to be extremely – and surprisingly – elusive. Despite that, it plays an almost equally important part in Lüdemann's account as, along with Paul's experience, an 'original' event, upon which the others are to be regarded as 'dependent' (*Resurrection*, 95). One reason for that is perhaps, as Vollenweider suggests ('Ostern', 42), the rarity of group-visions in the history of religions (although cf. the example cited by Broer, '"Seid stets bereit"', 55 – the alleged collective vision of Niklaus von der Flüe). Nevertheless, as Grass notes (*Ostergeschehen*, 107), it seems rather to have been the appearance to the Twelve which was of greatest importance to the early church, of greater importance than all others, including the appearance to Peter.

276. §7 in Schneemelcher, Vol. 1 (quoted from Jerome, *De viris illustribus* 2 [*PL* 23, 641B–643A]; cf. de Santos, 38).

277. Cf. Perkins, *Resurrection*, 89.

278. Rightly, therefore, Pannenberg (*Jesus*, 89) contends that 'the intention of this enumeration [in vv. 5–8] is clearly to give proof by means of witnesses for the facticity of Jesus' resurrection'. That is not quite the same, however, as Bultmann's claim, over against Karl Barth, that Paul seeks here 'to make the resurrection credible as an objective historical fact' ('Resurrection', 83) – for one thing, 'objectivity' is not at issue here.

279. Dodd, 'Appearances', 30.

280. Cf. Wedderburn, *Baptism*, 6–37; 'Problem'.

281. Dahl, *Resurrection*, 37, cites as the 'traditional view' the belief 'that the physical organism which we now possess, namely the body, is to be restored fully and completely at the Last Day' and finds this enshrined in the Fourth Lateran Council's declaration (in 1215) that '*omnes homines in fine sæculi cum suis propriis resurgent corporibus quæ nunc gestant*' (cap. *Firmiter*). But he finds just the same stress in the Anglican Thirty-Nine Articles (§4), in Luther's *Small Catechism* (Q. 195 [I have

been unable to check this reference]; at any rate Luther criticizes the phrase *'resurrectio carnis'* in his *Large Catechism*: see *Bekenntnisschriften*, 659: Art. 3 §60]) and in Calvin's *Institutes* (3.25.8). To these may be added Calvin's *Catechism* Q. 108 as quoted by Barth, *Faith*, 139 – and, although the *Catechism* speaks of 'resurrection of the body', Barth speaks consistently of the 'flesh', as the translator notes (136 n. 1), as also in *Dogmatik*, 180 (but not in the ET!). See also Badham, 'Meaning', 23–4, 26.

282. Kelly, *Creeds*, 165; cf. Robinson, 'Jesus', 16, 20. However, many Gnostics, doubtless anxious to seem still to belong to the Christian fold, did speak of 'resurrection', even though it proved difficult to accommodate this term, with its usual corporeal connotations, within their world-view; cf. Wedderburn, *Baptism*, 212–18.

283. Tertullian, *De res. mort.* 50 (2, 992–3).

284. Cf. Dunn, *Partings*, 254–8: he concentrates here solely upon the question of 'priesthood and ministry', but it seems to me that there are a number of other areas of early Christian life and thought where one could speak of some early Christians abandoning an earlier, less characteristically Jewish position in favour of a reversion to their Jewish heritage, and the concept of 'resurrection' may well be one of them.

285. Irenaeus, *Haer.* 1.30.13 (ed. Harvey 1.28.7).

286. Cf. Wedderburn, 'Body', 92–4.

287. Epiphanius, *Panarion* 31.7.6, tr. Foerster, 237.

288. Cf. Lüdemann, *Resurrection*, 77f.

289. Cf. Grass, *Ostergeschehen*, 71: the critique of the evangelist is directed against the *demand* for such proofs. So Bultmann argues that Thomas's doubt is representative of the attitude of those who cannot believe without seeing wonders (John 4.48): just as wonders are a concession to human weakness, so the appearances of the risen Jesus are a concession to the weakness of the disciples. Basically there should be no need for them, the word of Jesus should be enough (*John*, 696).

It is also interesting that, in effect, Lindemann's explanation of the enigmatic ending of Mark's Gospel (see below) comes to much the same thing as John's depiction of this scene with Thomas: 'faith in Jesus Christ is [for Mark] not the result of a seeing of the risen one . . . Faith in the sense of Mark's Gospel is the result of hearing the message that the crucified one is risen (16.6)' ('Osterbotschaft', 317).

290. Cf. Verweyen, 'Sache', 76: the appearances in Luke and John give the impression of concessions to weakness of faith.

291. Selby, *Look*, 167, 174.

292. Ayer, *Concept*, 82–128, here 115–16; Nielsen, 'Faces', 12–19. See also, on the whole range of philosophical problems touched on in this section, Flew, *Logic*.

293. Cf. e.g. Küng, *Christian*, 351. As Cupitt notes (*Christ*, 141), 'our criteria for continuing personal identity necessarily include bodily continuity'.

294. See Geach, 'Immortality', esp. 28–9.

295. Nielsen, 'Faces', 3.

296. Muddimann, '"I Believe"', 135–6.

297. Badham, 'Meaning', 28, mentions the problem of the clothes worn by the risen Jesus in the appearance stories; that is perhaps even more of a problem than his brief discussion reveals, for Jesus had presumably little or nothing on when crucified. Hence the rationalist solution of H.E.G.Paulus, according to whom Jesus 'stripped off the grave-clothes and put on a gardener's dress which He managed to procure' and hence Mary of Magdala's mistake in John 20.15 (in Schweitzer, *Quest*, 54).

298. See the discussion in Flew, *Logic*, ch. 1, in particular his quotations from Augustine's *Enchiridion on Faith, Hope and Love*, where Augustine expects (ch. 87) that those deformed from birth will be restored to 'the normal shape of man' (whatever that might be!). And one might think it a wholly unnecessary sophistication when he affirms (*Civ. Dei* 22.15) that all will be raised neither young nor old but at the same age as Christ was at his passion.

299. Cf. Geach, 'Immortality', 18; Phillips, *Death*, 2–3.

300. Tillich, *Syst Theol* 2,155–6.

301. Vollenweider, 'Ostern', 52.

302. Hick, 'Life', esp. 2–4, and *Death*, 265–396. Cf. also Badham, 'God'; Griffin, 'Life'.

303. Hick, 'Life', 13; *Death*, 279–95, 399–422, 450–64.

304. Ryle, *Concept*, 15–16.

305. E.g. Phillips, *Death*, 44.

306. E.g. Fischer, *Ostergeschehen*, 52.

307. Although Linnemann, 'Markusschluss', argues that Mark originally ended with 16.1–8, followed by an equivalent of Matt. 28.16–17 and then Mark 16.15–20. But then why is this version of the ending contained in no text of Mark? And *is* either the vocabulary or the style of 16.15–20 particularly characteristic of Mark?

308. Creed, 'Ending', 5, referring to 'Conclusion'.

309. That is the conclusion reached, forcefully, by Aland, 'Bemerkungen' and 'Schluss'.

310. Cf. also the speechlessness of Joseph's brothers in Gen. 45.3, ἐταράχθησαν γάρ.

311. Cf. Magness, *Sense*.

312. Demetrius, *On Style*, §253, tr. D. C. Innes, W. R. Roberts.

313. Cf. Bultmann, *History*, 285; Paulsen, 'Mk XVI 1–8', 150 (391).

314. Paulsen, 'Mk XVI 1–8', 153, 155 (393, 395).

315. Cf. e.g. Schenke, *Auferstehungsverkündigung*, esp. 88: an aetiological cult legend composed to accompany a yearly remembrance of Jesus' resurrection at sunrise in (how large was it?!) or by the empty grave. (Does that presuppose that they knew where the grave was? Cf. here Carnley, *Structure*, 50. But we have seen reason to ask whether they knew that at this stage.) Or Albertz, 'Formengeschichte', 265: behind the angelophany lies a christophany (assuming that the 'young man' is meant to be an angel). (Would one not expect the tradition to develop in the opposite direction, if anything, as indeed Grass argues that it demonstrably has [*Ostergeschehen*, 87]? But Albertz's surprisingly modern-sounding suggestion is that the later church, concerned to keep women in their place and silent, suppressed a more favourable estimate of their spiritual experience here, namely an account of an encounter with the risen Lord himself. Yet neither Matthew nor John eschewed reports of such encounters. On the other hand Grass's suggestion that the silence of the women guaranteed the independence of the apostles' witness and of the Easter faith [*Ostergeschehen*, 22] is rather surprising when there is no mention of the apostles' witness or of the Easter faith! Cf. Lindemann, 'Osterbotschaft', 309–10.) Or it can be regarded as the equivalent of a regular component of stories of various heroes and heroines being taken up to heaven; that they had been so exalted or 'translated' is proved, *inter alia*, by the absence of the (dead or live) body of the person in question: cf. e.g. the texts gathered by Berger and Colpe, *Textbuch*, 89–95 (esp. Diodorus Siculus 4.38.5; Plutarch, *Romulus* 27.5; Chariton, *Callirhoe* 3.3.1, 4–6; Testament of Job 39.11–12; but also in the OT: Gen. 5.24 LXX; II Kings 2.16–17). Bickermann, 'Grab', esp. 278, draws a basic distinction between accounts of exaltation, which merely require proof of the disappearance of the Exalted One, and stories of resurrection, which require proof that the Risen One has appeared again. But although there is undoubtedly a distinction to be drawn here, the account of Jesus' ascension in Acts 1 presents problems, for there the negative motif of the absence of the

proof that the exalted one is no longer on earth is missing (it is enough that the disciples have seen him going). Friedrich, 'Lk 9,51', also detects elements of exaltation stories in the accounts of the resurrection appearances (e.g. in the ἄφαντος ἐγένετο of Luke 24.31; see also Hoffmann, 'Auferstehung', 499). In short, the boundaries between these different categories of story are not hard and fast, nor would one expect them to be when the 'resurrection' being described was such a religio-historical novelty.

316. Robinson, 'Jesus', 12, goes further: in order to counter the dangers of purely 'luminous' resurrection appearances, Mark omits them and tells only of the empty grave which implies a bodily, tangible resurrection (similarly Goulder, 'Jesus of Nazareth', 64). But it is hard to imagine that Mark could not and would not have included apologetic features like those of Luke 24.39–43 had he really wished to make precisely this point. In complete contrast to Robinson, N. Q. Hamilton holds that Mark probably created the story of the empty tomb as an 'anti-resurrection story': the empty tomb points instead to 'translation', which, unlike the appearance stories, does not distract the reader from what Mark considers most important, the awaited parousia ('Resurrection Tradition'; cf. also Crossan, *Who Killed Jesus?*, 200: 'Mark wants nothing about risen appearances here and nothing about confessions of faith generated by them. Jesus is present to the Markan community only in the pain and suffering of absence, pending, of course, the imminent parousia'). Similarly Merklein (*Auferstehung*, 16–17; see also his 'Mk 16,1–8', 225–6) sees here Mark's attempt to free the kerygma from the framework of the empty tomb story and to point away from the empty tomb to the symbolic world and the meaning bestowed by the kerygma. This thwarts the desire of the reader to find confirmation of the kerygma in the empty tomb. But all of that has a very existentialist ring to it, and one must ask whether this is not, after all, an anachronism. Does not the enigma of Mark's ending compel us to be somewhat venturesome in attempting to explain, however tentatively, why he ended in so remarkable a way? On the other hand, von Campenhausen's suggestion ('Easter Events', 71) that Mark wished by this ending to demonstrate that the disciples had nothing to do with the empty tomb, and so to disarm the Jewish charge that they had removed the body, like both these other two accounts fails to carry conviction because too much weight is laid on an argument from (a deafening) silence. Wilckens, *Resurrection*, 33, argues that Mark omits any account of appearances because he knew of none – he knew of the fact of

appearances, but no more than this. See the critique of Lindemann, 'Osterbotschaft', 301–2, both of this and of Pesch's explanation that Mark's source ended here (*MkEv*, 2, 520).

317. Bousset, *Kyrios Christos*, 65; Bultmann, *History*, 284f.; cf. Lindars, 'Resurrection', 131. Hamilton, 'Resurrection Tradition', 417, goes further: the story did not exist at all till Mark created it (similarly Badham, 'Meaning', 32; Crossan, 'Tomb'; Goulder, 'Jesus of Nazareth', 65). Von Campenhausen, 'Easter Events', 60, traces this tradition of interpretation back to Wellhausen, but doubts whether it will hold water: no reader would imagine that a permanent or long silence is meant. Or this explains why the disciples remained in Jerusalem despite the command to go to Galilee: Schenke, *Auferstehungsverkündigung*, esp. 51.

318. Wilckens, 'Auferstehung Jesu', 114.

319. Cf., e.g., Crossan, 'Tomb', 149; Hengel, 'Maria', 253; Lincoln, 'Promise', 286; Paulsen, 'Mk XVI 1–8', 172 (413); Perrin, *The Resurrection Narratives*, 32.

320. Cf. Mark 4.41; 5.15, 33, 36; 6.50; 9.32. As Grass notes (*Ostergeschehen*, 16), a similar reaction to the more than natural or the unusual can also be expressed with similar terms: θαμβέομαι (1.27; 10.32); ἐξίσταμαι (2.12; 5.42; 6.51: cf. the ἔκστασις of the women); ἔκφοβος (9.6); cf. Koch, *Bedeutung*, 29 n. 17. Even Herod Antipas' fear of John the Baptist (6.20) is probably of this kind, for John's righteousness and holiness are mentioned; the 'fear' of the disciples, too, as they accompany Jesus on his way to Jerusalem (10.32), may also stem as much from their awareness that some purpose unknown to them drives Jesus on as from their anticipation of the physical dangers awaiting them there. The Jewish authorities' 'fear' of Jesus and the crowd (11.18, 32; 12.12) is another matter, more one of being impressed by the weight of public support that Jesus could muster. The disciples' fear is therefore in itself no failure in Mark' eyes, although the lack of understanding that sometimes occasions it (e.g. 9.32; 10.32) may be. Cf. also Bode, *Morning*, 37–49; Linnemann, 'Markusschluss', 257; Pesch, *MkEv* 2, 152.

321. So Theissen and Merz, *Jesus*, 491.

322. That would tell against the suggestion of Wengst, *Ostern*, 47–8, that since the command to go to Galilee means a return to following Jesus in earthly obedience, the women's fear is correspondingly occasioned by the dangers attending such a following in the first century. Merklein, *Auferstehung*, 13, regards the trembling and consternation of v. 8b as part of the pre-Markan source used here, and

comments: 'Their flight in consternation shows that they viewed the rolled-away stone as a sign which they could no longer explain from their world of experiences and which ran counter to and invalidated the human verdict that Jesus' history was now finished.'

323. Houlden, *Backward*, 72.

324. E.g., ibid., 56.

325. Vermes, *Gospel*, 6.

326. Watson, '"He Is Not Here"', 101.

327. And probably of Luke, too, even though he only refers to 'men' in shining garments (24.4; cf. the description of the transfigured Jesus in 9.29 and the two 'men' who re-appear in his story at Jesus' ascension in Acts 1.10).

328. Karl Friedrich Bahrdt in Schweitzer, *Quest*, 43.

329. For the symbolic interpretation, linked to Mark 14.51–5, cf. Crossan, 'Tomb', 147–8 and nn. 30–32 (he himself sees the young man as symbolic of the Markan community).

330. Cf. Lincoln, 'Promise', 290.

331. Cf. Bode, *Morning*, 43; Gnilka, *MkEv*, 2, 344; Hooker, *Mark*, 387; cf. also Merklein, 'Mk 16,1–8', 223–4 (although he doubts the aptness of the explanation of this phenomenon of 'inversion').

332. Nineham, *Mark*, 447–8.

333. See n. 2 above.

334. Cf. Houlden, 'Resurrection', 203.

335. Cf. also ibid., 205.

336. Josipovici, *Book*, 230, quoted by Young, 'Mark', 148.

337. Perrin, *The Resurrection Narratives*, 26–7: he notes how three-fold repetitions combined with variations within the repetitions are characteristic of Mark, and points to the three references to the women at the crucifixion, burial and tomb. Cf. Lindemann, 'Osterbotschaft', 311, who sees in 8.32–33 a rejection of any misunderstanding of the message of the resurrection which would separate it from suffering.

338. Or did the pre-Markan tradition contain a reference in v. 6 not only to Jesus' having been raised, but also to his having appeared to Peter (Gnilka, *MkEv*, 2, 339)? In that case the suppression of this appearance, according to Gnilka in order to direct attention away to Galilee, is all the more striking and calls for an explanation.

339. Gnilka, *MkEv*, 2, 343 and n. 29, rightly notes that (a) it would be unparalleled to speak of the parousia as an event involving only Peter and the disciples and (b) there is no express reference to Galilee in Mark 13. Perkins, *Resurrection*, 120, also comments that 'several elements in

the passage do not lend themselves to a parousia interpretation' and cites the absence 'of the vocabulary of the glory associated with the parousia' and of clear evidence that Mark associated the parousia with Galilee.

340. One may doubt whether Mark's readers could really be expected to see in 16.7 a reference to 'seeing' Jesus in the Gentile mission (*pace* Perrin, *The Resurrection Narratives*, 30); cf. e.g. Pesch, *MkEv*, 2, 540.

341. Lindemann, 'Osterbotschaft', 316.

342. Koch, *Bedeutung*, 191; Koch gives the example of the 'nature' miracles as raw demonstrations of power, which nonetheless have no effect on outsiders, in contrast to the popular appeal of the healings, and run up against the utter incomprehension of the disciples.

343. Perrin, *The Resurrection Narratives*, 40.

344. And yet Küng, *Credo*, 112, maintains that Paul was interested in both continuity and discontinuity.

345. Edited and translated by A. F. J. Klijn in *OTP* 1, 637–8.

346. Vollenweider, 'Ostern', 50. This would find confirmation in the passage from Ps. -Plutarch (= Aëtius), *De placitis philosophorum* 5.19, which quotes the opinion of Anaxagoras and Euripides that nothing in fact dies, but that rather a sort of recycling of existing matter takes place (cf. Berger and Colpe, *Textbuch*, §461). Against that one may quote the comment of Plutarch himself in a fragment of his commentary on Hesiod's *Works and Days* to the effect that 'the seed, after being cast in the ground, needs first to be hidden in the earth and to rot and then to transfer its power into the earth that has covered it, so that from a single grain of, say, wheat or of barley there may come a quantity' (*Moralia*, LCL, 15, 212–15, frag. 104; cf. John 12.24; also Braun, '"Stirb"', 140–5).

347. Grass, *Ostergeschehen*, 163.

348. At least that seems implicit in the parallelism of 'your limbs . . . yourselves' in Rom 6.13 (cf. Bultmann, *Theology* 1, 194, who particularly stresses this identification).

349. Cf. Badham, 'Meaning', 29–33: his interpretation at least means that a completely new form of existence is created (and thus the corpse can remain in the tomb, indeed had better remain in the tomb if Jesus' fate is to be the model and pattern for our destiny, for our corpses remain in the tomb, if that is where they have been put).

350. Cf. Wedderburn, *Baptism*, 165–6, 241–8 (the latter section dealing with the problems of the equivalent Greek adjective in I Cor. 10.1–4).

351. Bultmann, 'New Testament and Mythology', 40.
352. Marxsen, 'Significance', 39; *Resurrection*, 125–6.
353. Dunn, *Partings*, 184.
354. See Ch. 4 above.
355. This qualification is included to exclude insignificant 'some-things' like Jesus' body getting cold in the tomb.
356. That way of talking would have ample precedent in some Jewish apocalyptic circles, particularly in some parts of Ethiopic Enoch. But at the same time it seems doubtful whether this existence as spirits would be spoken of as 'resurrection' rather than as an interim stage awaiting a still future resurrection; cf. Wedderburn, *Baptism*, 173–80.
357. Cf. Hengel, *Charismatic Leader*, esp. 8–15.
358. Cf. here Dawes, *Freeing*, ch. 3.
359. Bruce, 'Epistles', 927.
360. There is an interesting parallel to this critique of Paul's argument in Traugott Koch's article on the resurrection of the dead ('"Auferstehung"', esp. 471, 478): he describes how Karl Barth denied the survival after death of the individual except in the memory of God, which he saw as a form of eternity, and how this stems from Barth's conviction that the human person only is what it is through God's gracious address and not of itself. But, protests Koch, does that then mean that my life is of no significance for God, that it is ultimately irrelevant? Must the human life in union with God be just a matter of self-surrender and forgetting of self, and not also a gain for one's self?
361. Cf. Selby, *Look*, 16: if I Cor. 15.35–39, 42–44 'states anything about the Christian understanding of death, it is that death is necessary. The life beyond death is apparently assumed; what is emphatically asserted is that it cannot be attained without the occurrence of death.'
362. Cf. Wedderburn, *Baptism*, esp. 342–56.
363. Cf. Col. 2.12; 3.1; Eph. 2.6.
364. Marxsen, *Resurrection*, 184.
365. That is certainly the case in Schweizer's (orthodox) glossing of 25b: God has already *begun* to build something new in Martha ('Auferstehung', 16). But this language of a process begun is foreign to the way in which the Jesus of the Fourth Gospel speaks.
366. Cf. Wisdom 3.1–3: 'But the souls of the righteous are in the hand of God, and no torment will ever touch them. In the eyes of the foolish they seemed to have died (ἐδόξασαν . . . τεθνάναι), . . . but they are at peace.'
367. Phillips, *Death*, 50.

368. See Bonhoeffer's letter of 30 April 1944 in *LPP*, 279.

369. Bultmann, *John*, e.g. 197–9; 'Eschatology'. Also Selby, *Look*, 103, 117. See, however, the discussion and critique of Bultmann's analysis in Frey, *Eschatologie* 1,86–157. Whether or not Bultmann's thesis of a later ecclesiastical redaction is correct or not does not greatly affect the argument here, for I would wish to follow the lead of the realized strand of thinking in this Gospel, whether it was the evangelist himself who counterbalanced it with a future strand or another, later redactor.

370. But in that case the work of Bultmann's ecclesiastical redactor and of the author of the Johannine Epistles, if they are to be dated after the Fourth Gospel, as seems to me the more probable (although this now quite widely contested), marks a step backwards in a more traditional direction as far as eschatology is concerned.

371. Schottroff, 'Heil', 298.

372. Cf. e.g. the reference to Jesus' having already ascended into heaven in 3.13; 'anachronistic', but not 'indiscriminate', as the argument of Frey, *Eschatologie*, 2 and 3, shows.

373. Hoffmann, 'Auferstehung', 508.

374. Käsemann, *Testament*, 15–16.

375. Cf. again Wedderburn, *Baptism*, 6–37; 'Problem'.

376. Cf. Wedderburn, 'Colossians'.

377. E.g. *IG* IX 2, 640; Kaibel, *Epigrammata græca*, §646a, tr. in Rice-Stambaugh, *Sources*, 243–4; see also the summary (and bibliography) in Klauck, *Umwelt*, 1,76; MacMullen, *Paganism*, 53, 55.

378. Vollenweider, 'Grosser Tod', 370, cf. 378; 'Ostern', 53: *'media morte in vita sumus'*.

379. Cf. Wedderburn, *Baptism*, 381–5.

380. Translated by S. K. Stowers in Malherbe, *The Cynic Epistles*, 257–9; cf. also *PGM* 4, 718–22.

381. The way in which Paul's corporate christology provides the basis of his thought here is a theme which I have explored more fully in my *Baptism*, esp. ch. 5.

382. Hick, *Metaphor*, 136.

383. Phillips, *Death*, 52–3.

384. Kaufman, *Theology*, 49.

385. Despite the contentions of those who wish to de-eschatologize Jesus; cf. especially Borg, *Jesus* (1994), chs 3 and 4. As Theissen and Merz (*Jesus*, 11) justly remark, such a picture bears the marks, not of (first-century) Galilee, but of California, although in deference to Borg

one should presumably take in more of the Western seaboard and include Oregon as well!

386. Lehmann, 'Frage', esp. 309. As far as the specific hope of 'resurrection' is concerned, A. F. Segal notes how references to it have been dropped from the liturgy of Reform Judaism ('Life', 90).

387. Segal, 'Judaism', 27.

388. See also Segal, 'Life', 91–6. However, Verweyen, '"Aufer-stehung"', 117–20, questions whether Israel in fact treated death as the final word before the rise of belief in resurrection, although he recognizes that his questioning of this is unfashionable. E. P. Sanders, too, holds that at the time of Jesus most Jews in fact believed in some form of personal survival after death and in the rewards and punishments that one would receive there, but grants that most may have conceived of this future life in rather vague terms (*Judaism*, 298–303). In the eyes of Anthony Harvey such vagueness is hardly surprising: a people that continued to use the Psalter would be accustomed to think of all descending at the end to a pit where the dead cannot even praise God (Ps. 115.17). For Schweizer ('Auferstehung', 3–4), 'the faith of the Old Testament is almost unique in the world of religions' in this respect, 'for here lives a people which lives with its God with the utmost intensity, yet without expecting a resolution of all problems in the world to come. Here lives a people which seeks to obey God in all aspects of its life, yet without any thought of eternal reward after death.' (This observation he uses as an argument against Feuerbach.) Harvey argues that alongside this belief that death was the end there existed the belief in rewards and punishments in the after-life ('Mark 9.10', 70). Fiedler, 'Vorgaben', 11, on the other hand, regards it as a well-known fact that not all Jews believed in a life after death.

389. Ollenburger, 'Mortals', esp. 30.

390. Christian theologians like Gordon Kaufman represent a very different interpretation of the Christian tradition here, for he deliberately tries 'to speak only in terms of *this world*, of the realities of *this life*' and avoids talk of the 'other world' (*Mystery*, 326, his italics); on a more popular level cf. Dawes, *Freeing*, ch. 4 and p. 68.

391. Watson, '"He Is Not Here"', 106.

392. To use the term made fashionable by Don Cupitt (e.g. *Sea*, 54, 229–68; in his *Taking Leave of God* the contrast to a 'realist' use of God-language was rather the 'expressive' use of it). Cupitt's non-realist programme seems, however, to be linked to an endorsement of Kantian epistemology in which the 'human mind is pre-programmed to construe

experience as being experience of an objective physical world'; the 'ordered world we see is the creation of our minds' (137–8) and without that ordering by ourselves it is chaos. To that one might object that experience in fact tells us otherwise and that the order, the formulae, the whole experimental basis of modern science exists prior to our discovery and analysis of it (contrast, however, p. 188). In other words, all that is here threatens to become 'non-real' apart, perhaps, from ourselves. That position is one that is hard to swallow, even if Cupitt finds it to be the essence of the thought of the later Wittgenstein (222); even Cupitt himself must hold together with this thesis the view that the 'thinking subject' is 'itself merely a product of nature and immersed in nature' (187). What nature is and, above all, why it is what is and how and why the human self can transcend it remain unexplained on Cupitt's account. At first sight Gordon Kaufman's talk of 'de-reification' of God-talk might seem to be similar (esp. *Mystery*, chs 22 and 23), but he is careful to insist that 'God' corresponds to a reality, albeit a mysterious one, in this world (but not in another). As applied to human history this may be near to Cupitt's view, but when applied to the movements of biological evolution less so. And Kaufman is keen to insist, as we shall see below, that 'God is a reality genuinely distinct from us and all our imaginings' (317). Similarly, Hick, for all his endorsement of the validity of non-theistic religious traditions, is keen to assert that 'to affirm the Real is . . . to affirm that religious experience is not solely a construction of our human imagination but is a response – though always a culturally conditioned response – to the Real' (*Metaphor*, 143). If the 'non-realist' stance means simply talking about 'life having the capacity for meaning and purpose' and 'God' is that meaning and purpose (Dawes, *Freeing*, 32, 48) or means that the only values are those *we* create (Cupitt, *Taking Leave of God*, 3), this could mean that *we* bestow a meaning and purpose upon it, but as soon as we start to speak of *finding* meaning and purpose in life, this gives the impression that they were there to be found before we started looking.

393. Cf. the discussion in Hick, *Evil*, 160–74.
394. Verweyen, '"Auferstehung"', 109.
395. Cf. Schrage, 'Theologie', 148.
396. Borg, *Jesus* (1987), ch. 6, esp. 115–16.
397. Theissen, *Faith*, 95.
398. Kaufman, *Mystery*, 76.
399. Becker, *Jesus*, 377.
400. Schoberth, 'Allmacht', 46; in this assertion he rejects the

reasoning of the American rabbi Harold Kushner in his book *When Bad Things Happen to Good People* (1981). Kushner, confronted with the dilemma of innocent suffering in the death of his son from an incurable disease that he had had from birth, opts for the denial of divine 'almightiness': God for him is no mere spectator or even cause of our sufferings, but is devastated by them and suffers with us; to such a God we can pray again and find comfort in so doing. To such reasoning, which appeals, after all, to the biblical story of Job, it is not enough simply to invoke the givenness of the biblical tradition as non-negotiable, particularly if 'the biblical tradition' does not speak with a single voice. By way of contrast, in the same volume Günter Altner refers to the 'dogmatically ossified formula about the almighty God' which no longer makes any sense ('Schöpfung', 95).

401. Feldmeier, 'Nicht Übermacht', 27.

402. Ibid., 29; τὸ ἡγεμονικόν, on the other hand, is used by Philo above all as an anthropological term, as is also the case in the Stoa (which viewed the cosmos and human nature as analogous).

403. E.g. Schobert, 'Allmacht', 60: 'What theodicy seeks to rescue is not the God of the Bible, but a metaphysical concept of God, which is not identical with the God of the Bible, although often enough it is superimposed on that God.'

404. Cf. e.g. the summaries by M. Rose in *Anchor Bible Dictionary* 4, esp. 1005, 1008–9 and H. Langkammer in *EWNT* 3, 25 ('in *šadday* the idea of the ruler seems . . . somehow to play a role').

405. Cupitt's remarks about the philosophers' God (*Taking Leave of God*, 7) are not unmerited: 'The philosophers are almost unanimous that the only God there can be is their god, the God of the philosophers, and that if *he* does not exist then talk of God has no useful job to do.'

406. Carnley, *Structure*, 304–15.

407. Ward, *Religion*, 135; cf. 163–71.

408. E.g. Tillich, *SystTheol*, 1, 235: it is not necessarily quite the same to speak of God as 'the power of being' (236; see also Keith Ward mentioned below); this could mean that it is God who enables being, makes it possible. A democratic constitution may make freedom possible, but would we therefore describe it as 'powerful'? Admittedly Tillich does also speak of the 'power of resisting nonbeing' (ibid.), which suggests something more is meant.

409. See Wedderburn, 'Paul and the Story of Jesus'.

410. See Kaufman, *Mystery*, 88, in criticism of Karl Barth.

411. Verweyen, '"Auferstehung"', 111; cf. 'Sache', 72.

412. Theissen, *Faith*, 181 n. 1 (my italics).

413. Perhaps one needs to differentiate here, since in between the process of biological evolution and that of the cultural evolution of human beings lies the development of a sort of 'culture' amongst animals in their behaviour patterns. Theissen recognizes patterns of learning by trial and error, by imitation and even, in some measure, by imaginative problem-solving, amongst the more intelligent lower animals (12–13). That would imply that one needs not only to 'speak of a hierarchical superiority of cultural evolution to biological evolution in humanity', but also of a hierarchy of various levels of evolution, graded according to their level of complexity and also according to the degree to which they are a matter of chance or of purposive, intentional change. See also Kaufman, *Mystery*, esp. 157–8, who depicts the process of biological evolution as developing into the evolution of culture and historical being. One misses here, however, the sense of a protest or reaction against the principles of biological evolution which is present in Theissen's account of cultural evolution (see below); the cultural process is for Kaufman far more a direct continuation of the biological, without the element of resistance, even reversal. And yet that element may be present – on the level of the individual agent at least (for although Kaufman often speaks here of the individual *and* communities these are treated far more as analogous: in other words, the interaction of the two and the responsibility of the individual for the shaping of society and culture needs to be further explored; Kaufman mentions the role of individuals in making society more restrictive and oppressive [215–16], but surely there is also a positive counterpart, individuals whose influence on society is for the better, liberating?) – in his account of 'the interpenetration of action with reflection' (ch. 13). For the shaping of culture, the interplay between the individual and the collective is vital, and here the ability of certain individuals to shape a culture may be decisive – in religious traditions (and yet not only in them, for there are also secular 'prophets') such a person would be called 'prophetic', whether the reflection and the resultant call to change is attributed to divine inspiration or not, and whether one views the resultant change as one for the better or not.

414. Ward, *Religion*, 120–1, in criticizing non-realist views of God, questions whether religion can be simply a matter of self-transformation 'as a personal policy, without participation in an empowering and transforming reality . . . without the theoretical belief that there is a personal

reality underlying the world which makes such attitudes [as reverence, gratitude, trust, and hope] appropriate'.

415. Would one not have to say that intolerant human beings would be, if not of less value, at least *less valuable in this process?*

416. Huxley, *Evolution and Ethics*, 81, 83 (139, 141 in the Princeton edition), quoted by Barbour, *Issues*, 96; cf. Altner, 'Schöpfung', 76.

417. Does that not imply a serious criticism of all talk of a divine election?

418. Perhaps it may nonetheless jar to hear Jesus spoken of as 'one "mutation" among many others' (87). See further below.

419. If one could speak of God's relation to nature solely in terms of persuasion and influence, as many process theologians do, then this would be no problem. But the world as we know it does seem to operate on the basis of more direct principles of causation, and not just those of persuasion; the analogy of the relation of a leader to a community may be an attractive one, but does it do justice to the workings of the non-human world? Even the courtship display of a pair of birds can only called 'persuasion' in a somewhat figurative sense of the word, let alone the natural processes of lower forms of life.

420. Kaufman, *Mystery*, 35.

421. The element of contradiction in Kaufman's account is, however, far more muted than in Theissen's.

422. 'Historicity' is defined as the 'process of grasping and understanding, of shaping and creating, through which a culture gradually defines and develops itself in the course of its own history' (103).

423. To my ears the word 'serendipitous' has a somewhat utopian ring that is rather out of keeping with the seriousness of the issues that are at stake in the struggle for our world and our existence. (Dictionaries speak here, in defining the word 'serendipity', of the making of chance, *happy* discoveries, but is all that has come into being in our world really to be described as 'happy'?) The image of the groaning and suffering spirit that echoes our discontent and disquiet with the world as it is is one which I at least find ethically more satisfactory and adequate. The impression that all in the world is not tightly under control, moving inexorably towards one goal without deviation, which Kaufman presumably wishes to explain by invoking the 'serendipitous' (and in view of the element of the fortuitous in the workings of evolution this is quite intelligible), seems to me to be more plausibly explainable by speaking of the strivings of a spirit or force within the world whose proddings and orderings are, over against traditional views of

God Almighty, in no way irresistible, either for inanimate creation or for animate, but are indeed often thwarted and frustrated.

424. See, e.g., Fiddes, *Suffering*, 221.

425. Other candidates for the one doing this submitting have been suggested (Adam, the devil), but it is hard to see Paul speaking in this way of any other than God.

426. Peacocke, *God and the New Biology*, 54–5, plays down the element of struggle and consequently suffering in biological evolution, but this seems to me to be undeniable, the higher up the evolutionary tree one advances.

427. E.g. Theissen, *Faith*, 108, 127–8.

428. This seems to exaggerate the gulf between the pre- and post-Easter Jesus movement.

429. Again, it must be asked, what happens to the conviction that it was (s)election which was the beginning of Israel?

430. Davies, *God*, 214; cf. viii. At the same time, it is to be noted that reflection on such questions is, as far as we know, something that distinguishes humankind from other life-forms. Other life-forms may perhaps show signs of puzzlement which may imply 'Why?' questions or, in their higher forms at least, may manifest adaptability and problem-solving which imply corresponding 'How?' questions, but there is no reason to suppose that apes reflect on why they are apes rather than lions or human beings or on how their habitat came into being.

431. Ward, *Religion*, 160.

432. Kaufman, *Mystery*, 329.

433. Davies, *The Mind of God*, esp. 194–222.

434. Kaufman, *Mystery*, 306–7, my italics.

435. Kaufman continues to talk of 'basic . . . historical trajectories' as if these all led in one single direction (*Mystery*, 336). There is here, it seems to me, a basic (over-)optimism about the way human civilization is developing, despite all his awareness of the monstrous threats to that civilization.

436. Sölle, *Mystik*, e.g. 122–6, esp. 123.

437. Fiddes, *Suffering*, 223, referring to Moltmann, *God*, 225 (referring in turn to M. Horkheimer).

438. Kaufman, *Mystery*, 333 (his italics).

439. Weder, *Hermeneutik*, 60–1.

440. Kaufman, *Mystery*, 21.

441. George Fox's reference to 'that of God' in every human person

(in a letter sent from prison in 1656 and contained in his *Journal* for that year) surely points in the same direction and awakes the same expectations.

442. Werbick, 'Auferweckung', 86.

443. Davies, *God*, e.g. 62–3, 84–6.

444. Kaufman, *Mystery*, 170: he also emphasizes, rightly, that 'free' is always a relative term, never an absolute one (172).

445. Dawes, *Freeing*, 106.

446. Sölle, *Mystik*, 147.

447. Cf. Weder, *Hermeneutik*, 131–3: 'Explanations [*Erklärungen* – he distinguishes *Erklären*, 'explain', from *Verstehen*, 'understand', however much the one may involve the other] have an inbuilt tendency to understand things *exclusively kata sarka* ['according to the flesh' – cf. II Cor. 5.16], on the level of worldly reality' (his italics); understanding according to the spirit of God, on the other hand, sees things with God's eyes, so to speak, sees God's truth within the worldly reality.

448. Moltmann, *God*, 246.

449. Cf. the critique of Fiddes, *Suffering*, 6.

450. Moltmann, *God*, 244.

451. E.g. Moltmann, *Trinity*, 110.

452. Fiddes, *Suffering*, 8.

453. See especially ibid., 221–9.

454. Peacocke, *Creation and the World of Science*, 246; yet much of the suffering in the world arises, not from the 'randomness' in the world, but from its inexorable orderliness.

455. Cf. Barbour, *Issues*, 452.

456. I have referred here to a 'reality', deliberately avoiding talk of '(a) being' because of the ambiguities inherent in that expression ('a being' may be a person or thing, 'being' on the other hand the existence of persons or things; nor does it greatly help clarity if 'Being', with or without the definite article, is written with a capital B); if 'being' is to be used at all, then I would prefer to identify the 'reality' of which I speak as the 'ground' of being; of the being, that is, the existence, of all things (all beings). But in all such language there is an impression of something static, immutable, and that is a way of talking of God which is (rightly) somewhat out of fashion today.

457. Even if we say that God's reality 'lies unknowably further along the line that characterizes us as persons' (so Grobel, 'Revelation', 159).

458. Cf. Griffin, 'Life', 90: 'how subjectivity can "emerge" out of

wholly objective things is as mysterious as how subjects and wholly objective things can interact.'

459. Hick, *Metaphor*, 141.

460. *Pace* Ward, *Religion*, 214. Contrast Altner's quotation of the South Korean theologian Chung Hyun Kyung's address to the Canberra assembly of the WCC in 1991 ('Schöpfung', 87).

461. Moltmann, *God*, esp. 47 (Moltmann describes 'the crucified God' as 'a monstrous phrase'), 65, 235.

462. In Davis, *Death*, 31, responding to Nielsen, 'Faces'.

463. Cf. Griffin, 'Life', 90–1: 'mechanistic materialism generally claims to be an empirical philosophy, yet it denies many of the most fundamental presuppositions of our experience. We presuppose that we are partially free while it says that our experience and behaviour are wholly determined by antecedent causes.'

464. Cf. Sölle, *Mystik*, 98–100.

465. Hoffmann, *Überlieferung*, 13.

466. Kaufman, *Mystery*, 378–9, reflects upon the way in which traditional reflection on Jesus' cross and resurrection has not only drawn 'the sting from the Christian motif of absolute self-sacrifice by transforming it into ultimate prudence and self-aggrandizement', but has also 'laid the foundations for later Christian imperialism'. See also Cupitt, *Sea*, 260–3, on 'the gradual fading of the expectation of an after-life'.

467. *Pace* Cook, '*Memento*', 155, who seems to me to underestimate gravely the numbers of those for whom death, so far from being 'the greatest of evils', in fact is a release from suffering or loss of dignity or of quality of life.

468. Houlden, *Connections*, 149.

469. Phillips, *Death*, 16.

470. Brecht, *Galileo*, Scene 8.

Index of Passages Cited from Ancient Literature

Index of Authors Cited